Whose Game Is It, Anyway?

Whose Game Is It, Anyway?

A GUIDE TO HELPING YOUR CHILD
GET THE MOST FROM SPORTS,
ORGANIZED BY AGE AND STAGE

Richard D. Ginsburg, Ph.D.
and Stephen Durant, Ed.D.
with Amy Baltzell, Ed.D.

HOUGHTON MIFFLIN COMPANY
BOSTON • NEW YORK

For information about permission to reproduce selections from this book,
write to Permissions, Houghton Mifflin Company, 215 Park Avenue South,
New York, New York 10003.

Visit our website: www.houghtonmifflinbooks.com

Library of Congress Cataloging-in-Publication Data
Ginsburg, Richard D.
Whose game is it, anyway? : a guide to helping your child get the
most from sports, organized by age and stage / Richard D. Ginsburg
& Stephen Durant with Amy Baltzell.
p. cm.
Includes bibliographical references and index.
ISBN-13: 978-0-618-47460-8
ISBN-10: 0-618-47460-9
1. Sports for children. I. Durant, Stephen. II. Baltzell, Amy.
III. Title.
GV709.2.G55 2006
796'.083 — dc22 2005020470

Printed in the United States of America

QUM 10 9 8 7 6 5 4 3 2

THIS BOOK IS INTENDED TO PRESENT THE RESEARCH AND IDEAS
OF ITS AUTHORS. IF A READER REQUIRES PERSONAL ADVICE,
HE/SHE SHOULD CONSULT WITH A COMPETENT PROFESSIONAL.

Throughout this book, we have gone to great lengths to protect the confidentiality
and privacy of our patients, athletes, and research subjects. To accomplish this
goal, we have disguised first names, athletic situations, defining characteristics, and
gender or have created stories that are a composite of more than one individual.

We dedicate this book to our children:
Brian, Claire, Jackie, Michael, Shayna,
Luke, Teddy, and Zoey Violet, and
to the wonderful children and athletes
engaged in sports.

Contents

PREFACE

"Enjoy them now, because it'll go by faster than you can imagine." Parents of young infants and toddlers often hear this refrain from the parents of grown children. Indeed, in the midst of the hard work, chaos, demands, and anxieties that accompany being a parent of growing kids, it can be easy to forget to enjoy the moment. But it can be done — and the following public example underscores just how significant such moments can be. On the morning of Super Bowl XXXIX, a father and his two young sons cavorted and playfully roughhoused on the perfect turf of the stadium. New England Patriots star linebacker Tedy Bruschi seemed blissfully ignorant of the pressure surrounding the championship game in which he'd compete in just a few hours. This great parenting scene was the best "ad" of the day. Putting aside the overblown hype of Super Bowl Sunday, Bruschi was clearly caught up in being a dad, and his sons shared his joy, creating the best advertisement of the day: "Enjoy the moment and enjoy your kids. That's what life and sports are all about!"

That episode seems even more poignant in retrospect because a few short weeks later, Tedy Bruschi experienced a medical emergency (a stroke), the kind that sends chills

> "Enjoy the moment and enjoy your kids. That's what life and sports are all about!"

up the spine, particularly for parents of young children. This event serves as a reminder that we need from time to time: Life is short. Our children are precious. We need to do our best to raise them, but we mustn't forget to simply enjoy life with them. (Fortunately, Tedy Bruschi is recovering nicely from his stroke. He returned to competition in the 2005 season.)

Physical activity and sports are a rewarding way to have fun with children. Yet many parents worry that organized youth sports aren't what they should be; parents fear an overemphasis on winning and a warped sense of priorities that undervalue academics and even basic common sense. Though sports form an integral part of Western culture, especially in North America, parents have seen children sidelined by unhappiness, adults overcome with rage, and an increase in emotional turmoil, loss of control, and bad, even tragically violent, behavior related to kids in competitive sports. For example, on a July day in 2000, at a suburban hockey rink outside Boston, two fathers exchanged words following some rough play among 9- and 10-year-old boys. Words became shoves, pushes, and then punches. A simple argument set off by one father's concern that another father, ostensibly in charge, had allowed play to become too rough, ended when the bigger man beat the coach to death.

Despite many problems, most parents fervently support the idea that participation in sports forms a crucial learning experience while it enhances a child's social skills, physical health, and happiness.

Most of us react to horrible news like this by denying the threat it poses to our own sense of safety:

"Tsunamis don't happen here."

"People in our family don't get cancer because we're not smokers and we don't eat much red meat."

"The violence shown by those two fathers at the hockey game would NEVER happen in our town's sports programs because we're different."

But the facts tell a different story. Almost every day, at all levels of sports — professional, college, high school, and youth — incidents ranging from the embarrassing to the horrific take place in North America. Not long ago, fans and pro basketball stars got into a full-scale brawl in Detroit. Every week, college and pro athletes — so-called role models — receive media exposure for drug dealing, drunk driving, steroid use, domestic violence, rape, assault, and even murder. Fans can also seem reckless and irresponsible—championship celebrations in major cities from Vancouver to Boston provide an excuse for rioting.

In fact, every community in America can cite examples of how adults (both parents and coaches) lose focus in supervising children's sports, causing physical and psychological damage to kids. Orthopedic surgeons and pediatricians see numerous teens, as well as younger children, who are emotionally burnt out and suffer from repetitive-use injuries because of an overscheduled, driven, quasi-professional athletic life. Violence and out-of-control shouting matches between adult fans at youth and high school sports events are only too familiar. In our better moments, we recognize that when we, as parents, lose control of our passion for sports, we often lose sight of our priorities for our children, which certainly include the fostering of good character and common civility.

Still, despite these problems, most parents fervently support the idea that participation in sports forms a crucial learning experience while it enhances a child's social skills, physical health, and happiness. In a country characterized by ever greater diversity, organized sports provide a community ritual in which most families can participate. If we don't meet at church, mosque, or synagogue, we may see one another at the Little League game. And in the hectic pace of life that we experience in the information age—with its demands for, and promises of, immediate results, instant gratification, and guaranteed success—the potential for community and team spirit and children's growth in physical health, mental sharpness, and emotional maturity makes sports an attractive activity. It seems to offer a way to instill values and take a break from the demands of school and work.

> We firmly believe that competition in organized sports and the pursuit of athletic mastery at the youth, high school, and collegiate levels can promote excellence in many areas of life, without sacrificing the development of character.

True athletes, both women and men, revel in the physical and emotional tests that sports offer but also embrace the deeper, life-affirming rewards of such activities. As they age, many adults more fully appreciate the sheer fun, the close relationships, and the insights forged in the crucible of athletic competition during youth. Frequently, wisdom gained in sports is readily applied to other challenges in life. Sports can be one of life's truly great experiences.

The three authors of this book remain steadfast in our hope that much physical and psychological good can come from children's participation in sports. We firmly believe that competition in organized sports and the pursuit of athletic mastery at the youth, high school, and collegiate levels can promote excellence in many areas of life, without sacrificing the development of their best character.

The death of a father in a hockey rink galvanized our interest in improving sports for young people. Two of us (Richard Ginsburg and Steve Durant), as practicing clinical psychologists at Massachusetts General Hospital, have dealt with problems occurring during childhood, adolescence, and adulthood, and we frequently have found that many patients lacked the kind of sports experience that had benefited our own development. We both reflected on our deep appreciation for our own athletic experiences and how much we had learned from them. By contrast, many children, adolescents, and adults reported unpleasant and even destructive experiences. We found ourselves asking parents and kids about their abandonment of athletic activities: "Why did you quit sports? What happened that made it no longer any fun?"

> From a biological, neurological, and psychological standpoint, our children are incredible works in progress . . . They are by no means mini-adults.

With disturbing frequency, we heard that children, teenagers, and college students felt miserable or bored by athletics or felt they had been treated unfairly, even abusively. They dropped off a team or simply quit all competitive sports or even most rigorous physical activity altogether. After doing so, some of these kids experienced difficulties with drug and alcohol use, obesity, and psychological problems such as depression. One might argue that at an outpatient psychiatric clinic, we encountered people suffering from major depression, trauma, bipolar disorder, or severe learning problems, and this would explain their difficulty with sports. Well, for a small percentage of our patients, this was true. However, what we witnessed both among most of our patients (often high-functioning individuals seen for brief treatment of less severe difficulties) and in the culture at large told us that something was terribly wrong with the practice of sports in this country. We wanted to help fix it.

So we immersed ourselves in the world of youth, high school, and college sports and sport psychology, and along the way we met numerous outstanding clinicians, sport psychologists, parents, teachers, coaches, and athletes who greatly enriched our understanding and knowledge. First and foremost is Dr. Amy Baltzell, a sport psychologist, a professor at Boston University, and a coauthor of this book. This book, a collaboration among the three of us, arises from decades of our work and experience as psychologists, athletes, coaches, and parents of athletes. We share a passion and vision for seeing sports done the right way. We believe that competitive sports, like life, are about passion, a controlled passion that must be placed in proper perspective, but a passion nonetheless, and we hope to share it with our readers.

Acknowledgments

While much of the inspiration for this book was generated from wonderful discussions over the years among the three of us, we wish to acknowledge many important contributors for their support, generosity, and wise counsel. These special people are the colleagues, coaches, teachers, parents, and fellow travelers who have guided us in our quest to make sports all it can be for all of our children.

Our colleagues, mentors, and teachers from the Massachusetts General Hospital (MGH), the Harvard Medical School (HMS), and Boston University (BU) have played an instrumental role. Through their guidance and expertise we gained valuable training that deepened our understanding of issues in psychology that underlie sports and human development. From MGH and HMS, we wish to acknowledge Dr. Bruce Masek, Dr. Paula Rauch, Dr. Mike Jellinek, Dr. Arnie Cohen, Dr. Paul Hamburg, Dr. Martina Albright, Dr. Stuart Ablon, Dr. Anne Fishel, Dr. Robert Reifsnyder, Dr. Jerry Rosenbaum, Dr. Tom Gill, Dr. Larry Ronan, Dr. Arthur Boland, Dr. Bert Zarins, Dr. Nicole Danforth, Dr. Harrison Pope, Dr. Jamie Wines, Dr. Dennis Norman, Dr. Fred Neff, Dr. Paul Levenson, and Mrs. Helen Kiddy. From BU, we wish to acknowledge Dr. John McCarthy and Dr. Len Zaichowsky.

We wish to give special thanks to our agents from the William Morris Agency, Suzanne Gluck and Jonathan Pecarsky, who were instrumental in guiding us through this entire process.

Bringing three authors together and finding a consistent voice was no easy task, and we are greatly indebted to our editor, Susan Canavan from Houghton Mifflin, who showed great patience, wisdom, and thoughtfulness in her work with us. We'd also like to thank our copy editor, Susanna Brougham, whose careful editing greatly enhanced our book. We'd also like to thank Justin Sharaf from Amherst College for his tireless work gathering references and keeping us organized.

While it is impossible to provide a complete list, we'd like to give special recognition to our wonderful teammates and opponents over the years, who taught us the beauty of teamwork, camaraderie, skill development, competition, and a lifelong love of sports.

We would each like to acknowledge those who helped us individually.

RICHARD D. GINSBURG, PH.D.: I've had some fabulous teachers and coaches. From my twelve years as a student at Gilman School in Baltimore, Maryland, I'd like to give special acknowledgment to Redmond Finney, Rick Snyder, William Merrick, John Schmick, Don Rogers, Shanti Kumar, and Peggy Simon. I'd like to thank my first great coach, Mr. Farnum, of the Mount Washington soccer team. From Kenyon College, I wish to thank Bill Heiser. From the Williston Northampton School, I wish to thank Rick Francis, Ray Brown, Tim Jaeger, Harris Thompson, Jay Grant, Todd Bucklin, Jen Fulcher, Andy DeRoche, John Fisher, Tom Carmean, Fred Koval, and Vince Heckel. From the University of Massachusetts, I'd like to thank professors David Todd, the late Jeff Lukens, and especially Richard Halgin, who is without a doubt the most influential figure in my development as a professional. From Harvard University athletics, I'd like to thank Scott Anderson, Bill Cleary, Bob Scalise, Bob Glatz, Jon Bernstein, and Ed Krayer.

I am deeply grateful to my family: the late Ted S. Decker and his wife, Marion (Sis); Hilda Stern and the late Leon Ginsburg; my parents, Bob and Wendy; and my big sister, Professor Emily Ginsburg. My wife's family, including Jack and Margy Kilduff, Scott and Denise Barker, and Jim and Chris Burke, have provided wonderful support and inspiration. And of course I wish to thank my wife, Teri. I could not have completed this project without her; she is my greatest supporter, a wonderful editor, an honest critic, and a great mother to our newborn son, Teddy.

STEPHEN A. DURANT, ED.D.: I want to extend my gratitude to the staff of the Daniel Marr Boys and Girls Club, especially Bob Scannell, Bruce Seals, Mike Joyce, and Danny Ryan; the coaches and players of Dorchester and Savin Hill youth sports, especially Joe Boyle, Chris Tomasini, Bill Cotter, Tom Whall, and Biff Leary; the faculty and staff at BC High; all the members of the former Beacon Hill RFC and the Boston Irish Wolfhounds RFC;

and finally, all the members of the Durant and Evans families, especially Laura, Brian, Claire, Jackie, and Mike as well as Doc, Freddy, Joe, and Sean.

AMY BALTZELL, ED.D.: I'd like to thank my college rowing coach, "Pat" Callahan, for sharing with me his compassion and kindness. He helped me understand what truly matters — doing your best, seeing your possibilities, and having the courage to go for it and accept whatever comes. I thank all of my U.S. National Team teammates who both supported and challenged me to become my best. Also, I thank all of my teammates from the crew of the A3 1995 America's Cup team. I am grateful for the love of my family, including my late parents, Aunt Martha, sister Laura, brother Mark, and my children, Shayna and Luke. And most important, I thank my husband, John, for his consistent love, support, and encouragement.

Whose Game Is It, Anyway?

INTRODUCTION: Character Counts

A 9-year-old Little League pitcher struggles mightily to hold back his tears. He has just walked a player, with the bases loaded, in the last inning of a one-run ball game in the playoffs. He is close to losing his battle to contain his anger and frustration at the umpire's calls and his humiliation at hearing the cheers and jeers of the opposing team. He had struck out the first two batters with ease, but then the ump made a few questionable calls and now it's crunch time. His father, the coach, has called time and is approaching the mound.

The boy is the team's best pitcher. His arm is a bit tired. He knows the team depends on him, but it is a struggle. He is too young to appreciate that the joy of competition takes place in the midst of that struggle. But deep down he knows he has to dig in, throw some good pitches, and get one more out. The tears quiver but hold at the rim of his eyes. He tugs his cap down low and keeps his eyes locked on his feet, waiting for his father's words. How can the father help his son face this challenge with confidence and spirit?

> Organized sports give children the opportunity to face challenges that will help them learn important lessons about themselves and the world.

Young athletes and their parents face situations like this one every day. This Little League pitcher embodies the worthy struggle that every athlete and, in fact, every person must endure: the attempt to master skill and control emotion in the face of adversity. In this way, organized sports give children the opportunity to face challenges that will help them learn important lessons about themselves and the world.

Some might hope that this young baseball player will use this opportunity to improve his technical skills under pressure — to gain control of his pitches and increase his ability to change both their speed and placement in order to fool the batter. Others might hope that he will learn something about handling adversity: "No matter what, son, keep your cool and be a man about it. There's no crying in baseball." Some parents genuinely might not care about the game itself but only about a son's emotional well-being: "It's okay, son. It's only a silly game. It's no biggie if they hit a walk-off grand slam. Don't be so upset." But others might teach the boy a darker lesson — he must learn to do whatever it takes to succeed, to win. "Son, success in sports and in life is determined by the answer to one question: did you win? That's all people will want to know. Life is unfair and that's the way it is."

What, then, *is* the right thing to say and do? The best response would take into account the child's age, gender, temperament, past history of performance, overall ability, the circumstances of the game, the child's level of fatigue, other problems the child might be experiencing, and his or her current emotional state, just to name a few factors. No magic words will guarantee a triumphant, strikeout performance. In a given situation, a coach or parent might use encouragement, passionate challenge, technical reminder, humorous distraction, sensitive support, or an "it's only a game" defusing of the pressure. However, certain approaches will more likely build confidence, promote a desire to improve, increase our child's overall enjoyment of sports, and reduce the risk of dropping out of athletics. Research clearly demonstrates that children who have fun and enjoy sports generally play longer, work harder at the game, and are more likely to have a productive athletic experience.[1] In the case of the 9-year-old pitcher, a good coach would likely reassure him and try to take some pressure off, perhaps by reminding the boy of a technical component of pitching success, such as

"Remember to lift your front knee above your belt before you push off your back leg." But most important, the best coaches and parents would see a single pitching showdown as a very small piece of a much larger mosaic. They would keep the bigger picture in mind.

Organized sports, perhaps more than any other typical childhood experience, with the possible exception of school, provides ample opportunity for the building of character because of the conflict inherent in competition, the necessary enforcement of rules, the threat of losing, and the demand to control intensely aroused passions. In our culture, parents are likely to be more directly involved in a child's sports activities than in the child's schooling. Sports give us ample opportunity to witness and potentially influence our child's character development as well as athletic progress. We are there when our 8-year-old son slams his batting helmet against the dugout wall after a strikeout, or when our daughter, a high school senior, loses a bitterly contested tennis match despite bravely mustering her best game ever, or when our Pee Wee hockey player taunts the opposition following a game-breaking goal. What, then, shall we do when events like these occur?

Here's where character comes in. The mastery of any sport requires the consistent control of body, mind, and spirit. Over the long haul, success in any endeavor demands the daily application of good habits, or good character traits, if you will. As parents, we should encourage our children to attend practice consistently, listen attentively to the coach, adhere to the rules of the game, and be a positive and supportive teammate. We should emphasize the importance of sacrificing individual accomplishment for the good of the team and controlling emotions and behavior in the face of conflict or potential defeat. Finally, we should remind our child of the importance of persevering and overcoming adversity while mastering a difficult skill, such as hitting a baseball or driving a golf ball straight down the fairway. Thus parents simultaneously promote a strong character and improved athletic performance. These goals are a joint endeavor; a parent must help a child reach them.

Turning a blind eye when our children indulge in behaviors that disrespect coaches, opponents, officials, or fans corrodes the mutual respect that makes the game meaningful. All competition demands that the individual willingly accept the rules and limits of the game. Three strikes and you're out. Hit the ball into the water, and you take a one-stroke penalty. Elbow the other player, and you get two minutes in the penalty box. The successful athlete learns to master the body and the emotions. Character helps us master emotions. When emotions get the best of athletes, they quit, take stupid penalties, skip good training habits, cheat to gain an edge, play for individual glory rather than team goals, and generally lose their cool. Poor character equals poor control and ultimately equals a poor performance.

Emphasizing the commitment to maximum effort, the building of skill and mastery of the game, and the willingness to accept and relish difficult challenges is a sound practice likely to succeed over the long haul. Accurate praise and positive reinforcement, not just for good plays or successful outcomes but also for virtuous behavior, will build skillful, resilient, confident, coachable, team-oriented kids.

As sport psychologists, we believe that striving to excel and win in competition is always important. For competition to bring out our best, wanting to win is vital. However, other crucial factors must balance this drive. One of them is character — caring about doing the right thing. But some Americans might privately say to themselves, "Who knows what 'doing the right thing' means for children? We just want our kids to be happy and successful, and in our society that means winning a lot more than losing." But deep down, we all know that we should care about teaching kids to do the right thing. Lack of character education can lead to destructive, even tragic, consequences, not just in sports but also in life.

As clinical psychologists who deal with depression, trauma, abuse, and emotional turmoil in children, as well as people of all ages, we observe the results of character flaws every day. A visit to the emergency room in any metropolitan hospital in America will demonstrate how flawed character leads to emotional and physical destruction in the form of substance abuse, risky sexual practice, sexual abuse, violence, murder, and suicide. Daily newspapers frequently report stories showing how character defects undermine athletes at a rate that more than keeps pace with the general population.

Character has been defined as "the ability to take rational control of passion or emotion on a consistent and dependable basis."[2] In general, character disorder is associated with an inability to consistently control emotion and behavior in an appropriate, nondestructive way. As parents we must address the character development of our children. Beyond providing food, clothing, shelter, and affection, our most important job is to teach kids right from wrong. The gift of a sound character is the best insurance policy that children can carry into the future.

BUILDING GOOD CHARACTER

A professor recently gave a talk about youth sports and psychology to a graduate school class focused on the sociology of sports. She posed this question: "Do sports build character?" The class, composed mostly of teachers, coaches, and athletic directors, vigorously nodded in assent. "Of course," they responded unanimously.

"But what about all the train-wreck stories you guys know from first-hand experience?" the professor asked. "The stories of childhood made miserable, ranting parents, and teenage athletes who have burned out and lost the joy of the game? What about the strained family relationships or the standards of good behavior sacrificed on the altar of the 'win at any cost' mentality that seems to be our American code of conduct? And finally, what about the attention-grabbing headlines of bad behavior among athletes, parents, and coaches — the hazing, the brawls, the teen steroid use, and the disrespect toward officials, coaches, fans, and the game itself?"

> Accurate praise and positive reinforcement, not just for good plays or successful outcomes but also for virtuous behavior, will build skillful, resilient, confident, coachable, team-oriented kids.

The professor's questioning hit home. The class had fallen into a trap that Americans frequently jump into with both feet — the unquestionable belief that sports are unequivocally good for our kids. Lately, however, horror stories associated with youth sports have given sober-minded adults pause for reassessment.

A particular temptation can undercut the many positive effects of sports: the addictive high that comes from winning. Mix desire for this high with the other emotions that parents feel as their deepest wishes and fears for their children emerge during competition, and you have a potentially dangerous drug. The highs and lows associated with winning and losing can get magnified, and all too often, as parents, coaches, and fans, we find ourselves yelling at 11-year-olds for not acing the serve, or hitting the cutoff man, or nailing that body check, or swishing the jumper. Even those of us who believe ourselves to be free of a "win at any cost" mentality may lose control in this way.

Over a decade ago, the psychologist Philip Cushman commented on the effect that the cultural landscape has on the development of the individual. His observations are still salient today. The self is "empty in part because of the loss of family, community, and tradition. It is a self that seeks the experience of being continually filled up by consuming goods, calories, experiences, politicians, romantic partners, and empathic therapists in an attempt to combat the growing alienation and fragmentation of its era."[3]

At times, parents, their lawyers, and school administrators undermine coaches who are trying to discipline athletes for poor academic performance or violations of the team code of conduct. These young athletes are allowed to indulge in bad behavior because of their ability to contribute to a win. As the cartoon character Pogo used to say, "We have met the enemy, and they is us."

Actually, sports don't build character — people do. Character development requires unselfishness, restraint, thoughtful reflection, and a stilling of the passions. Parenting or coaching to form good character means at times that winning takes a back seat to fairness, safety, the good of the group, and long-term growth. As parents, we must make the joys and lessons of competitive sports readily available to our children without tainting sports with our own unrealistic expectations or emotional outbursts, or those of other adults.

> Good character in a child is painstakingly built through ongoing relationships. No one activity or sport magically confers the reward of good character.

In our experience as psychologists we find that even the best parents and coaches tend to zone out when the terms *good sportsmanship, virtue,* and *good character* are brought up in the context of organized sports. Those ideas have somehow become marginalized as platitudes that everyone publicly acknowledges but have little meaning in the heat of competition. Yet we value the diligence required to stay after practice to do the painful wind sprints that will improve fitness, the discipline required in getting good grades to stay academically eligible, the refusal to cheat by using steroids, the willingness to change positions to improve the team, and the courage to play hard until the last moment in a hopelessly lost contest. Believe it or not, these sports behaviors are all about character.

BALANCING CHARACTER, SKILL DEVELOPMENT, AND FUN

Play is child's work; it's a kid's job to play. It's how they naturally explore, learn, and grow. The essence of good play involves a joyful immersion in activity, with freedom, a lack of critical observation, and even a loss of the sense of time. Organized sports are, in reality, just a serious form of play. Sports structure play; there are rules to obey, skills and positions to learn, and plays to follow. The demands required to become good at any sport, combined with the intensity of competition, introduce our children to the pursuit of excellence. In their demand that children channel their behavior according to rules, organized sports provide a natural place for many life lessons. The hunger for mastery and worthy achievement, the willingness to accept one's own strengths and limitations, as well as the recognition of the needs and rights of others are all crucial aspects of responsible, mature adulthood. Sports can help develop these areas of competence, but it does not happen without guidance, direction, and strength from caring parents and coaches.

Children must be taught. There is a right way and a wrong way to spell, to play the piano, and to swing a baseball bat. The learning of new complex behavior, such as riding a bike, frequently tests the patience, will, and endurance of teacher and pupil alike. However, learning and playing at one's best can coexist with the ability to enjoy the moment. Practice involves discipline, long hours, and hard work, but it also engages joy of movement and freedom of expression. The challenge for all adults involved in youth, high school, and even collegiate sports is to preserve the enjoyment of playing while introducing the structure and discipline of proper teamwork, skill, and technique. Because children are vulnerable and still growing, they need our ongoing help in mastering this struggle.

Yet as parents, we face our own struggles: knowing when to push our child and when to back off, when to stick to principle and when to be flexible, and when to maintain control and when to let go and let a kid simply play. Many of us have heard the following complaint from a 9- or 10-year-old child: "Mom, I don't want to go to practice. I'm too tired." It takes discernment, and some trial and error, to sense when to be firm in honoring a commitment and when to prevent a child from physically and emotionally burning out. As parents, we must live with the anxiety and uncertainty of those decisions while trying to teach our kids the crucial lessons of life yet allow them the freedom to make mistakes.

Today's Youth Sports Culture

The seductive pull of achievement and winning that permeates sports in our society can easily overwhelm entire athletic programs and communities. As a wise parent of five athletes of ages 10 to 22 recently lamented, "This league used to focus on developing good kids who were good athletes. Now we're all about winning regional or state titles. If you can't help them win, they really don't care too much about you. They'll take a kid from another town over one of our own kids if they think it'll help them win." Choosing the right teams and programs for our children is particularly difficult because the sports culture has changed so much since we were kids. We didn't specialize. We didn't have many travel teams. (Travel teams are composed of better players of a town or community who travel to play other town teams. Frequently, tryouts and cuts are required to build these squads.) Many of us didn't start playing organized sports until we were 8 or 9 years old, if then. These days our kids are playing on organized teams as early as age 5. Many of us are not entirely familiar with the myriad teams, programs, and athletic opportunities, nor the administrators and coaches who run them, nor the history or mission of our own town leagues, let alone the specifics of what makes up an elite travel team. This makes decision making harder. Either we follow the tide so our children can participate, or we bail out, leaving our children potentially out of the loop, off the team, and even socially ostracized.

It can be extremely difficult to arrange for children to participate in youth sports on our own terms. Practice times, tournaments, and playing time are dictated to us. Sometimes we feel forced to make painful compromises, such as signing up our children for teams knowing that they won't play as much as we would like, since the alternative seems to be no team at all.

Parents can, however, be more proactive and let their thoughts and feelings be known. Ultimately, our sports culture will take its direction from the decisions of families like our own. If we join with other parents and clearly demand a balanced approach to organized youth sports, others will follow. Parents must see that a child's abilities, level of maturity, and values are recognized and respected by those who train and coach them.

> Sports don't build character — people do.

If we take time to articulate and promote reasons for equal support of skill development and fun in the pursuit of competitive excellence, always honoring our children's physical and emotional needs, the culture will follow.

CONTENDING WITH OUR OWN EMOTIONS

Another challenge to teaching our children how to play well, have fun, and be a good kid is our own emotional baggage, which we parents carry from our past and project onto the future. The desire to see our kids achieve what we ourselves couldn't or didn't often makes it difficult to remain under control. It can be troubling to observe our children perform in a public arena, where they may experience the euphoria of victory, the agony of defeat, the humiliation of publicly making an error, or the pain of injury — they're on display at very vulnerable moments. Competition can also trigger memories and the feelings that accompany them: "That coach sucks; he screwed me my senior year too. Now he's screwing my son." Some parents become vocal and combative as spectators, but others withdraw and watch in isolation, standing off to the side. Others will cheer and use every ounce of emotional energy to support their children. Occasionally, parents can't bear the tension of watching and won't attend competitions at all. Add to the scenario parents' own daily pressures and problems, and you can see how parents and youth sports can become a volatile mix.

In one example of an unhealthy interaction, the parents relentlessly quiz and critique a child in the car, following a game:

> "Why didn't the coach play you more? Did he say anything to you? I don't understand that guy."
> "Why did the ref call that penalty on you? Did you mouth off?"

"Why didn't you shoot more? How come you're not being more aggressive?"

"You looked exhausted out there. Why did you stay up so late last night?"

"You guys played like you didn't even want to win. You're not going to make varsity if you don't get in better shape."

"When are you going to listen to me? I told you repeatedly: you need to work much more on that part of your game."

"Are you feeling okay? You sure didn't look like yourself out there today."

The "post-game quiz and lecture" during the car ride home might not contain twenty questions, but it is one of the corrosive ways in which we, as parents, can suck the joy out of sports for our children. There is no need to list the number of times that otherwise rational parents have overstepped the boundaries of proper behavior in their zeal to protect, promote, or exalt their child in the heat of those competitive fires. Some parents make their displeasure public. In fact, as this introduction is being written, a daily metropolitan tabloid shouts the headline SCHOOL BANS FANS. In this unfortunate incident, parents, players, and fans had engaged in a major brawl following a high school hockey game; subsequently, the athletic director banned all fans from the upcoming rematch. As parents, we must find the will to present ourselves as role models for young athletes. Sometimes the first step is slowing down, catching our breath, and reviewing what we really want our children to experience in sports participation. We can replace the question "Did you win?" with other questions that reveal our values:

"Did you have fun?"
"How did you play?"
"Did you learn anything new?"
"Did you give your best effort?"
"Did you play as a team?"

These emphases give more than lip service to character building.

FAMILY GOALS AND MISSION STATEMENT

One key tool of effective sport psychology for performance enhancement is goal setting—the mapping and measuring of sports success. But even before setting goals, successful athletic departments and sports programs begin with a broad statement of purpose and intent, a mission statement, to guide their goal setting. Parents and children can greatly benefit from a clearly articulated family sports mission statement. The first step is to answer the following questions.

> "When my child is 21 years old, what kind of person do I want him or her to be, and how will sports help us, as parents, get our child there?"
> "What are the three most important virtues or lessons that I want my child to learn through involvement in sports?"

Families might need some courage to articulate their own values and goals for their children. Their idea of sports may run counter to a consumer culture driven by the values of profits and success. The demand for speedy results and instant gratification has certainly colored sports culture. Televised highlights on ESPN's *Sports Center,* where flamboyant individualism and self-promotion are on display, emphasize the glamour of stardom and make fame and fortune look effortless. Exposure to such media, and the advertisements that accompany them, can skew the expectations of young athletes — and even parents. Some families have made extensive, even risky sacrifices of time and money to invest in a child's athletic talent. Painful emotional injuries can follow when results fall short. A well-crafted family sports mission statement can help family members keep their balance in a sports culture that often fails to value character, patient practice, simple pleasures, and the rewards of teamwork.

It takes discernment, and some trial and error, for parents to sense when to be firm in honoring a commitment and when to prevent a child from physically and emotionally burning out.

It's up to parents to choose the virtues that their family will hold most dear, as their family code. The psychologist Kenneth Kaye, in his excellent book *Family Rules,* states a basic tenet simply and elegantly: "responsible behavior earns freedom and privilege."[4] Parents must define what responsible behavior is in their own home and set appropriate, consistent, and fair rules with clear and firm consequences to help kids build good character.

Dr. Kaye challenges parents to start by articulating and prioritizing the values of their particular family. The following list might serve as a starting point.

lifelong health	ability to be a loyal friend
physical fitness	self-control
discipline	ability to sacrifice for others
mastery of skill	compassion for others
pursuit of excellence	honesty
perserverance	integrity
love of competition	courage

Many other possibilities exist as well. For example, the Smiths may value education and therefore give high priority to the completion of homework and good school performance. The Jones family may focus more on completing family chores or family loyalty. Values lay the foundation for a clear, consistent, and fair approach to children's behavior.

In youth sports, certain values are especially important. First, though sports can involve serious play, especially as children get

> "When my child is 21 years old, what kind of person do I want him or her to be, and how will sports help us, as parents, get our child there?"

older, it is play nonetheless. It isn't war. It isn't a life or death matter, and it shouldn't be made into that. But a consideration of values can lead to some sticky questions. Parents may worry that their children must learn to survive in a competitive world that does not forgive setbacks or mistakes, and these parents may push their kids to win at any cost at sports, to toughen them up for life. Yet at the same time, parents may feel uneasy about compromising their values of fairness and sportsmanship. We believe parents don't need to make this compromise.

What about families whose first priority is to see their children become collegiate or professional athletes? For some families facing economic hardship and limited opportunities, athletic talent may seem to be the ticket to higher education and economic success; rags-to-riches stories apparently abound in the world of sports. However, the odds are long indeed on even getting an athletic scholarship at college, let alone becoming a professional athlete. The National Alliance for Youth Sports cites this statistic: less than 1 percent of high school athletes receive any form of athletic scholarship.[5] Gambling the happiness of children on their athletic talents is a huge risk. Investing in strong character is far likelier to offer a healthy return.

All too often, parents, coaches, and fans find themselves yelling at 11-year-olds for not acing the serve, or hitting the cutoff man, or nailing that body check.

Ultimately, raising a healthy child who demonstrates good character is neither immediately gratifying nor guaranteed. We know it cannot be purchased. It cannot be measured by daily results like some sort of stock report. The path to this goal is neither easy nor well traveled. We have to live with and manage our own anxieties, disappointments, fears, and frustrations while staying the course with our children.

PART ONE

KNOWING
YOUR CHILD ATHLETE

1

Your Child's Development
and the Three-Step Approach

MOST OF US don't like being defined by just one aspect of our lives. We are not just "John the plumber" or "Mary the lawyer" or "Billy's sister." Our relationships with friends and family, our spiritual beliefs, our political views, our jobs, our bodies, and our interests and activities outside the workplace form crucial components of our identity. Being mindful of this complex variety of roles in a child's life is an essential part of parenting. Our kids are sons and daughters, brothers and sisters, grandchildren, cousins, friends, students, neighbors, citizens of communities, members of religious congregations, budding artists and musicians, future voters, as well as ath-

letes. We must be vigilant to ensure their growth as a whole person, physically, psychologically, and socially. Too much emphasis on any single aspect of a child's life can cause instability and difficulty.

> Too much emphasis on any single aspect of a child's life can cause instability.

To a far greater degree than mature adults, children are biological, psychological, and social works in progress. Good parenting involves a solid, at times intuitive grasp of what children can handle physically, emotionally, and mentally at a given age. We don't expect 8-year-olds to enroll in algebra classes, we don't allow 12-year-olds to drive, and we wouldn't expect a 6-year-old to baby-sit for a 6-month-old infant. We understand that growing bodies, developing minds, and evolving egos can only gradually accept greater, more complex challenges. Unfortunately, this understanding of child development sometimes gets lost in the pursuit of athletic goals.

17

A coach can become exasperated at a 9-year-old quarterback who doesn't remember the play that the coach yelled from the sideline only if that coach fails to understand that a 9-year-old's ability to memorize a string of terms (such as "Pro set left, Z out, slam 36, on 2") is not yet well developed. That coach is ignorant of the developmental realities of the age group he is coaching; he misapplies adult norms of behavior to the bodies, minds, and psyches of youth. This mistake can have sad consequences.

One of the most celebrated cases of misunderstood childhood development involved Todd Marinovich. From birth, Todd's father raised his son to be an NFL quarterback. Todd received rigorous instruction and training throughout his childhood and adolescence. He was forbidden to drink soft drinks or eat fast food. His father carefully scripted his life, controlling Todd's daily schedule and hiring consultants to provide state-of-the-art advice regarding nutrition and physical conditioning.

> By age 10, Todd was working with a throwing coach and weight-lifting became part of his pre-teen preparation to become a professional quarterback. He had the arm and the size, but ultimately he did not have the character. For a while, his father's champion-building strategy worked. Todd set a national record with 9,194 passing yards while at Capistrano Valley High in Mission Viejo, which led him to a scholarship to play quarterback for USC, where he was arrested for drug charges and suspended from the team twice. He was eventually drafted by the Raiders and played one season before his drug problems ended his career. For parents who like to see their children get involved in athletics, the lesson learned of Marinovich is to focus on the character building, not the champion building.[1]

Later, Todd Marinovich was arrested on drug-related charges.

Like Tiger Woods, who was trained in his sport from an early age by his father, the story of Todd Marinovich represents an extreme case. Not every kid who gets pushed too hard will end up like Todd, just as every kid who gets intense specialized instruction will not become a Tiger Woods. But the story still offers an important cautionary tale: as parents, we easily see the future Tiger but overlook the more likely Todd. Yet there is a way to help our children get the most out of sports without sacrificing their emotional development and the values a family holds dear. We can start by gaining an understanding of their specific needs at different ages and stages.

THE THREE-STEP APPROACH

Our three-step approach to navigating youth sports is derived from the developmental approach we just described. The three basic steps are (1) know your child, (2) know yourself, and (3) know your child's sports environment. This process reviews the physical, emotional, and social landscape of our children, our parenting, and our sports community. The steps sound deceptively simple, yet they can map pathways to athletic excellence, emotional health, character building, and real teamwork and community spirit. These steps need not be taken in a specific order; rather, the three areas of observation and reflection will together produce positive results over time.

Know Your Child

Understanding the unique needs and abilities of each child is essential. This knowledge should include appreciation for the biological, psychological, and social realities of his or her life. No two children are alike. One 8-year-old daughter may thrive on a Pop Warner football team, while her 10-year-old sister worries more about how her hair looks as a member of the cheerleaders. One brother may embrace the individual challenge of golf or tennis, while another may thrive on the speed and hitting of lacrosse. An individual's interests may also change as time passes. A rabid baseball player at ages 6 through 12 might drop the sport altogether at age 13 or 14. A child who felt extraordinarily exposed, self-conscious, and vulnerable in the water at 2 years of age might be a totally carefree water lover by age 5. Kids are different, and their abilities and interests change over time.

When taking a child to the first day of school or, more pertinently, the first day of mini-hockey, swim class, T-ball, or mini-soccer, parents might make faulty generalizations and set expectations based on these initial encounters.

> "Trevor didn't really get in there and act as enthusiastically as his cousin did last year, so maybe he's just not as athletic."
> "Jenny got grouped with the less talented kids; it looks like she'll always be in the slow group, and they get less attention."

"Manny was dominating; maybe we should get him into an accelerated program."

Yet many factors influence a child's behavior on a given occasion. Temperament, place in the family, the ebb and flow of the day, how much sleep the child got the night before, and whether friends are present are just a few possible influences. The child might behave quite differently on another day. Observant parents learn to revise their interpretations of a child's actions. As a child grows in mastery of a skill, a parent may raise the level of challenge. When a child shows frustration or fatigue, the parent may introduce fun or soothing activities, always attuned to the child's level of development and unique characteristics. They do not treat children as mini-adults or as some idealized perfect child they would prefer to deal with. They come to know the reality of the precious person whom they love.

Though specific developmental markers can help parents gauge their children's growth, the markers do not appear in a uniform, lockstep way. For example, boys don't slowly and incrementally grow adult facial hair in a predictable pattern from ages 6 through 14.

> We don't expect 8-year-olds to enroll in algebra classes, we don't allow 12-year-olds to drive, and we wouldn't expect a 6-year-old to baby-sit a 6-month-old infant.

Puberty bursts on the scene with relative quickness, biologically speaking, and brings a host of changes, including peach fuzz and then stubble. Likewise, certain athletic skills run parallel to certain stages of development; they can't be introduced earlier. For example, prior to puberty, lifting weights will not increase muscle mass in boys because that result requires the increase in testosterone that accompanies puberty. A misguided program for prepubescent boys, which attempts to increase boys' strength by building muscle mass with a scaled-down, "mini-adult" version of weight-training principles, will not only fail, but also risk injury.[2] Kids are not just smaller than adults; they are physiologically and psychologically different.

To measure your child's emotional health, consider these areas individually: confidence, judgment, interests, relationships, emotional control, and sports-related skills. Each will help you know your child better. In a way, it will complicate how you think about him or her and avoid simplistic, black or white answers. The "one size fits all" book of parenting rarely works over the long term, and few pat answers universally apply to all children. A focus on core abilities — essential skills — will help in negotiating children's different ages and different stages. The chapters on specific developmental stages will explore these categories in more depth.

CONFIDENCE

Confidence is our children's hopeful belief that they are capable of acting successfully on their own behalf. Some psychologists refer to this as a sense of agency: "I can be an effective agent of action for myself" or "I'm pretty sure I can do this." This differs from self-esteem ("I feel pretty good about myself"). This active, positive, and hope-filled view helps our children face challenges and uncertainties. Competitive youth and high school sports provide numerous opportunities to build up or tear down this core ability. Whether a kid hears "Great effort, you're really hustling!" or "Another mistake! What the hell is wrong with you?" will strongly affect his or her experience. Confidence comes from increased exposure to and mastery of a task. Good Little League coaches have their favorite story of the persistent player who didn't get a base hit until the very end of the season and beamed the broadest smile imaginable when that hit finally came. When we as parents and coaches focus on positively rewarding effort and skill building, we set the stage for growth in our children's confidence.

> Know your child, know yourself, and know your child's sports environment.

JUDGMENT

This is the age-appropriate ability to do, learn, and know what's right and wrong; to know what is safe, correct, or morally right; and to know whom to trust in times of need, stress, or threat. The growth of cognitive abilities resulting from normal brain development plays a major role in the acquisition of judgment. Parents and coaches easily lose sight of what our kids can effectively handle, judgmentwise, at different ages. We can't expect a 10-year-old quarterback to "read" the field the same way a 20-year-old would. Judgment develops over time.

INTERESTS

Our children, even as infants, naturally seek physical and intellectual stimulation and increased mastery over both their bodies and objects in the world. As our children grow and attend school, their interests and competencies explode. It is their job to play, learn, and take delight as their abilities increase in different activities. Sports should be viewed as just one of these rich areas of exploration and discovery. Even if we as parents passionately enjoy watching our children compete, increasing sports activity is not always best. We wouldn't limit our children to math classes only even if they showed great promise in addition and subtraction. Similarly, a narrow focus on one sport can be detrimental; instead, allow kids to explore sports in general. Moreover, having a variety of activities and interests stimulates brain growth in ways we are just beginning to understand. The parent who balks at a child's request to take up the drums or some other musical instrument might want to consider this. Taking those drum lessons might increase intelligence and skill in areas that have a direct impact on athletic functioning as well as the overall development of the child.

> Kids are not just smaller adults; they are physiologically and psychologically different.

RELATIONSHIPS

The age-appropriate ability to successfully interact with and be emotionally connected to parents, siblings, teachers, friends, and coaches and other authority figures is perhaps the most vital skill of all. The emphases of these relationships will change as our children grow. Sports afford opportunities for both positive and negative experiences in building our children's interpersonal abilities. We as parents must faithfully pay attention to how our kids, and we ourselves, treat teammates, coaches, opponents, fans, and officials, because relationships are the ultimate testing ground of character. Likewise, we must consider how we allow our children to be treated. Do we tolerate a verbally abusive, sadistic coach because he is a winner and will improve our daughter's or son's chance for a college scholarship? If so, at what age, or in what circumstances, might such coaching behavior *not* be tolerable? What do we say to our daughter when the star player on her team is given preferential treatment and allowed to break the rules? Our child's capacity for successfully dealing with other people may be the single most important aspect of his or her growth and deserves ongoing attention.

EMOTIONAL CONTROL

Judgment allows us to learn and eventually know what is right, safe, and moral. Emotional control is the capacity for restraint and discipline that allows us to get our needs met without resorting to inappropriate or even destructive behavior. Self-soothing — that is, self-initiated and self-controlled behaviors that reliably and appropriately reduce tension and stress — is a facet of emotional control. Not all self-soothing behaviors (such as use of drugs and alcohol) are healthy or appropriate. Skills in emotional control are acquired through observation, an enriched, caring environment, and good parenting and teaching. As our children mature, they must exercise greater control in more complex situations. What do they do when they get hit with a cheap shot? Do they smash their batting helmet into the dugout when they strike out? How do they handle an umpire or referee who gets in their face? If a coach unfairly benches them, how do they act? For both adults and children, competition routinely tests the ability to control emotions.

SPORTS-RELATED SKILLS

Biological, psychological, and social aspects of child development directly relate to participation and performance in athletics. Until they reach a state of "developmental readiness," kids cannot perform certain physical and cognitive tasks. Also, talents emerge at different ages — children do not have a fully developed adult brain until well after age 18. Mental facility also changes over time.

QUESTIONS FOR KNOWING YOUR CHILD

Here are some key questions that parents should address about their child when contemplating his or her involvement in sports.

1. How does my child approach new experiences and people?
2. How is my child faring in the six essential skills (confidence, interests, relationships, judgment, emotional control, sports-related skills)?
3. How does my child compare with peers in regard to size, speed, coordination, strength, and sports skill?

4. Is my child improving in relation to his or her peers in the development of physical abilities? Is my child falling behind or leveling out?
5. What is my child's usual activity level?
6. How well does my child accept limits and take instruction?
7. What is my child's learning style? Is my child a doer or a listener? How coachable is my child?
8. What are my child's attention span and level of distractibility?
9. How well does my child transition from one activity to another?
10. How well does my child get along with peers?
11. Can my child ask for help when it's needed? Can he or she speak up to get needs met?
12. How well can my child contain anger, frustration, or disappointment? What self-soothing skills does he or she have?
13. What are my child's interests outside of sports?
14. How balanced is my child's range of activities (including schoolwork, time with friends, and sports and other interests)?
15. How often does my child complain about participation in certain activities?

Know Yourself

A well-respected psychologist we know often uses the following pet statement: "Psychologically speaking, we're all six-foot bodies trying to stay warm with a four-foot blanket." No one successfully deals with all their emotional needs and conflicts; we all have unresolved emotional wounds. When these hurts lie buried and undetected, they can cloud our ability as parents to see our child's present needs. If those hurts touch on issues of achievement, physical ability, and competency, they can blur our vision of our children, triggering what Dr. Dan Siegel calls the "low road approach." Dr. Siegel states, "In the absence of reflection, history often repeats itself, and parents are vulnerable to passing on to their children unhealthy patterns from the past."[3] An unconscious, impulsive, emotional overreaction can result in irritable, unproductive interactions between parent and child, parent and coach, parent and official, parent and administrator, or parent and parent. Unrecognized emotional

> "Psychologically speaking, we're all six-foot bodies trying to stay warm with a four-foot blanket."

baggage is the likely culprit in situations where adults react in over-the-top, explosive, destructive ways during youth sports events. As parents, we serve our children and ourselves well by becoming aware of our own emotional history, particularly as it pertains to issues of competition, achievement, and athletics.

QUESTIONS FOR KNOWING YOURSELF

Here are some key questions that parents should address about themselves when reviewing and assessing their child's involvement in sports.

1. Can I articulate my ultimate goals for my child's sports participation?
2. What character traits do I want my child to demonstrate by age 21?
3. Have my spouse or partner and I discussed and agreed upon an overall philosophy of sports participation for our child?
4. Have I defined three to five virtues that I see as essential to a positive sports experience for my child?
5. What sports-related behavior or event (such as showing apathy, crying, unfair outcome, unfair playing time, physical threat or injury, errors, defeat) sets me off emotionally?
6. Can I link anything in my own past to the child's behavior that sets off these feelings?
7. Here's how I rate my own sports experience as a child, adolescent, and adult (0 = lowest satisfaction; 10 = highest):
   Before age 6 _____ ; ages 6–12 _____ ; ages 13–18 _____ ; ages 19–22 _____ ;
   ages 23–30 _____ ; ages 31–40 _____ ; age 41+ _____
   For ratings under 4, describe the circumstances of the poor sports experiences.
8. What was my best experience in sports? What factors made it rewarding and positive? What good parts of my experience can be handed down to my children?
9. Do I have a family history of depression, substance abuse, anxiety disorder, panic attacks, attention deficit disorder, or learning problems?
10. Is anything happening in family life that causes significant stress for any family member (job loss, move, separation/divorce, death of relative or friend, loss of friend, problem at school, problem with boyfriend or girlfriend, transition to new school or phase of life, death of pet, drug or alcohol use)?

Know Your Child's Sports Environment

No child is raised in a vacuum, and no family is immune to the positive and negative effects of the wider culture. As we've noted, our society places an unhealthy emphasis on immediate gratification, speed, convenience, and outcomes that benefit the individual at the expense of the group, and there is an addictive quality to this desire for instant, total satisfaction. Sports are deeply affected by this trend. Even in youth and high school sports, cheating, steroids, rage at umpires and referees, and out-of-control fans can overwhelm the positive aspects of athletic competition.

> As parents, we serve our children and ourselves well by becoming aware of our own emotional history.

We must know the community we live in and its approach to sports. Inquire about sports activity programs just as diligently as you would ask about the quality of schools or houses of worship in a town. It's easier to accomplish the goals of your family mission when other parents and coaches are like-minded. It's worth the effort to find the right sports programs, coaches, administrators, and fellow parents.

QUESTIONS FOR KNOWING YOUR CHILD'S SPORTS ENVIRONMENT

Here are some key questions that parents should address about sports programs when reviewing and assessing their child's involvement in sports.

1. Does the program have a mission statement? Does it include the promotion of virtue or values? How specific is it?
2. Is there an explanation of how the program implements its goals?
3. Do clear policies address playing time, physical and emotional safety, skill building, and disciplinary matters? Are the rules clearly stated and consistently enforced?
4. By what mechanism is new leadership, ideas, or policies considered and implemented in the league, activity, or team?
5. What do other parents (past and current) say about their children's involvement in the program?
6. Does the program regularly screen coaches by implementing background checks?

7. How much emphasis is placed on championship banners, trophy displays, and travel team awards? What type of behavior does the program formally reward? Is most of the formal recognition given for winning, performance, and achievement?

8. Observe a game or practice unannounced. How much fun do the participants seem to be having?

9. How organized, knowledgeable, accessible, and emotionally in control are the coach and the administrators of the league? Is there a mechanism for certification or upgrading of coaching skill?

10. What's the retention rate of eligible players returning to the activity or program from season to season?

THE THREE-STEP APPROACH IN ACTION

Kat, a 14-year-old highly ranked tennis player, groans as she realizes her next match in the tournament is against her best friend. She turns to face her mom with a look that practically accuses her mother of high treason. This is the one sports situation that causes sheer panic for Kat. Although she recognizes that she is a better player than her friend, Kat always plays her worst against her. She can't really find the words to explain it, but the gnawing in the pit of her stomach speaks volumes. Kat hates to lose and really hates to play poorly, but this is her best friend, and it's just so hard to beat her. Kat's mother gets tense, fearing an angry, racket-breaking tantrum; she hates these situations as well. "This is not what sports should be about . . . fear and loathing at the net," she says to herself. "It's supposed to be fun." Kat's father fumes and mutters with a clenched jaw, "Just go out and beat her!" Their daughter struggles about whether to beg off, using a phantom injury as an excuse.

> Confidence comes from increased exposure to and mastery of a task.

> It is children's job to play, learn, and take delight as their abilities increase in different activities.

The three-step approach breaks down this complicated, painful situation into three manageable areas. First, *know your child*. What particulars of temperament and ability, risk factors, and extenuating circumstances exist for this girl? Kat is 14 years old. For most female athletes at this age, the tension between maintaining close friendships and competing at one's best is a common hot-button issue. Some girls will tank a performance on purpose rather than jeopardize a close friendship. For a girl saddled with a limited social network or an anxious temperament, this scenario is more loaded and might contribute to a loss of emotional control or confidence. Informed parents might find a way to limit the amount of direct competition with friends their daughter must face by temporarily switching their daughter's club affiliation or playing venue. They also might implement supportive strategies, based on sound sport psychology, for bolstering their daughter's confidence and ability to control her emotions.

> Our child's capacity for successfully dealing with other people may be the single most important aspect of his or her growth.

Second, *know yourself.* What circumstances are the parents facing in this situation? Are there emotional, logistical, financial, or other causes for concern? For example, parents who have unresolved emotional baggage (such as an intense sibling rivalry between the mother and her sister during their teens) might have a hard time recognizing their own investment in seeing their daughter beat her friend. If the parents have devoted considerable time, energy, and money to their daughter's training, they may have a difficult time when she experiences a dip in performance, especially if the problem seems related to emotional issues. Identifying our own emotions can free us to see our child's situation more clearly. It can allow us as parents to reassess whether possible solutions to the performance slump are in keeping with the family mission statement outlining what truly matters in sports.

Third, *know your child's sports environment.* What is the nature of the program and those who run it and participate in it? Is it an elite program, in which winning is the only focus? Is it a nurturing program, done just for fun? Does it promote mastery and skill building in both tennis and relationships? Some coaches have sophisticated insight about a young teen's needs; they might be more adept than others at helping female athletes work through issues of competition and friendship. This knowledge can help parents tailor the right fit for their child and facilitate development of ability and character.

2

THE EARLY YEARS (AGES 1–5)

Safety and the Joy of Movement

MANY OF OUR PARENTS and grandparents would likely dismiss the very idea of organized sports for preschool children. Our grandparents might say something like this: "In my day, we'd take a baseball bat and a ball and go down to the park and play until our mothers called us home for supper! But we didn't do that until we were 7 or 8 years old. The younger kids played in the backyard at home and stayed with their mothers, where they belonged. We didn't need organized sports to teach us how to play and have fun."

There may well be great wisdom in these words of our elders, making us long for simpler bygone days. As parents today, we are faced with a more complex and competitive set of circumstances. As the intensity of competition increases in all areas of life, from the business world to college admissions, the trickle-down effect is felt during high school, grammar school, and even preschool. As parents, we feel pressured to expose our children, at the earliest possible age, to the best training and broadest range of experience available. So if we enroll our children in French immersion classes at age 3 or piano lessons at age 4 (and some scientific evidence suggests that there may be some benefit to such practices), doesn't it make sense to look for ways for children to get an early jump on athletic development? If swinging golf clubs at an early age worked for Tiger Woods, couldn't it work for our sons and daughters? It's natural for us as parents to seriously search for the athletic equivalent to the Head Start program.

> "In my day, . . . we didn't need organized sports to teach us how to play and have fun."

Indeed, this book contends that we can help our children begin with a strong foundation for life in and out of sports. However, the means for doing this are not always obvious, nor are they always what we would intuitively expect. As we have noted, our fast-food culture, with its emphasis on immediate results and instant gratification, does not always provide the building blocks of strong character and a robust athletic life. The process of fostering these capacities really does start when our children are very young, and it's up to us to lay the groundwork. Consciously or not, we as parents set in motion patterns and expectations that could affect our children for years to come.

Children of ages 1–5 undergo a bewildering amount of growth and face a wide range of challenges. What are their most essential needs? If we can articulate them, then we can create a sports environment specifically attuned to our children.

Typically, the basic needs related to trust and control characterize this period in a child's life. Trust is important because children are so vulnerable at this age and completely rely on their parents to provide, protect, and guide. The consistent loving presence of us as parents gives our child a foundation for growing up to be emotionally healthy. Predictable, comfortable routine and our practice of consistent good habits will build our child's trust: "When I'm thirsty, Mommy brings me a drink. When it's bedtime, Daddy reads me a story; then I brush my teeth, say my prayers, and go to bed with my teddy bear. Mommy and Daddy kiss me good night, and then I wake up and see them in the morning."

That predictable routine forms a bedrock of trust that frees a child to start to master the basics of physical and emotional development and self-control. Exercising control is another focus of children at this age. With their explosive growth in the ability to move their bodies and to speak, the motto of this age group could be "I did it!" The learning of new skills also entails a fair amount of trial and error, accompanied by emotional ups and downs, including experiences of stubbornness, fear, and frustration.

> The consistent loving presence of parents gives children a foundation for growing up to be emotionally healthy people.

Consider Brian Martin, a 2½-year-old boy who hates going to the swimming pool. Everyone else in his family, including his 5-year-old sister and his parents, loves swimming; it is the family's main recreational activity. Brian's refusal to get into the pool has caused tension, particularly between his mother and father. Both parents have tried coaxing, bribing, and literally forcing Brian into the pool. But he has become

> "Watch me, Mom! Watch me, Dad! Watch me do this!"

even more entrenched in his attitude, ready to throw a tantrum at the mere suggestion of taking a swim. The Martins feel as if Brian is ruining a favorite family activity. They can't decide whether to push him through this aspect of the "terrible twos" or give up on the family swim. (During the "terrible twos" children want to exercise control, and parents' best efforts can't always get them to comply in trying new activities.)

By contrast, some young children refuse to accept normal limits and reasonable caution. Four-year-old Tyler Austin is that type of go-go dynamo. He never stops moving full throttle, rarely putting on the brakes. He appears fearless, having a high threshold of pain; he rarely cries after head bangs and body crashes. Ty has a relentless desire to play, and to play *his* way. Ty's father revels in his son's brave, physically tough, adventuresome spirit, but his mother fears that Tyler gets too aggressive too quickly and too much. She cringes at the level of physical intensity that Tyler seems to crave and worries that he is going to hurt someone. Broaching the topic with her husband often results in a dismissal of her concerns or an argument. Is Tyler's mom overly concerned?

What about the child who is neither stubborn nor overly active but simply not active enough — the child who appears timid and hesitant? Wendy Thomas is a painfully shy wisp of a girl, considerably tiny for her age. Her mother enrolled Wendy in the community soccer program, which has competition for ages 5–7. Wendy is 5 years old. Shy and anxious, she barely utters a word at practice. The coaches have to make a special effort to get her to even attempt to kick the ball or run. In games she generally stands rigidly in one spot. Her mother wonders whether she's being unfair by insisting that Wendy participate, but she is equally worried that allowing Wendy to quit will teach her that quitting is a way to avoid tough challenges.

How do we as parents help children like Brian, Tyler, and Wendy? Each has an experience fairly common to his or her age group, which is entering the world of organized sports for the first time. We as parents must take many new variables into account. What types of behavior should we insist upon? What limits should we set, and what questions should we seek to answer? The following section may help illuminate the way.

ESSENTIAL SKILLS FOR CHILDREN OF AGES 1–5

From searching for the correct word, to walking up and down the stairs, to no longer needing diapers, small children relish mastering their bodies and the world about them. They can also become frustrated at the trials and tribulations associated with the many challenges they face: learning a language, mastering toilet training, getting dressed, using eating utensils, walking, running, learning to use hands for drawing with crayons and playing with toys, going to preschool, and sharing toys with others. As the psychologist Erik Erikson often noted, a basic sense of trust and a basic sense of control and mastery are the goals for this age group.[1]

Confidence

"Let me do it myself, Mom!" is an exclamation heard early and often in a child's life. Children take great pride and joy in basic accomplishments, and they look for constant parental approval and praise. Parents often hear their child excitedly call out, "Watch me, Mom! Watch me, Dad! Watch me do this!"

As good parents, we clear the path of potential obstacles as our toddler wobbles and falls repeatedly while learning to walk. It takes great patience and it's time consuming, but we provide whatever support is needed so that our child can gain confidence and skill.

Confidence is a rope woven from several cords, including children's biological strengths and weaknesses and what they experience psychologically and socially as they grow, and these differ a great deal among children, as the examples of Brian, Tyler, and Wendy show. Some children, like Tyler, are born with a sense of fearlessness and a high need for physical activity. Others, like Wendy, are physically and emotionally sensitive. Most children are more like Brian, somewhere in the middle level of confidence. With time, support, trial and error, and the scaffolding provided by good parents and teachers, most children grow confident that they can master the skills they need to survive and thrive.

Interests

Children of this age group are naturally preoccupied with their own bodies, sensations, perceptions, and will. It's natural for them to be egocentric. Through love and care, they become socialized and attuned to pleasing their parents. However, their focus is centered on mastering basic body functions and skills. Walking, running, talking, controlling bladder and bowels, getting dressed independently, and transitioning from a crib to a bed are special areas of interest at 2 and 3 years of age. In fact, Brian's dislike of swimming may be related to discomfort about not having completely mastered bowel and bladder control just yet; he is not developmentally ready for this element of the swimming experience. Just because siblings or same-age peers might appear to enjoy an activity such as swimming, skating, roughhouse wrestling, or climbing high on the playground jungle gym does not mean that another child will, or should, easily take to these activities.

Children of this age group are also interested in what feels immediately pleasurable, and some typical recreational activities aren't. Many require the ability to tolerate and overcome fear, lack of control, the sense of being vulnerable or physically exposed, and other physical or emotional discomforts. For example, when learning to swim, children have to overcome the unpleasant sensations caused by swallowing water or breathing it in through the nose, holding the breath underwater, and the fear of sinking. When learning to ice-skate or ski, children have to deal with hard falls, feeling cold, lack of control over feet and legs, the discomfort of wearing helmets and bulky snow pants, and the inevitable missing glove or mitten! Even wearing a baseball glove or a football helmet for the first few times can cause uneasiness. Should we be surprised that our children might not initially find these activities tons of fun? Sometimes our kids require time to adjust. Certainly at this young age they need an abundance of patience, confident support, and unflagging encouragement.

For older children in this age group, transitioning from home to nursery school and kindergarten and further mastering language skills to set the stage for reading are not just developmental tasks affecting their sense of safety and control but also major areas of interest. While they might fear the unknown, older children in this age group also can delight in their accomplishments as they demonstrate to themselves and to parents that they did it! "I'm a big boy now, Dad. I'm going to school!"

Relationships

For children at this age, relationships are all about Mom and Dad. Both boys and girls start by being more focused on Mom, the original source of warmth, protection, and food, and that bond changes only gradually. Fathers can feel a bit left out because infants, toddlers, and preschoolers seem to prefer their mothers, particularly when they feel stressed. The plaintive cry "I WANT MOMMY" isn't always what dads want to hear. (Sometimes mothers flinch too.) The fathers of Brian and Tyler focused on their son's ability to act physically and assertively without fear. Therefore Brian's fear of swimming and his desire to stay close to his mom and far from the pool might be especially galling to his father, who might misinterpret this behavior as an indicator that Brian will grow up "soft." Not to worry. Early in this stage, oppositional, rigid behavior toward parents is quite normal, as is preference for Mom. As they reach ages 4 and 5, children will become more invested in pleasing and imitating the parent of the same sex, frequently adopting their mother's or father's behaviors as well as their likes and dislikes: "Look, Mom, I have a baseball glove just like Dad's." Parent-child relationships evolve a lot in a child's early years.

Judgment

Children at this age rely solely on their parents for guidance and protection. They can't tell the difference between good and bad and certainly can't differentiate between rules of basic safety (such as "Do not put your hand near that hot stove!"), rules that aren't crucial to physical safety but are important to health (such as "Eat up your vegetables!"), and simple parental statements of preference (such as "Put on your red coat because it looks so much better!"). Children cannot make adult judgments. They are supremely egocentric at this age. Furthermore, if they *feel* bad, then they conclude that they *are* bad. Recall that Wendy, our reluctant soccer player, consistently appears miserable on the field. It is likely that in turn she feels miserable about *herself.* Feeling bad does not build trust and confidence. Rather, it leads to outbursts or avoidance behaviors meant to make the bad feeling go away. Adults must see that such negative self-assessments are countered, not reinforced. Small children don't yet have the judgment to do this for themselves.

Emotional Control

Since children at this age are struggling to master basic control of their little bodies, it stands to reason that they struggle even more to control their emotions. Although children can experience great pride and joy in their accomplishments and triumphs, they also experience heaping doses of frustration. Children can be overwhelmed and fatigued by the amount of trial-and-error learning in their daily lives. For most children, meltdowns and difficulties arising from loss of emotional control are short-lived. Persistent problems that occur regardless of time of day, situation, the child's level of fatigue, or the people involved may indicate that something is amiss with the ability to pay attention and appropriately control behavior. But most parents learn to identify, anticipate, and avoid their child's emotional meltdowns, recognizing them as the byproduct of a long day of bumps, bruises, spills, admonishments, frustrations, and missed naps. Children rely on their parents' ability to control their own emotions as well as create a reassuring environment of predictable routine and soothing habit. This structure sets the stage for a child to gain greater control over emotions and related behavior.

Sports-Related Skills

Remember one word, *JOY!* It is sheer joy to master the ability to run and jump and slide and skip and do all kinds of neat things with the body. As parents, we need to avoid deflating the joy of glorious movement. Providing experiences that are fun will ensure that memories and thoughts associated with swimming, skating, playing catch, climbing, wrestling, and all sports-related activities are pleasant ones. If after several attempts on several different days with some gentle coaxing and prodding, a young 2- to 4-year-old clearly seems miserable in the pool or swinging the Wiffle bat or falling all over the ice on skates, then we as parents might wisely give it a rest, switch to a less-conflict-ridden activity, and revisit the sport or activity in question at a later date. Don't worry about teaching a small child perfect or even the basic form of a new skill; just keep it simple and keep it fun.

In terms of reasonable expectations regarding sports skills, early in this stage, children should be able to run and kick a ball. Through ages 2 and 3 they progress to riding a tricycle, jumping off steps, and climbing. Through ages 3 and 4, children may engage in some cooperative play with other children. By ages 4 and 5 children may spontaneously engage in competitive play and tend to prefer play that is (as they see it) appropriate to their gender. Children can vary greatly in the acquisition of these skills.

A Closer Look: Wendy, the Anxious Soccer Player

Wendy, the reluctant 5-year-old soccer player, remains painfully anxious. Gretchen, Wendy's mother, is a single parent who has recently ended a difficult relationship with her husband, a man who was not Wendy's biological father; Wendy's father left shortly after her birth and has had no contact with his daughter. Gretchen agonizes over her daughter's welfare. At times, she struggles with guilt about her recent separation as well as other aspects of Wendy's history but feels that she has done what's best for both herself and her daughter. Gretchen has observed that Wendy frequently gets a stomachache or headache when it's time for a soccer practice or game. Games especially seem to be a source of anxiety, and Wendy frequently just refuses to play. Gretchen wonders whether it is right to force Wendy to continue with soccer. She is pained by her daughter's anxiety and is determined to help Wendy become more resilient.

> Children are supremely egocentric at this age. If they *feel* bad, then they conclude that they *are* bad.

Know Your Child

Some children are temperamentally ill-suited to competitive sports, at least early in life. It may make them feel vulnerable, expose their fragility, and amount to an exercise in fear and shame. Wendy's level of anxiety and shyness indicates that she may be one of those children. Competitive team sports are not for everyone and certainly not a requirement for a 5-year-old. Many other avenues exist for learning to appreciate physical activity and gain confidence. At age 5, Wendy has plenty of time to learn those lessons. Her shyness and anxiety affect her participation in several activities, not just soccer, and have persisted from an early age. Those plaintive cries before literally every practice and game — "Do I have to, Mom? Do I have to go?" — are heart wrenching and would cause any parents to question themselves. At this young age, it is unlikely that being on this soccer team will magically increase Wendy's hardiness. Given the physical complaints associated with playing, her grim and frightened demeanor, and her lack of meaningful participation, this activity does not seem to be in her best interest. Continued forced participation runs the risk of increasing her anxiety, her sense of isolation, and her future aversion to anything resembling sports or physical activity.

As parents, we frequently wish to impart the important lesson of finishing something that has been started. In general, this is a worthy guideline, but it must be applied judiciously. Many children at this age feel a good deal of anxiety prior to a new experience. Tears or displays of anger may accompany this phase. The anxiety may be likened to the first day of school, which requires for most children a major emotional adjustment. We parents need to reassure our children that

Competitive team sports are not for everyone and certainly not a requirement for a 5-year-old.

they can master the new task or experience. However, some children do not naturally transition out of this state of unhappiness and anxiety. Sometimes, for some children, leaving a sport, team, or activity is necessary to protect their physical health and emotional well-being. Despite the best intentions, sometimes the fit between a child and a sport, team, coach, or program simply isn't right. A pattern of persistent unhappiness, physical complaints, attempts to avoid the activity, angry or tearful outbursts, a total lack of enjoyment in any aspect of the activity (even the social off-the-field friendships), or minimal participation over a two- to three-week period suggests that the child may be in a "bad fit" situation. This intensity of negative feeling stands in contrast to the temporary emotional difficulty children may experience while working through initial anxiety about trying something new.

It's worth noting that sensitivity is not a negative trait. It does not necessarily go hand in hand with weakness or being "thin skinned." It can be a strength in developing empathy for others and creating compassionate relationships; many people with artistic talent would describe themselves as sensitive. Parents of a child who is physically and emotionally sensitive should make a special effort to find an enjoyable sports experience for him or her.

Know Yourself

Wendy's mom has just endured an extremely difficult emotional trial and transition. Possibly she has been sensitized to her daughter's anxiety and fear due to recent events. The mother may hope that Wendy's success in soccer will confirm that "all is well" after this emotional upheaval. Also, Gretchen might view Wendy's sports participation as a remedy to a problem that she perceives — Wendy doesn't stick up for herself enough. She may fear that her daughter might feel powerless and trapped, much as she did until becoming empowered to cut off a relationship. These may be valid concerns, but urging Wendy to stick with soccer might not be the proper strategy for strengthening this girl. Perhaps Wendy's shyness and anxiety are biologically based as well as psychologically fueled by changes in her home life. A consultation with a pediatrician would serve both mother and daughter well as a way to determine the nature and extent of Wendy's anxiety and whether she needs further professional help.

It's imperative that we as parents have a good working relationship with our child's pediatrician. Refer to this doctor as a source of support and information about the parameters of healthy physical and emotional development, including your child's sports participation.

Know Your Child's Sports Environment

For Wendy, a huge green field flanked by yelling and cheering parents is not an anxiety-reducing environment. Her league is fairly competitive and scoreboard oriented, despite the young age of the participants. Winning matters; success in playoffs and the championship is the goal of the season. Also, the two factions that run this local league clash. One group favors fun and total participation, while the other is focused on preparing for playoffs and becoming the winners of the championship. Competing for the championship means that hesitant players such as Wendy hurt the team's chances; they are also subjected to critical comments from older kids on the team. These conditions don't improve Wendy's comfort level.

> It's imperative for parents to have a good working relationship with their child's pediatrician.

In Wendy's case, even if the league had placed more emphasis on participation, most likely the activity still would have been too much for her.

Wendy ultimately benefited from going to the local boys and girls club. There she was able to build relationships with caring adults and take part in a wide range of individual, paired, and group activities in the arts, music, homework help, and even team sports. This environment proved a much more appropriate fit. Boys' and girls' clubs can be great for any child but ideal for those who need a structured environment closely monitored by caring adults. Because of the breadth of activities available at a well-run club, children can find a good fit between their abilities and a particular sport, in their own time and at their own pace. Some children, though uncomfortable with the social demands of team sports, thrive in individual sports, which may involve more one-on-one support from coaches. Caution should be used, however, in concluding what sport is best for children before they reach the age of 14.

> Parents may fear that clingy, stubborn behaviors and unwillingness to try new things will last throughout childhood, but such concerns are usually unfounded.

A Closer Look: Brian, the Reluctant Swimmer

Brian Martin's stubborn refusal to jump into the pool is throwing cold water on family fun. Becky Martin is the mother of both Claire, a 5-year-old burst of confident energy, and Brian, a 2 1/2-year-old healthy yet slightly cautious and anxious boy. Claire has always been eager to try new things. At 6 months old, she readily took to playing in the water and always delighted in the pool and the lake. Even at the beach, Claire was remarkably daring and almost exhausted her parents in her eagerness to pull them into the water. She had to be watched carefully at the water's edge. As Claire's father says with obvious pride, "She is the kind of kid who will stay in the water until she turns purple."

Younger Brian is a different kind of fish. In fact, he's not much of a fish at all. His parents had expected that he'd take to the water as easily as Claire did. Whereas Claire is rarin' to go, Brian is a clingy, stubborn foot-dragger. Jake Martin, the children's father, has always been a good athlete, and he's getting increasingly irritated by Brian's reluctance: "Shoot, in our family we all love the water; what the hell happened with him?" The Martins have tried bribing ("I'll get you a Happy Meal afterward"), pleading, modeling the behavior ("Bri . . . watch me, it's easy . . . IT'S FUN!"), and enlisting Claire's help, all with little effect. Brian seems to enjoy riding in the car a hundred times more than going to the pool. At the pool, he cries. He whines. He pouts. He stays in the stands and calls for his mom. Once, when sensing her husband's irritation, Becky used a bit more physical effort to get Brian into the pool, but the boy threw a tantrum, and later the parents argued about how to get Brian to start swimming.

When Claire was younger, little discussion took place about activities—everything came easily to her. The Martins are stumped about Brian. It makes them dread new family activities, such as ice skating or skiing, and especially that future day when Brian will have to face going to school and other new challenges. They wonder, "Is this behavior normal? What should we do? Should we just push him to overcome his reluctance and fear?"

Know Your Child

It's important to remember just how much Brian is accomplishing in other parts of his life. Also, it is not uncommon for girls to be slightly ahead of boys in development. For example, Brian has taken longer than his sister did to become toilet trained and still hasn't completely mastered bowel and bladder control; some of his anxiety near the water could be related to this. He may not yet be able to correctly and consistently read the physical signals. Being in the open space of the pool might heighten anxiety about safety and control. Also, it is common for children of ages 2 to 3 to experience fear of separation, especially from their mother, and to exhibit clingy, dependent behavior. Tantrums are not unusual—children of this age can rigidly insist on maintaining their comforting routine.

Parents may fear that such behavior and unwillingness to try new things will last throughout childhood, but such concerns are usually unfounded. Brian's behavior a year down the road may little resemble his current hesitations. Parents may overreact to a child who is frightened and whiny, but the problem usually passes.

Fathers especially may fear that such behavior means that a son will lack courage and spunk in later years: "If he's this way now, what will happen when he has to stick up for himself?" To be sure, some children are consistently shy, sensitive, and anxious throughout the course of childhood.

This temperament is not to be confused with temporary emotional set-backs that can accompany the "terrible twos." And in the case at hand, Claire's robust behavior has spoiled the Martins to some extent, for it is a bit out of the ordinary. She bypassed some of the typical difficulties that char-acterize this age range. It is also quite possible that Brian's folded arms and pout stand as his own statement that he is different from his sister, the star swimmer. It could be an unspoken but understandable expression of sibling resentment.

Know Yourself

Brian's parents to some degree are victims of the rat-race pace of life in America. With complex logistics to juggle (two jobs; housework; chauffeur-ing kids to school, after-school care, and day care; setting aside time for in-dividual pursuits and social life and so on), there isn't much extra time for family activity. Swimming had been a convenient, relatively effort-free way to spend time together and have fun. Claire's love of the water neatly fit into the family legacy of athleticism, love of the ocean, and swimming. Her joy enhanced the parents' pride and their own enjoyment in a mutually rein-forcing way. Brian's behavior, though fitting the norm for his age, simply doesn't fit the family routine. When family sports and a child's capacity for enjoying them don't mesh well, parents should adjust the family routine to accommodate the young child. Forcing an activity that is meant to provide pleasure and fun is almost sure to backfire, especially with a child of this young, typically obstinate age.

The Martins would do well to tone down the pressure on their younger child. It is leading to frustration for them and likely causing Brian's behavior to become even more entrenched. They also may be unintention-ally communicating a negative message to their son. Although children at this age can differentiate basic facial expressions for anger, sad-ness, and joy, they cannot interpret their subtleties. Therefore they may misread the emotions that par-ents and others are communicat-ing. Brian could easily mistake his

> Our aim should be making a child's memories of physical activities as happy as possible.

parents' expression of frustration as being severely critical, the equivalent of them saying, "Brian, you're a bad boy." It's unlikely that this message, and the feeling it engenders, will make Brian feel more at ease and eager to swim.

Know Your Child's Sports Environment

The Martins run the risk that Brian might associate playing with his parents and sister with the prospect of feeling bad and being labeled as a bad boy. The goal for us as parents of toddlers is to create an environment where physical contact and activity are associated with safety, joy, and fun. Our aim should be making our child's memories of such activities as happy as possible. For example, this might mean that Brian gets to bring his favorite toy and play with it at the pool, perhaps wearing clothes rather than a swimsuit, while his parents share time with him without urging him to swim. Favorite stuffed animals, blankets, and toys provide emotional comfort and a sense of safety. Even during outdoor physical activities, a child's motto might be "My blankie — don't leave home without it!" If children are having fun and see that others are having fun too, it's far more likely they'll eventually join in the new activities. Finally, perhaps Brian would enjoy wrestling with his dad in the safety of his own living room rather than being expected to enjoy himself in an unfamiliar activity at an unfamiliar location. Parents can be creative and resourceful in thinking of such alternatives.

A CLOSER LOOK: TYLER, THE FEARLESS DYNAMO

Four-year-old Tyler Austin is like the nonstop Energizer Bunny, and he's starting to cause problems with his roughhousing and aggressive play. Lately Mrs. Austin has noticed that mothers and their children slink away when she and Ty arrive at the playground. She has received fewer calls for shared play time at others' homes as well. Then last week Tyler was asked to take a week off from the Learn to Skate ice hockey program after he slammed a child from behind into the boards because the child had beaten Tyler in a race. Mr. Austin feels that the program director may be overreacting, but he acknowledges his wife's concern. Mrs. Austin witnessed the incident, and she is worried. Previously, both parents had felt a slightly different degree of concern about Ty's aggressiveness (Dad was more likely to dismiss the problem), but now suspension from the hockey program has forced the issue to a head.

Know Your Child

It is not unusual for children at age 4 to increase their level of competitive play. (Interestingly, evidence suggests that fearlessness in young children is associated with future success in team sports.)[2] So too, children naturally gravitate to play that they consider appropriate for their gender; for example boys want to play tackle football. Boys prefer to play with their father, often want to be "just like Dad" in as many ways as possible, and joyfully engage in rough, wrestling play. These phenomena are generally viewed as healthy components of male child development. Boys do tend to play longer, more aggressively, in larger numbers, and outdoors more than girls do.[3] Therefore parents must be vigilant about helping their sons control emotion and aggression. However, Tyler has recently gone beyond the limits of acceptable aggression.

More than his love of and need for physical activity, Tyler's trouble with self-control, especially when he's angry or frustrated, has caused this difficulty. In general, 4-year-olds take pride in following rules; they enjoy cooperative play and socializing with other children. It is cause for concern, then, that Tyler has begun to alienate other children and that he has trouble containing his aggression and following the rules. In addition, Tyler seems easily distracted, which may indicate some form of attentional weakness as well as impulse-control problems. A consultation with Tyler's pediatrician would be highly recommended.

Know Yourself

Different parents may exhibit significantly different tolerance levels for certain behaviors, such as children's aggressive play. Mothers are usually associated with more conventional play (dolls and games); fathers are more typically associated with unpredictable, rough-and-tumble play with their youngsters of ages 2 to 4.[4] Boys seem to favor this type of play with their fathers more than girls do.

Fathers in general tolerate, even encourage physically rougher play. Within certain parameters, this can be a healthy interaction between father and son. Play-time wrestling and affectionate physical contact are highly recommended because they help children bond with their father, help sons identify with the parent of the same sex, and also can teach the limits of aggressive play.[5] However, when safety rules are broken, play should stop, or a time-out should be used. The lesson should be reinforced: "No punching in the face and no kicking, especially below the belt!"

Tyler's parents disagree about the limits of roughhousing and physical play. Mr. Austin initially had to struggle to accept his wife's concern as legitimate because he loves it that Tyler is physically tough. In the past he's said to his wife, "Would you prefer he be some little wimp? Boys will be boys. He's a real boy." Both parents now flinch at the idea that Tyler has some type of problem. They both hope he will just grow out of this phase, but special care and monitoring are required to ensure that Tyler's behavior does not undermine his development. Tyler is not in the "terrible twos." He is 4 years old. And it appears that his high energy, his failure to listen, and his "no breaks" impulsivity have been evident for some time. He is becoming ostracized — avoided by kids, parents, and, potentially, coaches — an unusual thing for a 4-year-old. As his mother states, "Too many mothers have given me that raised-eyebrow look. They pack up when we arrive."

These factors are a red flag indicating possible attention deficit disorder with hyperactivity (ADHD). Tyler's parents would be wise to consult their pediatrician as soon as possible. (In fact, because of his parents' opposition to medication treatment, Tyler went on for five more years without treatment. He continued to experience significant difficulties at home, at school, and in his athletic and other after-school activities. Eventually, he was successfully treated for ADHD when his parents felt his academic problems had reached a critical stage, in the fourth grade.)

Know Your Child's Sports Environment

The environment played a small role in Tyler's difficulties. It acted as a window, which revealed his problems in controlling his behavior. Oversensitive or defensive parents might have waged heated battles with other parents or a sports program director, blaming Tyler's problems on them. Luckily, Tyler's parents realized that the environment did not cause Tyler's difficulties. (When we cultivate a good working knowledge of our community, sports programs, and coaches, we can readily sift useful, accurate feedback about our children from less helpful information.) Eventually, Tyler's parents had the strength to recognize their son's possible problems and seek appropriate help.

USEFUL TIPS

- Prepare your child for a new sports experience by playfully introducing aspects of the activity in a safe environment, prior to opening day.

Walking and talking the youngster through some of the particulars can make the activity seem more familiar and less frightening. For example, if your young child is entering a youth soccer league for the first time, buy a new soccer ball in his or her favorite color and frequently kick it around together in the backyard a few weeks before soccer season. This can set the stage for an easy transition.

- Older siblings or slightly older peers in the neighborhood can be great allies in helping an anxious child try new activities.
- In the weeks before your child starts a new sports activity, introduce yourself to league administrators or coaches, and sound them out about their philosophy and how they run their program. If you have concerns about your child, talk to coaches and administrators before teams are set and before the chaos of opening day; generally, this is when they'll be receptive to special requests.
- Parents of older children can be useful sources of information about the most patient, supportive coaches or other clues that can make your child's experience easier.
- If it seems that your child and a given activity or program are not a good fit, provide a dignified exit strategy before things reach the meltdown stage. Misery doesn't build a child's joy in sports. Don't prolong a miserable experience.
- Be wary of reading too much or too little into your child's current abilities. Enjoy the discovery process. Let children enjoy themselves and try a lot of activities. Perfect form and correct understanding of the rules of the game are not that important at this stage. Joy of movement is.

3

THE ELEMENTARY SCHOOL
YEARS (AGES 6–12)

Building Competencies, Exploring Interests,
and Making Friends

ORGANIZED COMPETITIVE YOUTH SPORTS begin in earnest at ages 6 through 12. At this age most of us who are currently parents were first introduced to sports through Little League baseball or girls' softball, Pop Warner football, youth basketball, hockey, soccer, or perhaps competitive swimming or tennis. The phenomenon of youth sports has exploded during our lifetime; almost 9 out of 10 children will play in an organized sports league before the age of 13. If the early years provide the "happy feet" of a child's journey in sports, ages 6 through 12 form the backbone and skeletal frame of athletic experience.

Psychologists call this age range the latency period because it is believed that many aspects of adulthood, especially sexual development, lie dormant in these years prior to puberty, a time of steady psychological growth and reduced emotional turmoil. In addition, during this period the physical growth rate is steadier and less explosive than it is in the stages preceding and following it. The greatest growth rate occurs from birth through age 2. Growth proceeds somewhat more gradually from age 2 through 12 for boys and age 2 through 10 or 11 for girls. Girls (at ages 10–12) begin their adolescent growth spurt somewhat earlier than boys (at ages 12–14). Prior to this surge, boys and girls are physically quite similar in strength, muscle mass, and overall range of physical abilities.[1]

The major psychological tasks of this period are twofold: the development of competencies and the ability to make and keep friends. Competency extends to many domains — not just reading and writing and arithmetic, but also a variety of activities in sports, music, and the arts, providing a wide range of learning opportunities.

Yet contemporary America seems to offer too many activities from which to choose. Overscheduling, overspecialization, and overemphasis on sports performance, as opposed to the development of the whole child, threaten to burn out our kids. By the end of this age range, a great many children will drop out of their team or sport. For some children, this will represent a reasoned move to more compelling interests: "I played softball until I was 13 but I really liked soccer better, so I dropped softball and focused on travel team soccer in the spring. It's what I was best at and what I enjoy the most." This situation does not bear the negative connotations of just quitting a sport. It's more accurate to call it moving on.

However, many other children leave organized sports because they are unhappy. Research cites the number one reason our children give for dropping a sport: "It no longer was any fun."[2] Unfortunately, many children are inclined to give up sports entirely because of unpleasant experiences in organized competition. This choice raises their risk of falling into unhealthy habits that

> **Research cites the number one reason our children give for dropping a sport: "It no longer was any fun."**

may result in juvenile obesity or even drinking, smoking pot, and engaging in other risky, self-destructive behaviors.

Studies show that children who play organized sports reap profound benefits. They get more exercise. They enjoy a healthier lifestyle, consuming more fruits and vegetables, and are less likely to smoke cigarettes, use drugs, or engage in early sexual activity (for girls only, that is).[3] It's crucial that as parents we ensure that our children enjoy physical activity, take pride in caring for their bodies, and desire to continue an active lifestyle. As parents, our first priority is our children's health. Therefore, we need to invest time, energy, and thought to help them adopt a lifestyle that will allow them to stay fit for life.

Many unhappy children who have quit sports for good by age 12 do so because adults make a big mistake. We impose adult standards of performance on youngsters who are still developing. As we have already noted, all too often, we find otherwise intelligent and caring adults foisting unrealistic and psychologically unhealthy expectations on young kids, based on collegiate or professional sports standards. The professional motto of the NFL team the Oakland Raiders, "Just win baby," sets a poor standard for children.

Furthermore, parents and other adults can make the mistake of seeing child and adolescent development as predictable, a series of uniform steps. If a child shows a high level of talent in relation to her friends at age 8, we tend to believe that this athletic dominance will continue and grow, given proper support: "If she is this good now, she'll be spectacular in high school." During ages 6–12, because of children's relatively stable physical growth, it is easy for parents and coaches to believe that outstanding performers will improve at a consistent rate and will naturally stay at the top right through the college years. From a physical standpoint, this is simply not the case. Continued growth in physical size and talent may or may not occur. Research shows that boys of ages 10–16 can differ from one another in size a great deal—as much as 15 inches in height and 90 pounds in weight![4] Boys and girls in a junior high classroom are a picture of disproportionately sized arms and legs, hands and feet, noses and ears, all attached to small but growing bodies. Some kids grow gradually, and some seem to sprout up overnight; their athletic skills also may grow and level off in unpredictable ways.

We realize expectations for constantly improving performance can make parents demanding and prone to disappointment when kids don't hit the mark. When adults display disappointment at children's failure to live up to unreasonable or uninformed expectations, they instill in kids a sense of failure. Young minds at ages 6 to 12, wired to see things as black and white, all or none, cannot help but blame themselves for their athletic "failures." In self-defense, humiliated kids might show anger at teammates or coaches or the sport itself for their sense of shame at not meeting unrealistic standards: "The coach is dumb and baseball is just a stupid game anyway." Drawing such conclusions is in part a function of children's cognitive skills at this age. Under the stress of competition, they tend to think in absolutes: "We lost and I played lousy, so I am a loser." Such unhappy, and completely unnecessary, athletic experiences can prematurely end sports participation.

Adults' unrealistic expectations of child athletes also pose physical risks. Orthopedic experts adamantly warn us that growing bones are vulnerable to repetitive-use injuries, such as those caused by too many serves in tennis or too many pitches in baseball. Overemphasis on sports, particularly specializing in one sport, as a path toward guaranteed high school or collegiate success is dangerous — the physical and emotional fallout could be serious. Eager parents of would-be sports stars would do well to remember that for every Tiger Woods, there are numerous Todd Marinoviches who suffer physically and emotionally because sports became too much, too soon.

Focusing on one sport during this age range may be tempting; it could produce a short-term boost in performance. But different experiences activate different areas of the developing brain of a child, and children are still discovering which activities suit them best. As one knowledgeable father said to another dad who was pushing him to get his son to play soccer year round, "I like steak, but we don't eat it every night. Why should I limit Jimmy to one sport? Maybe three years from now, he'll be golfing or playing lacrosse or some crazy sport I know nothing about, like rugby. Why limit him now?"

But the one-sport focus dominates the life of Patrick Tremblay, an outstanding hockey player at age 11. His 11- and 12-year-old opponents are overshadowed by his remarkable ability. Like many who parent talented athletes, Patrick's father has aspirations that extend beyond Patrick's current level of play; he believes that his son has the potential to play hockey at a very high level. Furthermore, he wants Patrick's talent to earn much-needed scholarship money for prep school and eventually for a Division I or Division II college, but his hopes don't end there: "Who knows, maybe pros if he gets a few breaks! That college coach said he was better than Mike Modano was at this age!" Belief in his son's supreme talent has provoked him to disagree with hockey coaches and program administrators. Mr. Tremblay is "team shopping" for a hockey program that will give his son maximum playing time and expert coaching. The Tremblays are considering changing teams for the second time in three years.

Childhood athletic excellence can be a double-edged sword. The label of "having great potential" can be a burden. Yet the potential tangible and emotional rewards for athletic success are seductive. How can parents ensure that they are doing the best thing possible for a child? No one wants to miss an opportunity, but we also want to avoid putting a child at physical or emotional risk.

For most children, however, the one-sport superstar problem is not an issue. Most parents will simply help their child learn the basic skills of various sports and how to compete confidently as an individual and as a team member. For most families, this effort will resemble other learning experiences, with its share of ups and downs, daily struggles, and differences of opinion among parents, children, coaches, teammates, and moms and dads. For example, Cheryl Walker is the mother of a sweet, eager-to-please, 7½-year-old boy named Jason. His father coaches Jason's Little League baseball team. Cheryl is concerned that the pressure on the father-son relationship is causing tension for the entire family. Jason seems to be enjoying baseball less and playing below his capability. She wonders, as most of us would, how she can help both her son and her husband without making things worse. What should we do when our young children struggle with their performance on the field? How can we resolve disagreements while acting in the best interests of our kids?

> As parents and coaches, we are frequently demanding a performance level in our children that their bodies and minds are not yet capable of producing.

Finally, some children at this age seem to succeed in many areas effortlessly. Parents might take it for granted that such children will continue to glide along from strength to strength: "She's never been a problem. She never causes us a moment of worry. She just does everything we ask so well." These "easy to parent" children almost seem to do our parenting for us. Yet the relative ease that these children enjoy should not mask the fact that they need help avoiding the pitfalls of organized sports.

Deidre Kelly is one such kid. An attractive, red-headed 9-year-old, she is quiet, determined, well coordinated, and athletic. She excels in most everything she attempts: school, friendships, and home life. She has been asked to join a highly successful swimming club, but this might mean quitting step dancing, an activity that means a lot to her parents and the extended family. In fact, Deidre has seemed to enjoy step dancing. How can her parents help her decide between these attractive choices? Would doing both be wise — or too much?

What wisdom and guidance will help the families of Patrick, Jason, and Deidre? The following section offers suggestions for dealing with issues that arise for young athletes of elementary school age.

ESSENTIAL SKILLS FOR CHILDREN OF AGES 6–12

Whereas a basic sense of trust and control is the psychological goal of ages 1–5, at ages 6–12 kids learn to make and keep friends, and they develop a wide range of skills as well. Good friends, good grades, and good play are the goals they strive for as they make further progress in the six essential skills.

Confidence

Throughout the latency stage of childhood, an emotionally healthy child will experience an ever-growing sense of usefulness and ability to influence his or her world — in other words, the child will have a healthy sense of agency, the capacity to act successfully on his or her own behalf. For example, Deidre knows she can do things well because, with support from her parents, teachers, and coaches, she has already done so. She has that hopeful belief that she can try something and expect positive things to happen: "Let me try that . . . I think I can do it."

During this age range, required tasks in and out of school grow in number and size, and the normal child will master crossing the street, going to the store alone, completing a school project, negotiating a sleepover with friends, and many other accomplishments. Sports can be a wonderful vehicle for promoting this sense of mastery. Sports make children face and overcome fear, anxiety, and frustration regularly, and this experience can build their confidence. Unfortunately, a pattern of bad athletic experiences can result in a lifelong sense of inferiority and diminished self-esteem, and too much of a good thing, such as Patrick's talent for hockey, can also undermine balanced physical and psychological growth. Sports-oriented parents need to remember that music, art, friendships, and schoolwork are equally compelling arenas for the development of confidence. Children need a variety of experiences involving different people, places, and activities to enhance their confidence as effective agents in their own life.

> Childhood athletic excellence can be a double-edged sword.

Interests

One chief psychological task at this age is discovering what you like and getting good at it. Different interests arise as children develop competence at school and in the arts, sports, and relationships. Whether they delve into baseball, video games, friendships, computers, pets, music, or stamp collections, children can surprise us with the breadth and depth of their interests and their rapid grasp of a variety of related skills.

Having a wide range of interests is a marker of healthy development at this stage. As previously stated, avoiding specialization in a single activity or sport is wise during the elementary school years. Encourage multiple interests, and you will likely have the rewarding experience of seeing your child express surprise or wonder at enjoying something you have urged him or her to try: "I didn't think I'd like it, but that vacation to Yosemite was pretty cool" or "Hey, this really does taste good! Can I have some more?" In sports, children deserve the same wide range of experience. Patrick's narrow focus on hockey at age 11 might limit his overall growth. Moreover, a lack of interests or friendships and a limited range of activities are cause for concern for children of this age.

Relationships

Making and keeping friends is a major focus for children of ages 6–12, as significant as school and certainly more important than the number of sports trophies they may win. Just as play is joyful work for the preschool child, friends are the lifeblood of later childhood. Friendships build on the trust learned in relationship to parents and sets the stage for moving beyond the egocentrism of childhood toward the capacity for mature love. Making and sustaining good friendships and good relationships with teammates require the ability to accept limits in oneself and others. Team sports are a great vehicle for learning to tolerate and accommodate people's varied needs and strengths and weaknesses. Parents and coaches of children in this age group must seize the "teachable moments" that reveal how to be a good teammate and friend.

It's just as important to recognize how team sports, particularly elite or travel teams, might jeopardize the development of friendships, which need free time in order to thrive. Overscheduling and pressure to perform can threaten children's growth in learning to relate to peers, siblings, parents, and other people. This constitutes a serious loss, and wise parents will see that children have the time and space to cultivate friendships.

Judgment

At this age, children are moving to a less egocentric view of the world. Not until age 12, however, can children accurately understand what caused them to perform well or badly on a given occasion. The tendency to see things in an all-or-none, black-or-white way is still prevalent. Especially for ages 6 through 10, producing a poor outcome means the same thing as being a bad player. Struggling young athletes like Jason can be prone to making sweeping, unjustified generalizations about their abilities: "I struck out with the bases loaded, so I am a lousy baseball player." Also, children of 6–12 years of age are very sensitive to what parents think about them so we need to be aware of messages we may be unconsciously telegraphing through tone of voice or facial expressions, and we should actively dispel kids' unfair assessments of their performance, skill, or worth. They still depend on adults to establish the rules and standards of performance and behavior.

By age 12, our kids should be able to make basic moral judgments of right and wrong. They should also evidence a growing capacity for distinguishing good friends from troublemakers, adults who can be trusted from those who can't, and safe situations from those that might cause trouble.

Emotional Control

An area of great concern, emotional control comprises a set of skills difficult to master for adults as well as children. Over the course of this age range, children should show increased ability to tolerate frustration, negotiate emotional needs, and seek help without resorting to destructive behavior. Because it can create intense emotional highs and lows, sports competition can bring out the worst in parents, coaches, and kids. When adults lose control of their emotions, they give children tacit approval for bad behavior. By age 12, our kids should be able to get mad, sad, anxious, frightened, lonely, frustrated, joyous — you name the emotion — without resorting to self-destructive, aggressive, or otherwise inappropriate behaviors. The occasional outburst is not a cause for alarm, but healthy 12-year-olds should express emotion without impulsive aggression, staging a meltdown, or withdrawing emotionally.

Sometimes sensitive, high-achieving kids like Deidre will protect their parents from the emotional difficulties they experience. This is especially true for girls in the upper part of this age range (ages 11–12) and for boys and girls in families facing emotional turmoil such as parental illness, divorce, or job loss. Younger girls may mask their feelings because of being both biologically wired and culturally conditioned to be more sensitive to the emotional needs of others than to their own needs. Smart, sensitive kids can sense when their parents' energy and resources are depleted and might therefore keep their own emotional difficulties to themselves; they don't want to overload the family with more problems.

Avoiding specialization in a single activity or sport is wise during the elementary school years.

As parents we need to state early and often that no matter what else is happening, our children should follow this rule, which we first heard from Dr. Paula Rauch, the head of the MGH Child Psychiatry Consultation Service: *Do not suffer alone.* If something is bothering you, make sure you come to Mom or Dad or someone else who we agree is a responsible person.

Sports-Related Skills

Tremendous growth and variation characterize boys and girls of this age; marked differences in the height and weight of the sexes are established by the end of this stage. And although basic competencies in many sports can be skillfully mastered by some young athletes, even the most gifted have not fully matured physically. For example, vision plays a significant role in athletic success, yet throughout ages 6–12 and even into the teen years, vision remains a work in progress. Depth perception and dynamic visual acuity (the ability to correctly judge the position of objects as they move, such as a baseball in flight) do not reach maturity at least until age 12. Peripheral vision ("Is that a teammate or an opponent that I see out of the corner of my eye?") and accurate figure-ground perception ("How close is that defender to my own player down the court?") continue to develop throughout the teen years. As for hearing ability, auditory memory ("What did the coach tell me to do?") and auditory discrimination ("Was that a ref's whistle or a noise in the stands?") are also not fully developed.[5] Touch and awareness of the body's movement in space are still evolving, yet it's not unusual to hear a football coach yelling at a 12-year-old Pop Warner quarterback to put some touch on a pass (which means to throw the football with less than full force to accurately place it in the hands of a receiver), another example of an adult's demanding use of a skill that a young athlete does not yet possess.

What is the proper athletic focus for children in this age range? Rather than work to beat the other guy, the best athletes should compete against themselves to bring out their best. According to Jim Thompson and his Positive Coaching Alliance,[6] the "scoreboard mentality" of youth sports should be replaced with the "mastery approach." Instead of planning to win at any cost, the emphasis shifts to improving skill through effort and learning proper technique. Mistakes are seen as a valuable part of the learning process, rather than a setback in the grand cause of scoring a victory. A coach having this mindset can say, "Yes, you missed that shot, but your form was great. Keep it up and you will succeed. I loved your effort, and your technique is sound." Success is measured against one's own personal best, not by comparison to another's performance. Striving to win is vitally important in the mastery approach as well, but it is coupled with an equal emphasis on something that can be controlled. We can't always control outcome — who wins — but we can always strive to give our best effort. Research shows that this approach reduces anxiety and improves self-confidence in young athletes,[7] and self-confidence promotes willingness to work harder and persevere.[8] A focus on effort and skill building during this stage will help our children become engaged in sports and derive positive benefits from the experience.

> Just as play is joyful work for the preschool child, friendship is the lifeblood of later childhood.

A Closer Look: Patrick, the Superstar

Patrick Tremblay is all about hockey. Approaching 12 years of age, he is slender and tall, but it is not his physical presence that impresses, but rather his dazzling skating skill and stick handling. He possesses the grace, explosive speed, and soft hands that make opponents and teammates gape in slack-jawed wonder as he swerves, darts, and drives to the net with the puck — which often lands in the opponents' net. It is not unusual for him to score two or three goals in a game. His father proudly attends every game and quietly sits in the stands, only occasionally commiserating with other fathers when a game is not going well. Patrick's father is deeply committed to his son, especially his development as a hockey player. Patrick plays for his town's travel team as well as an elite side team. He plays in summer ice hockey leagues as well. Patrick's mother died when he was 5, and he has no siblings. His life and his father's life revolve around sports, especially hockey.

Patrick's dad argued long and hard with Patrick's coaches about his son's playing time: "My son is the best player in the league. He should be skating extra shifts or at least on all power plays and penalty kills. If you don't use him as you should, then we'll go somewhere else. You're depriving him of earned playing time and stifling his development!" Coaches and administrators have countered Mr. Tremblay's demands, admitting their delight in Patrick's skills but reminding Patrick's dad that hockey is a team game, and Patrick should develop a team approach that emphasizes passing and helping his teammates improve. They have explained that the program's stated mission is the development of the entire squad, with fair playing time for all: "Yes, we want to win, but we want to accomplish a few other things too, both for Patrick and the team."

Mr. Tremblay eventually pulls Patrick from this town travel team at the end of the season; now he plays for another town travel team, in addition to his elite team. This new travel team has presumably agreed with Mr. Tremblay's philosophy regarding playing time for his son: "My first obligation is to make sure that my son is in a program that will help him get the most out of his abilities!" Patrick has changed programs twice in three years. This represents yet another change.

What effect will being on a team that grants him superstar status have on Patrick's long-term interests? What risks attend this strategy?

Know Your Child

Patrick's specialized involvement in one sport is indeed perilous; the blessing of exceptional ability can come with less visible curses. As many Hollywood child stars know, good sense and good parenting can fall by the wayside when a child's glorious talent emerges. We all know that the rules are often broken for exceptional athletes, even in grade school. It's harder to acknowledge that parents themselves can be swept up in the bright lights when the talent is one of their own.

Patrick's father might mistakenly believe that his son's development and dominance as an athlete will continue at the same rate as he grows up. But his son has not yet reached puberty, and it's impossible to assess whether he will maintain his advantage; Patrick could conceivably hit a ceiling in size and in talent. He may be an early bloomer who is already close to his full height. His peers certainly will make gains in size, speed, strength, and numerous visual, auditory, cognitive, and motor skills at a rate that could cause them to catch up with or surpass Patrick's hockey talent.

A growing body of research confirms that we cannot accurately predict the future athletic success of a child before age 12. Experts view early sport specialization, harnessing a family's time, energy, and money because a child is viewed as a "can't miss" prospect, as folly. Bob Bigelow documented his studies and counseled parents and coaches on this topic in his book *Just Let Them Play.* Countries of the former Soviet bloc, once intensely focused on the idea that elite athletes could be identified at an early age and perfected in youth sports academies, have moved away from that practice. Development proceeds at a discontinuous rate and is a river fed by a lot of different streams, making prediction of future athletic success a risky bet indeed.

Patrick's dad is, however, fostering his son's growth in some areas of psychological health. Patrick's confidence is quite robust; he KNOWS he can play well, and he certainly is developing his interest in hockey. But other measures of healthy development suggest that Patrick is lacking in academic focus, the enjoyment of friendships, and other nonathletic pursuits. Moreover, moving from team to team has potentially negative effects. The idea that individual talent trumps the concerns of building teamwork and friendships means that Patrick is missing positive lessons in the use of individual ability to help others, the ability to sacrifice for the greater good, and the willingness to adjust to the limitations of others as well as one's own. When a parent consistently gives the message that it's okay to circumvent the coach because the coach is wrong, the child is locked in the selfishness and egocentrism that should be left behind as one matures. The "hockey above all" mindset could significantly undermine other important areas of growth.

> Children should follow this key rule: Do not suffer alone.

Balance and diversification are key. Research shows that young athletes who avoid specialization in a specific sport until after they reach puberty become more consistent performers, play sports longer, and sustain fewer injuries.[9] And ironically, a single-minded focus on talent development may produce results that Patrick's father never dreamed of. It may well be a talent killer instead of a talent builder. The concern for wins, statistics, playing time, and specialized training turn a sport into a numbers game. The athlete loses the flow and ease of playing—the release that occurs when the critical brain takes a back seat and focus moves to the here and now, an experience marked by great enjoyment. But a hyperintense, hypercritical approach inhibits such performance. When statistical outcomes become the measure of success, play becomes willful and feels suffocating—what athletes refer to as "pressing" or not "playing within themselves." ("I had 3 goals so I'm happy with my game. Why should I listen when the coach says I should be back checking more and helping out defensively, we're winning? Why should I change how I'm playing?") Down the road when the goals or wins start to dry up, frustration, overthinking, playing tight, and blaming teammates, referee's calls, and coach's decisions can often follow quickly on the heels of an outcome-driven approach that is not producing the desired results.

> A growing body of research confirms that we cannot accurately predict the future athletic success of a child before age 12.

Any approach to youth sports that becomes dominated by measures of outcome, be it for team ("You guys didn't win, so you failed"), individual ("You didn't get a hit or you didn't score, so you failed"), or scholarship or monetary gain ("You HAVE to succeed! It's our ticket out of this crappy neighborhood!"), runs the risk of undermining the joy *and* the performance of the young athlete. If kids like something, they will work to improve at it. If they do not like it, they will eventually quit or burn out. The danger for Patrick is that playing sports for the purpose of winning a scholarship might become joyless and eventually unproductive.

Know Yourself

If Patrick's father becomes more aware of the dynamics of child development, he'll be able to reassess his strategy for achieving his goals for his son. At this point, Mr. Tremblay is operating on the premise that his son's athletic talent is the boy's best shot at both a good high school and college education. Because of a work-related injury, his wife's death, and limited economic resources, Patrick's dad knows he cannot afford the best schools for his son. There is no "frustrated jock" in Mr. Tremblay; he is a hopeful, caring, but financially strapped parent. He believes hockey will offer scholarship money for both prep school and college. After all, his son loves hockey; certainly, this father and son are entitled to establish and pursue their own family goals. But caution is required.

Financial constraints and a desire for top-notch educational opportunity are legitimate concerns. Any reasonable person would acknowledge the anxiety, frustration, and guilt that Patrick's father might feel because of the death of his wife and his own physical disability. However, he could strive for a deeper understanding of the emotional landscape that he and his son inhabit together and a more balanced approach to his son's athletic, academic, social, and extra curricular life. Basing all their hopes on Patrick's future success may set them up for yet another cruel blow.

By investing so much time and energy in one activity, father and son may be masking pain and emotional needs. In a family of only two people, pressure is put on father and son to cover all bases; whether they acknowledge it or not, they must feel the absence of Patrick's deceased mother. Although she died some time ago, children in a sense mourn the death of a parent over and over again as they develop a more adult understanding of life. For a child to successfully manage this revisiting of grief and loss, the surviving parent needs to be able to handle his or her own emotional replay of the painful loss. Patrick's father may need help with this. Sports can be a wonderful distraction and bonding ritual; however, an overblown family immersion in sports can postpone the grief, mourning, and readjustment that families suffering death, divorce, or some other loss must go through.

Know Your Child's Sports Environment

Parents aren't the only ones who get caught up in the overzealous, no-holds-barred pursuit of developing young athletic talent. Many coaches, team administrators, and sports business owners push the envelope, getting kids to specialize in one sport at an ever earlier age. It's not uncommon for select soccer teams to require prospective players to play both fall and spring soccer, with an implicit demand that indoor soccer during the winter is necessary if you're really committed to improving. Hockey can have similar pressures. Elite leagues and select side teams can cherry-pick the best talent, to the detriment of local teams.

These elite leagues foster a hypercompetitive, "every kid for himself or herself" mentality, with little regard for anything but winning and the development of individual talent in one sport. These leagues and teams are sophisticated enough to paint a rosy picture of their character-building goals in their mission statement: "We're dedicated to the overall development of your child." But all too often, these are empty promises. In practice, many elite youth teams are cutthroat about winning and promoting superstar talent. One hockey parent describes the situation: "My son was told he made the team, but then two kids came to the attention of the coach at the eleventh hour. They were even too late for the regular tryouts, but the coach had heard of them and knew they were tremendously talented. They were. So at the last minute, my son [age 12] got bumped. After being told he was in, he was out. That's just the way it is with these elite teams. We had to scramble to get a place on another select team."

Winning and trumpeting the elite few who go on to college teams make these programs more marketable to prospective families who want guaranteed results for their kids. Such programs add to the pressure that parents misguidedly place on young kids. In many ways, Patrick's father could be described as simply trying to work within a flawed, manipulative system that is geared to promote individual talent.

Patrick's father would do well to limit his son's exposure to this warped sports culture. Permitting his son to seek other forms of recreation purely "for the fun of it" would be a sound investment in Patrick's emotional bank. Perhaps requiring that Patrick limit hockey during the summer would provide a good break. Stable membership in a boys and girls club, another

> The key to success is focusing on the process and the development of good habits, as opposed to just winning or excellent individual outcome alone.

sport, or a religious or neighborhood summer program might stabilize Patrick's social development and counterbalance an overblown sense of his own importance based on his hockey talent. Talented children are sometimes less likely to suffer the slings and arrows that afflict mere mortals and therefore may take longer to shed childhood egocentricity and self-preoccupation; too many people never quite accomplish this crucial task in character development. As parents we can make sure our children know they are loved but also help them learn that everyone has weaknesses, and this is acceptable. Patrick needs situations in which he does not stand head and shoulders above his peers and can experience his own limitations. This type of struggle allows perseverance, discipline, and empathy toward others to develop.

A Closer Look: Jason, the Coach's Son

Jason is a 7 1/2-year-old boy who plays on a Little League team coached by his father, Jack. Slightly above average height and weight for his age, Jason is the oldest of three, with a younger brother, age 5, and a baby sister, age 2. Jason plays for the Astros in the B League (primarily 8- and 9-year-olds) of the town's Little League program. Because the league has been hurting for coaches, Jason was allowed to play in the B League on his father's team, even though he's slightly under age. Jason's dad was a better-than-average high school player whose career got cut short by a knee injury in his junior year. He is a bit of a demanding "hard marker" on his kids but deeply involved in their lives. Jack and his wife, Cheryl, occasionally disagree about how much to push Jason. Jason is an average player. His younger brother is an active dynamo who may be the most naturally gifted athlete of the family.

At this stage of the season, Jason probably could be playing better. He seems to struggle at the plate and has made errors in the field. Most troubling to his mother is the fact that in virtually every game, Jason visibly tears up after a mistake or a strikeout. His shoulders slump, and he hides his face in his glove or pulls his hat down low over his eyes. When this occurs, she sees her husband's anxiety level rise. Despite her husband's best efforts and the constant reminders not to be overly critical, Jason and his father seem to interact in an unsatisfactory way. Dad tries harder to coach the finer points of the game immediately following Jason's latest "failure": "Just relax, Jason! Take a deep breath. See the ball, hit the ball!" Unfortunately, Dad's coaching tips are delivered in such a charged atmosphere that they send Jason into a funk. And funks don't produce good baseball for Jason or any children. Cheryl occasionally frets that her husband feels extra pressure as the only African American coach in the league. She wonders how to help her son without setting off a major misunderstanding with her husband. Jason and his mom and dad face a typical struggle for parents who coach or are the spouse of a coach.

Know Your Child

Jason may be suffering from multiple sources of pressure. In a sense, because the Little League needs coaches, Jason is being forced to perform at a slightly accelerated pace, moving up to the B League somewhat earlier than is typical. He is being asked to do a bit more than he is wired to do at his age. It's easy to think that all children benefit from being exposed to a better level of play, but frequently the opposite is true. Some kids develop a greater sense of confidence as the older, "veteran" player in, for example, a T-ball league. In fact, some parents purposely hold their child back a year from school, even lying about a birth date so a kid can benefit from the extra growth advantage.

Jason is in over his head just a bit. By the end of the season, things may work, but right now he is struggling. He may feel pressured by a hotshot younger brother, a father who is also his coach, older players with whom he must compete, and finally, his own ideas about how well he should be doing. That's a lot of pressure.

Jason adores his father and hangs on every word and gesture he makes as father and coach; he picks up on every sign of his dad's disappointment and frustration with him. Then he puts extra pressure on himself to do better. He is well aware that Dad was a very good athlete who is still in excellent physical shape, and Jason wants to live up to this standard. He feels the pressure that oldest children naturally feel to please both parents, especially the father. He doesn't have the insight or cognitive ability to recognize that he's really doing unbelievably well to even be playing with the older kids in the B League.

Know Yourself

Cheryl Walker can help her son and husband by focusing on their family goals and articulating the pressures they are under as parents. In short, the Walkers need to become aware of what they want and what they are doing. First, Cheryl can model how she wants her husband to treat her son by curbing her criticism and perhaps her anger toward her husband, particularly in the immediate aftermath of the game. Just as Dad's emotionally charged approach to Jason has been unproductive, an emotionally charged criticism of her husband probably won't defuse his tension and lead him to a more relaxed coaching style.

Second, Cheryl and Jack should plan ahead. They could sit down before the season and discuss their ultimate goals and specific expectations for

Jason in sports, including the values and behaviors they hope he will continue to develop throughout his life in sports, even into adulthood. If they don't already have one, they could craft a family sports mission statement as discussed in this book's introduction. This will help the family stay on course during the ups and downs of competition and keep small setbacks and disappointments in perspective.

Since she has noticed the problem, Cheryl might be the one to open a discussion with Jack, keeping the tone level and noncombative. Timing is important too; she might wait a day or two following the last game, then say, "I noticed that Jason gets awfully down on himself when he strikes out or makes an error. Do you notice that? I know you're doing a good job coaching him, but he seems to get so down that he doesn't even take in the pointers you give him. What do we want

> Studies show that successful Little League coaches use accurate praise much more frequently than direct criticism.

him to get out of this? I mean, besides having fun and being happy? I know I just want him to try his best and to be a good teammate. What qualities do you hope he learns from baseball?"

Jason's mom can do even more to improve this situation for both her son and husband. Since pregame overcoaching and postgame analyses can create unproductive and unnecessary tension for a child athlete, mothers can help defuse postgame criticism in the car ride home: "Win or lose, we go for ice cream!" And Jason's dad can apply sound coaching principles as he works with his son. Studies show that successful Little League coaches use accurate praise much more frequently than direct criticism to develop talent and keep kids in baseball.[10] Also, good coaches (and good parents) break down athletic skills into small, manageable bits of behavior, accentuate the positive, and avoid focusing on the negative. To begin a more positive approach to coaching Jason, his father might say the following after Jason's next strikeout: "Gee, son. Your balance was great. You swung at good pitches. Your batting stance is steady and correct, and your swings weren't bad at all. Next time, try setting back a bit deeper in the box. Don't worry. You'll hit. Your mechanics seem very good. Even though you struck out, that wasn't a bad at bat. I'm very happy with your effort."

There's a 4:1 ratio of accurate praise to constructive criticism in this coaching moment. Kids also read the body language and facial expression of the speaker, so they must fit the positive message. Kids both learn and feel relieved by such interactions, which contrast sharply with the dread of postgame critiquing: "Dad's upset we lost and feels bad that I didn't play well, and he's going to tell me what I did wrong now that we're alone in the car." This dread does not promote love of the game or improvement in skill.

If postgame talk can't be completely avoided, Jason's dad should be encouraged to ask open-ended questions that elicit Jason's view before launching into his own critique:

"What do you think about the game?"
"What did you enjoy most about today's game?"
"How do you feel about how you did?"
"What do you think was the best part of the game?"
"What do you think you did well today?"

These questions elicit information on how Jason is processing the game and allow his parent to attend to what he needs. For example, Jason might respond to a postgame question with this tearful rant: "I totally SUCK. I hate baseball and I don't want to play any more! I shouldn't play infield EVER again, and I can't hit worth a damn!" At this point, criticism of Jason's play will corrode his love of the game and his trust in his dad. It surely will do nothing to improve his performance.

Yet this tearful mode may be hard for parents to handle. It might stir up a parent's own failures, humiliations, and losses. This "gut memory" may not be traceable to a single event, and the parent may not be aware of the deep emotional scar rubbed raw by the child's present pain. Recall that Jason's dad was robbed of a more promising career by an injury. Recall too, the pressure of being the only black coach in town. Might Jason's struggle and temporary "underachievement" fire up a deep-in-the-gut, unconscious body memory of loss as an athlete and the ever-present stress of being a person of color in America? Such wounds can cloud parents' ability to see a child's present needs clearly. They can also trigger an impulsive emotional reaction during competition. Harsh, unloving, unproductive criticism can make kids like Jason come to this conclusion: "I suck." They might not always say it, but the tears and slumped shoulders and tummy aches attest to it. As Dr. Shane Murphy has written in *The Cheers and the Tears*,[11] too little

attention is paid to what produces children's tears. Adults can be too preoccupied with making sure kids get the cheers.

Parents who are impressed by hard data might be interested in a study
done by the U.S. Navy in the early 1970s. An in-depth psychological assessment of elite navy pilots showed that the highest-rated fighter pilots had
significantly closer relationships with their fathers than did the lower-rated
pilots. These relationships included shared interests and were described as
"unusually close."[12] Apparently these fathers found a way to instruct their
sons in a positive, affectionate way without being overly critical. Accurate
instruction, coupled with a positive, affectionate approach, really can promote excellence.

Know Your Child's Sports Environment

Jason's predicament somewhat resulted from the understaffed coaching
ranks of the Little League. The children of coaches frequently are asked to
sacrifice for the good of the team or the league. Frequently in youth sports,
decisions are based on what's good for the adults rather than what's good
for the child. Mr. Walker was moving up from T-ball to fill a need for
coaches, and his son Jason came with him. In this case, the league bent its
own rules about age limits because Jason was an older 7-year-old just under
the cutoff date. Youth sports programs deal every day with arguments about
rules, eligibility, and the choice of being rigid or flexible. This effort requires
constant work and revision. As parents we must be aware of how the rules
and regulations or an exception to them will affect our child. Will the choice
be in the best interests of his or her development? Because the Walkers decided to move up, they should have taken steps to lessen the pressure on
Jason, especially early in the season. Such parent-to-parent discussions can
ultimately influence a sports program. The more that families articulate
clear goals and values related to sports, the greater the likelihood that sports
programs will reflect similar ones.

One Little League in Boston articulates its mission with the acronym
SHARPP. S is for *spirit. H* is for *hustle. A* is for paying *attention. R* is for *respect. P* is for *positive* approach. And the final *P* is for *practice.* (See chapter
15 for a further elaboration of this code.) Just like a good parent, the people
that run this league have tried to articulate core virtues and good habits that
they seek to promote. Every coach and player does not always succeed in living up to the code, but these goals hold everyone to a standard and help re-

solve conflicts when they arise. Families, coaches, and administrators can be allies in instituting such a mission.

A Closer Look: Deidre, the Irish Step Dancer

Deidre Kelly is a 9-year-old athletic girl. With three older brothers, she's learned how to fend for herself, and she enjoys competing in a number of sports. A vibrant member of the local boys and girls club, she has regularly played soccer, softball, and basketball. She's won a number of awards for her athletic ability and team spirit. A good student, she has several friends at school and in the neighborhood. In addition to her involvement in school and sports, Deidre has been an Irish step dancer since the first grade, an activity that runs for eight to nine months during the school year. Her mother is particularly happy about Deidre's dancing. In her opinion, as a form of art it balances her daughter's sports activity, and it's a link to the family's ethnic heritage. Quietly, Mom is also pleased about the dancing because it resolves her mild but persistent worries that Deidre might be too much of a tomboy.

The highly regarded coach of the swimming team, considered one of the best programs in the boys and girls club and indeed in the whole region, has asked Deidre to join the team. Mrs. Kelly knows this coach to be a wonderful young woman with a great approach to sports and life; no doubt Deidre would benefit from the swimming program. Deidre is initially excited, as she usually is, about taking on a new endeavor, but Deidre's parents worry that she will be spread too thin. Then Deidre offers to quit step dancing. Mrs. Kelly knows that Deidre's dance teacher is a "wee bit of an old-school task mistress" who has recently criticized Deidre, somewhat harshly, for what the teacher thought was a lackadaisical approach. But in general, the dance teacher is wonderful, and deep down she's a softie. Deidre's parents sense that their daughter has taken great pride and joy in performing well, and both are re-

> Children can be relieved and comforted when parents exercise their authority by setting clear, protective guidelines and consequences for straying from them.

luctant to see Deidre give up dance. Deidre's grandparents would be especially grieved by the change. How should they proceed?

Know Your Child

Deidre's case represents an embarrassment of riches; the child, the parents, and the programs have a lot to offer. Deidre does many things well, and she enjoys life. She has good friends and succeeds academically and socially in school. By any measure, she is a healthy, well-adjusted kid. She carries herself with an air of confidence that some girls her age do not possess. Her home life is warm and supportive, reflecting the family's easygoing style. Deidre's mom calls her husband "the reasonable one," and she trusts his organizational skills to manage the family's schedule. This is fortunate for Deidre. Because she is friendly, likable, and successful, Deidre is a popular child much in demand for social events, sleepovers, sports teams, and other activities. Frequently, young children (perhaps girls a bit more than boys) who have flourished in a loving, nurturing environment have difficulty saying no to well-intentioned offers and proposals. Such children can be relieved and comforted when parents exercise their authority by setting clear, protective guidelines and consequences for straying from them. The Kellys prevent Deidre from overscheduling herself.

Know Yourself

The Kellys benefit from having a clear family mission. From the time their children were old enough to participate in sports and other extracurricular activities, the Kelly family has articulated a pretty consistent sports mission statement. They want their kids to try varied activities in sports, music, and the arts in order to get along with different types of kids and learn a range of skills. They expect Deidre to work hard, respect her teachers and peers, and have fun.

Based on their experience with their older boys, the parents try to limit their children to one sport per season, while tolerating the occasional seasonal overlaps. They also prefer to balance their children's sports activities with time spent learning a musical instrument, attending dance lessons, or participating in an after-school arts program. Generally, the kids choose these activities themselves, though the father insists that every child, including Deidre, learn to swim and ice-skate. The parents have worked well as a team. The programs their children have selected have, for the most part, been aligned with the family's values and mission. Solid communication between father and mother and their clear goals can help them negotiate Deidre's options.

Know Your Child's Sports Environment

The parents know both the Irish dance program and the boys and girls club and their missions well, and they have excellent relationships with the programs' directors, coaches, and teachers. In fact, each program has been flexible with regard to occasional schedule changes that accommodated other activities in Deidre's life. For example, the Irish step dance teacher has occasionally changed a practice time to allow Deidre to participate in a soccer playoff.

In the end, after discussion with her parents, Deidre decided to stick with step dancing and forgo swimming. Her father had stated his strong preference for this option, based on the fact that swimming involved extensive travel, meet, and practice time. Both parents did explain that although they preferred to eliminate swimming, they would accommodate Deidre's choice if she herself would rather choose swimming, provided that she give up step dancing and quite possibly basketball. Because of potential schedule conflicts with that winter sport, swimming and basketball together would break the house rule of one sport per season. Deidre went along with her parents' wishes and didn't seem to harbor resentment about it. Her parents did an excellent job of giving Deidre some freedom of choice within a framework that reasonably controlled her total activity level. Coaches as well as parents can benefit from this style of decision making. Research shows that coaches who employ a more democratic coaching style (letting players make some choices about team practices, rules, and relationships) have a lower dropout rate, and their players display greater self-esteem and overall satisfaction.

Deidre took three more years of Irish step dancing and went on to play junior varsity and varsity high school soccer, basketball, and softball. She eventually gave up soccer to play in a rock band. She continued to be a good student at a very competitive high school and enjoyed rewarding relationships with her friends and family. In this situation, experienced parents sent a clear message about what they expected from their daughter's participation in sports. They set clear guidelines but allowed for some choices. They set limits as needed, and they knew their daughter well — her talents as well as her weaknesses. They had developed a good understanding of and work-ing relationship with the people who staffed their daughter's programs. Fi-nally, through raising their children, Deidre's parents had gained a balanced view of the role sports can play in developing the whole person.

USEFUL TIPS

- Encourage children not to suffer alone. Urge them to come to their parents or another trusted person when they are in emotional pain, confusion, or doubt.
- Preserve a balance between organized sports and free, unstructured play. Kids need free time for spontaneous creative play by themselves and with their friends; it's critical to healthy emotional development.
- Create and preserve quiet time each week, ideally at least twenty min-utes a day, at least three times a week. This time should be free of radio, TV, videos, and other distractions. Quiet time allows the child to de-compress from the daily bombardment of stimulation. It lets children practice calming themselves. For families so inclined, prayer or medi-tation is an ideal form of quiet; reading might be offered instead. Prac-ticing this habit as an entire family and introducing it at an early age increase the likelihood that a child will be able to express feelings and meet emotional needs appropriately. This skill can be translated into the athletic domain as the ability to calm oneself and refocus in the face of distraction.
- Create positive postgame rituals and avoid critical analysis. Nothing kills a child's joy in sports more than negativity and criticism. Try to keep at least a 5:1 ratio of accurate praise to constructive criticism, and avoid all criticism for at least an hour following games. Even better, leave the criticism to the coach, and focus on your supportive role.
- It's never too early to help your children practice or play at their best and compete hard — while following the family code of behavior. Focus on and praise instances in which children persevere, overcome adversity, or demonstrate discipline, courage, responsibility, cama-raderie, and good sportsmanship. This approach is preferable to prais-ing only wins, base hits, goals, touchdowns, or trophies. This practice emphasizes and rewards behavior consistent with good character and the virtues of effort, proper technique, and enjoyment of sports. This is the best way to enhance performance in the long run.

4

THE TEEN YEARS (AGES 13–18)

Identity Development, Independence, and Achievement

MANY OF US can honestly say that we would never want to relive our adolescent years. Pimples, puberty, and peer pressure are a few of our most often cited pains. Some of us remember feeling rejected after being dumped by a first love or cut from the school team. Others recall a pass we dropped in a devastating loss to a school rival or a test we failed that caused a drop in our GPA.

Adolescence is also a time when many of our teens blossom and shine: making a crucial play in a hockey game that leads to a huge win, acing a challenging chemistry exam during junior year, being elected captain of the varsity team after years of hard work and dedication characterize some of their accomplishments. At such moments, we can almost see them being transformed into confident, well-balanced young adults. But the ups and downs of adolescence cause many of our teens to become overwhelmed at one time or another. As our teens ride the emotional highs and lows of success and failure, we as their parents are often taken along for the ride. We hold our breath, hoping they will not become discouraged by failure or endangered by the wrong group of friends or experiments with drugs and alcohol. We hope they survive adolescence in one piece, embrace their successes, and march confidently toward adulthood, but the uncertainty along the way can be taxing and painful for all involved.

While many of our teens experiment with dating, going to parties, and asserting themselves in school and sports, others may not find these activities appealing or easily accomplished. Teens may still feel closely connected to us, preferring to stay home and watch a movie rather than go to the school dance. Their bodies may not mature as quickly as those of their peers, making it difficult to fit in socially or compete effectively in sports.

Some of our adolescents feel clumsy, awkward, and uncoordinated. We find ourselves trying to understand exactly what our teens want and how to help them. Often this task feels daunting because the needs of teens seem to change frequently and unpredictably.

Adolescent children are preoccupied with two all-consuming, essential tasks: discovering their identity and establishing their independence. It is quite common for teens to be immersed fully in this quest. Joining teams, participating in community service groups, and becoming engaged in school politics all serve their self-discovery. And as they get involved in various activities, they wonder how others perceive them: are they smart, funny, friendly, talented at athletics, and attractive to the opposite sex? Questions about who they are and what they stand for buzz in their developing minds, often creating anxiety and uncertainty.

> As teens mature, they still are quite fragile emotionally.

At the same time, adolescents begin to assert their independence. They will pull away from us and rely more on friendships, romances, and relationships with teachers and coaches for emotional support. Relationships with peers and adults will help them gain the strength to function on their own as they move toward adulthood. This transition can be painful for many of us parents; we are unprepared for the abruptness of our kids' change in behavior. Suddenly, we cramp their style. They don't want our advice about school or sports. It's as if we don't matter much to them anymore. But though teens are excited to explore the world, learn about themselves, and become more independent, they still need their parents more than they recognize. Sometimes adults can forget this because our kids may act as if they don't need us. Yet we continue to play an important role throughout their adolescence and young adulthood, though the ways in which we support our children will change.

During early adolescence, our teens begin to experience significant changes in mind and body, though at varying rates. Some boys will begin to grow facial hair and become increasingly muscular, while others will look like fifth-graders more interested in playing with toys than being a middle or high school student. Our daughters develop at varying rates as well. Some, in their physical growth and overall maturity, seem ready for the varsity basketball team; others are more tentative about sports and teen social life.

On a similar note, sports intelligence, or an athlete's capacity to understand field play, game strategies, and coaching instruction, may come into bloom during this stage of development. For example, some athletes suddenly know just what to do in a game situation. The shortstop makes the right throw to first base. The basketball guard slows down the offense. The hockey player understands the proper positioning when defending a power play. Or, even more exceptional, the athlete shows leadership when the team is down or rises to a challenge when others fear failure. By contrast, some athletes who are physically gifted may lack the sophistication, game smarts, or confidence to excel. Some skills cannot be taught, and during adolescence athletes may discover mental talents and abilities, such as concentration under pressure, not previously experienced.

But even as our adolescent athletes reach their senior year in high school, their brains may still not be fully developed. The frontal lobes, which influence the ability to organize, sequence, and attend to information, are crucial in athletic performance and can continue to develop well into the young adult years. Therefore, it is quite possible that some of our teens may not reach their full potential until the college years or even their midtwenties.

It is difficult for many of us to assess accurately our teens' abilities and their need for our guidance. Consider Alex, a 14-year-old freshman in high school who is trying out for the varsity soccer team. Although he is one of the best players in his class, and many have told him that he has a chance to make the team, Alex has one major disadvantage. Standing five feet, five inches tall and weighing only 135 pounds, he is much smaller than the juniors and seniors with whom he is competing. Alex's parents are proud of their son's abilities but worry that he is setting his hopes too high. When the news arrives that Alex has not made the team, he becomes enraged and then inconsolable. Knowing that their son is devastated by this news, Alex's parents struggle to figure out how to help him. They want to talk to him more about it, though it appears that he wants to be left alone.

The confusion Alex's parents are experiencing resembles the challenges many parents face during their kids' adolescent years. As our teens mature, they still are quite fragile emotionally, sometimes surprising us by how ill-equipped they are to handle seemingly manageable setbacks on the athletic field. As they move toward middle and late adolescence, the stakes rise. Making the team and playing are becoming harder to do. Some teens will have to face the reality that they cannot compete with their peers in the realm of sports; this may lead them to quit or change sports. Increased academic challenges only add to the stress. Teens begin to worry about applying to college. They fear they won't get a scholarship, or even worse, they won't get in. These uncertainties can make them irritable, unpredictable, and at times overwhelmed.

Sarah is a 17-year-old midadolescent cross-country star. At 16, Sarah was ranked in the state in cross-country running. In her junior year, just after her seventeenth birthday, a talented freshman joins the team and beats Sarah by 20 seconds in the second race of the season, quite a difference for a 3.1-mile race. Sarah's performance declines in the following meets, and her parents think that she is on the verge of quitting the team — a poor decision, in their opinion, since she is a candidate for a college scholarship. Every attempt Sarah's parents make to support her seems to exacerbate the situation. They want to help her get back on her feet, but they can't seem to identify how to do so. Parents of adolescents often find themselves second-guessing their actions and words because their kids don't respond in ways that make sense. This phenomenon often persists well into the young adult years. We want to help, but our role is becoming increasingly unclear. Even as our kids mature and advance to higher levels in sports, we still may think we know what's best for them. But as they grow older and more knowledgeable about their sport, we may know less about it than they do.

David, an older adolescent, has just turned 18 and is in his senior year of high school. David is uncertain about whether to try out for the varsity lacrosse team. Having played lacrosse for many years and served as a backup goalie on the junior varsity team in his junior year, David knows that his chance of getting playing time as a senior is remote. To his surprise, an opportunity arises for him to be the lead in the school play. When David's father hears that his son is planning to quit lacrosse to do this, he becomes angry. He vows to his wife that he will not support David's decision.

All three of these adolescents are becoming more independent as athletes and individuals. At the same time, making the team, getting playing time, and being successful become increasingly difficult for them because competition levels rise greatly during the high school years. It's difficult to know how much emotional support Alex needs in managing his feelings of rejection and disappointment. It seems that every time Sarah's parents try to help, they make things worse. And it is quite evident that David's father is strongly against his son's quitting lacrosse. How do we help teens develop emotionally and perform to their best ability while providing enough distance to allow them to establish greater independence from us?

ESSENTIAL SKILLS FOR CHILDREN OF AGES 13–18

Because adolescence is often unpredictable, it is difficult for many parents to identify what is normal and healthy behavior in the context of sports. Despite this uncertainty, there are core traits that we hope our adolescents develop by the time they reach age 18.

Confidence

Adolescence marks the period in which boys and girls learn about their strengths and weaknesses, an important aspect of self-discovery. Teens must learn to manage negative feelings and setbacks caused by their weaknesses — which may be hard to acknowledge. This task can evoke powerful responses: "Damn it! I suck at this!" "What's the point of this dumb game?" "I want to quit." Discovering strengths and confronting weaknesses can be both rewarding and painful, particularly in sports. Sarah's confidence is shaken when she loses the cross-country race to her freshman teammate. Working through this blow to her self-esteem is critical, for she is clearly talented and needs to remind herself of her ability. David, on the other hand, recognizes both his limitations in lacrosse and the promise of a new opportunity in an activity outside of sports, even though such a decision challenges his parents. Younger adolescents, like Alex, may have a more fragile sense of themselves; Alex's confidence is shattered when he fails to make the varsity soccer team. But failure for adolescents offers an opportunity to learn from mistakes or setbacks and improve so that they are better prepared for the next opportunity; however, watching our adoles-

> The key is to reward adolescents with more freedom and independence as they demonstrate the capacity to learn from their mistakes.

cents fail is painful for us as parents as we worry that our children will become discouraged and despairing. Developing confidence during adolescence is a dynamic process with many highs and lows. Ideally, as parents, we look forward to seeing our teens take chances in sports and other arenas such as the arts and academics, make decisions about what activities they like and don't like, and gain the strength and experience to manage success and failure as they progress toward adulthood.

Interests

Many of us may recall adolescence as a time of a huge influx of new interests and passions. Sex, preoccupation with their bodies, parties, time with friends away from parents, and identification of academic, athletic, and professional goals make up teens' major interests. At this stage in life, their bodies are changing dramatically. Girls are developing breasts and beginning menstruation. Boys' racing hormones increase their sex drive, making it hard for them to sit still and concentrate. These changes demand much of adolescents' attention, often distracting them from participation in sports. Adolescents must learn to balance these interests wisely, so one does not eclipse another. Of course, this is easier said than done. For example, in the movie *Blue Crush*, the lead character is a female surfer who begins to lose her focus in surfing competition when she starts to date a professional quarterback. As she spends more time with her new boyfriend, she practices less, ignores her surfing friends, and watches her confidence for an upcoming competition drastically drop. Her challenge, like that of many adolescents and young adults, is to strike a balance between the time she needs to practice and the time she allows for her boyfriend. Only after she recognizes the importance of practicing and training can she perform to her ability while also developing a better, more supportive relationship with her boyfriend. Parents of adolescents want to ensure that their children have a variety of interests, including relationships, sports, and academic activities, while maintaining a balance.

> Talent and maturity emerge at uniquely different moments for each child.

Relationships

It should come as no surprise that adolescents direct much of their energy away from parents and toward their peers. Our daughters and sons may begin to date and devote hours of time to talking on the phone and contemplating their romantic interests, much of which they share exclusively with their friends. Using cell phones and instant messaging, teenagers chat or type on their computers into the wee hours. We hope many families have unlimited-minutes plans with their phone companies.

In any case, this frequent contact with friends and potential romantic partners serves adolescents' need to develop strong relationships. When not on the phone or on the computer, they can develop particularly strong friendships with teammates on the athletic field. For example, boys on a football team develop a tremendous bond as they weather the physical and emotional challenges of preparing for each game. Relationships with coaches also play a critical role. As our kids get older, they look more to their coaches and teachers for advice and guidance, a process that can be uncomfortable and surprising to many of us parents but necessary if our teens are to become independent. Sarah's cross-country coach may be more effective than Sarah's parents in helping her recover from a series of disappointing losses because she is helping Sarah learn to manage her feelings on her own, specifically *without* relying on her parents. Strong, positive relationships with other adults and peers help adolescents like Sarah develop a sense of independence and confidence in their own abilities. By age 18, it's a good sign if our adolescents use sports and other areas of interest to experiment with developing strong relationships with coaches, teachers, and peers, including romantic interests. They can carry what they have learned into positive relationships in adulthood.

Judgment

Unlike children in the stage of latency (ages 6–12), young adolescents can develop the capacity to evaluate, judge, and act on their own. They can choose not to drink and drive. They can decide that cheating during a game is not worth the risk of getting caught, even if it means they might lose.

Providing adolescents the space to make decisions on their own, however, can provoke anxiety for us as parents. We fear that without our input and direction, our children will make poor decisions; perhaps they will quit the sport that would have led to a scholarship, which is the concern of Sarah's parents. Our kids will spend time with friends who we believe will have a bad influence on them. Or even more frightening, they will try that harmful drug or take a risk such as going to a late-night party in a dangerous part of town or having sex impulsively. Although as parents we will always want to protect our children, it is precisely this freedom to make mistakes that teenagers need in order to learn and grow. The key is to reward our adolescents with more freedom and independence as they demonstrate the capacity to learn from their mistakes and act in responsible ways.

However, our adolescents are not adults. They will still need our support and guidance when they make mistakes and poor decisions on and off the athletic field. By the age of 18, our adolescents should demonstrate an ability to evaluate their decisions and behaviors and deal with the consequences of their actions responsibly.

Emotional Control

It is hardly a challenge for many of us parents to remember the emotional roller coaster of adolescence. We might like to forget how hard it was to manage immense hormonal and other physical changes and the overpowering feelings associated with a first crush or being cut from a team or excluded from a group of close friends. We will watch as our adolescents scream incessantly, cry uncontrollably, punch a wall, or verbally lash out at others when failing to manage strong feelings. Even though our adolescents are becoming more sophisticated intellectually, often their thinking has not caught up to their emotions. Frequently, they don't understand why they feel angry, frustrated, sensitive, or agitated. This uncertainty can make them feel out of control or lost at times. For example, Sarah is devastated when she loses a race to a freshman; it feels as if her world is crashing down. Yet the beauty of sports is that it provides adolescents with opportunities like this one to manage emotional highs and lows by facing competition. When faced with a setback, they are challenged to find ways to manage their feelings, get back on their feet, and keep moving forward. Younger adolescents like Alex may have a harder time controlling emotions and will need more support and guidance from parents. As adolescents approach the age of 18, they should start to get a better handle on their feelings so that setbacks and disappointments do not incapacitate them. Even when they become overwhelmed with feelings, they recover more quickly and use their own resources to do so.

Sports-Related Skills

During adolescence, most athletes come into their own. Unlike the previous stage, in which it is difficult to evaluate athletic ability and potential, most of our 18-year-old adolescents will reach full height and gain a more accurate sense of their physical skills and hand-eye coordination. Even within this period, however, great variability exists. A 15-year-old boy might stand at five feet, seven inches one year and then shoot up to six feet, two inches the next. Coordination and agility will obviously be affected by such remarkable changes. Alex the soccer player is only a freshman; fortunately, he will have future opportunities to try out for the varsity team as he gets older and stronger.

The fully developed, well-rounded athlete possesses a composite of physical and mental skills and abilities that are influenced by the genes inherited from parents and the environment that helps to shape their athletic identity. Some athletes struggle in high school with a certain degree of clumsiness or limited strength but later turn out to be superior athletes when their bodies fully mature. This phenomenon is not unusual. One year, a senior basketball player is tall and skinny, with feet so big that she often trips over them. No matter how well coached she is, she continues to falter over the same physical mistakes. The next year, as a freshman in college, after growing more muscle and getting more comfortable in her adult body, she begins to use her strength and size to her advantage, surpassing players who previously appeared to be much more skilled.

Kids who develop physically at older ages face some disadvantages; some athletes who have great potential are overlooked or cut from a team at the moment they are physically evaluated; future development may not be taken into account. Imagine if Michael Jordan quit basketball after being cut as a sophomore in high school. It took him only one year to develop from a below-par high school varsity player as a 15-year-old to a future superstar at age 16. Though few individuals have the natural ability and athletic intelligence of Michael Jordan, we must recognize that talent and maturity emerge at uniquely different moments for each child. We cannot predict when and if this will happen, but can create positive, encouraging sports experiences for our children so they have the opportunity to achieve their potential.

Ideally, by age 18, our adolescents will reach most of their growing capacity, develop greater hand-eye coordination, and have an enhanced ability to understand the more tactical, complex aspects of sports, including individual performance and team strategies. Confidence in their ability is also crucial as they play at higher, more challenging levels.

A CLOSER LOOK: ALEX, THE SOCCER PLAYER

Fourteen-year-old Alex is waiting for his mother to pick him up, and it seems to take an eternity for her to arrive. Alex's mother is surprised to see tears in her son's eyes.

"What's wrong, honey?"

"Nothing," Alex replies. Silence follows, but about halfway through the ride home, Alex shares that he was cut from the varsity soccer team that day and is in shock.

Knowing that Alex had anticipated making the team, his mother responds thoughtfully. "Oh, Alex, I'm sorry you didn't make the team. I know you really wanted it. Do you want to talk about it now?"

"Not really." Alex sighs. "I'm just pissed I didn't make it. I know I am good enough, but I didn't get a lot of chances to score. I had one pass from that senior guy, but it was too far out of my reach. It's just not fair. Now I have to play with the JV guys."

> Learning to fend off negative thoughts can help teens stay focused on the positive in the moment of play.

Alex's father is more matter-of-fact. He has just returned from an exhausting business trip and has hardly unpacked his bags when he hears the news. "Hey, Budso, I guess you just weren't ready yet. Don't worry about it. You'll have a good experience at the JV level. You'll get a lot of playing time, and you'll have fun with your friends."

"Come on, Dad! That's not what I want to hear. I should have made team!"

"Well, maybe you should have, but you can't do much about it now except make the best of the situation."

Alex doesn't answer. With tears in his eyes, he sulks off to his bedroom.

Perhaps Alex's father is too tough, or perhaps his mother is overly supportive. It is difficult to know when to commiserate with teens and when to push them to look on the bright side. To address this concern, we must first assess the situation. How mature is Alex emotionally and physically? Is there a good fit between Alex, his coaches, and the sports program? Answering these questions will help guide Alex's parents to a suitable course of action.

Know Your Child

Alex is clearly upset. As parents, we can certainly understand the pain of being rejected. Younger adolescents like Alex are just beginning to manage a huge change in emotional makeup, and they are often unprepared for how strong their feelings are. For Alex, soccer is the one thing that makes him feel good about himself, even when other parts of his life feel uncertain. He has always been a star in soccer; he recalls scoring a goal in almost every game during his eighth-grade season. Classmates regularly remind him that he should make varsity, and even the coach made a special gesture, pulling Alex aside to ask him to try out for the team. His getting cut crushes his dream of being the only freshman on the varsity squad.

Other factors contribute to Alex's strong reaction. He is entering his first year of high school and feels anxiety about how well he will adjust to harder classes, older students, and intense athletic competition. Failing in his first high school experience feels like he is getting off on the wrong foot, even though making junior varsity is a wonderful accomplishment. As parents, we often need to remind ourselves how sensitive our adolescents can be to failure and how ill-equipped they are to cope with these powerful feelings. In our research and clinical work with high school student athletes, we are often struck by how negative and self-critical they are. They distort minor mistakes and setbacks, inflating them into huge disappointments. Caring parents can help them correct these misperceptions to protect their sometimes fragile self-esteem. Also, our support can help teens become more mentally tough competitors. Learning to fend off negative thoughts can help them focus on the positive in the moment of play, a crucial element for successful performance in sports at any level. Not many kids score goals when saying to themselves, "I suck."

Alex initially resists sharing his disappointment with his mother but eventually tells her how angry and hurt he is. By contrast, older adolescents, when faced with similar disappointment, are less likely to share their feelings with parents — they want to handle it on their own. Alex is not quite ready for that level of independence. He needs his mother's support and reassurance, even if he doesn't act that way. Without this safe environment in which to express his feelings, Alex might have felt even worse. Having this opportunity to vent his negative emotions and feel support may well give Alex the energy and confidence to get back on his feet and keep fighting.

The push and pull parents feel when dealing with an angry, disappointed adolescent can be confusing and exhausting. But it is crucial to persist in finding ways to check in with our irritated, angry, and troubled young athletes, even if they seem resistant to help.

Know Yourself

Alex's parents want to help their son manage his disappointment and gather strength for a positive season playing on the JV team. Obviously, Alex's mother finds it easier to be supportive and nurturing to her son. She wants him to succeed in sports, but she is more concerned that he be happy and enjoy his experience. Having played sports only until junior high school, she is less tuned in to the importance of making the team. Her nurturing approach, however, fits well with Alex's need to feel understood and supported. Often, our adolescents just want parents to be there for them and listen. Giving advice is often more effective after the emotional tension has died down, when our child is more receptive to guidance.

Alex's father falls into the trap of providing advice too quickly. More dismissive of Alex's disappointment, he is focused on Alex's future. This approach angers Alex because he is too hurt and disappointed to think about the future. As a former athlete, Alex's father recognizes that his son's setback is minor in the broad scheme of things and in fact is likely the best

Adolescents need understanding, but they also count on parents to help them maintain their confidence and keep trying.

outcome for Alex. Tired from a long business trip, Alex's father perhaps lacks his more typical patience and ability to communicate sensitively. His response sounds blunt, and Alex lacks the perspective to understand the important message his father is sharing with him.

Often as parents, we feel frustrated when we have wisdom and experience yet our children just don't want to gain from us. As parents, we might think, "If we could just take our knowledge and place it in their heads, they would be so much better off." Athletic fathers can at times be wise about how to encourage their children. At other times, they can be bullies at pressuring their children in sports. We often find that athletic fathers push their sons to be tough in the face of adversity, but sometimes this approach backfires, even if the intentions are good. Clearly, Alex's father is trying to build his son's confidence to tackle the challenges of JV soccer, which will help him become a better player. Alex will need this type of support from his parents, and their belief in his ability will increase his confidence so that he can compete. Ideal parents possess a bit of Alex's mother and his father in dealing with our athletic children. Our adolescents need understanding, but they also count on us as parents to help them maintain their confidence and keep trying. The yin and yang of the nurturing but encouraging approach works well for Alex; however, one feature without the other might not be as effective.

Know Your Child's Sports Environment

Fortunately, Alex is participating in a good sports program. Though the level of competition is often extremely high, the coaching staff takes into consideration athletes' overall development. Instead of bringing Alex up to the varsity level, his coaches chose to protect his development and future confidence as a player. As parents, we cannot protect our children from failure. Giving Alex the opportunity to try out for the varsity team created an opportunity to test his skills.

While there is some risk that this setback will damage Alex's athletic confidence and development, the opposite will more likely prove true. Through positive experiences on the junior varsity level, he will have the opportunity to build skills and get more game experience, a good way to bounce back after a disappointment. Waiting a year before playing at varsity level actually enhances his potential for improved performance down the road. In fact, the following year, he made the varsity team and won a starting position on a state-ranked team. The additional training and athletic competition readied Alex physically and emotionally to tackle the challenges of more competitive play.

Other coaches might have assessed a freshman like Alex and said, "Hey, this kid is going to be a star. It may be a risk to bring him up now because of his size, but we'll take our chances." The player would have been pushed hard before he was prepared, which can lead to quitting the game, missed opportunities for friendship, and the risk of getting injured. Many parents naturally don't want this to happen, but how can we tell whether a program will pace our kids, adding challenge as young athletes are ready to face it? It isn't easy to find out. Talking to other parents, teachers, and even kids can make a difference. Parents may be the best judges as to whether their child has the physical and emotional stability to handle more intense, competitive environments. A slow pace entails far less risk than pushing a young athlete too hard.

Of course, every parent believes his or her children are exceptional, so maintaining a slow pace can be a struggle. Although it is good for kids to know that their parents think they are great (it builds a sense of self-worth), parents easily overestimate their children's level of ability and maturity, and this puts pressure on young teens, who might in fact have a better sense of their level of performance. Even more problematic is the teen who shares the distorted view of his or her parents. When the reality of this kid's limitations becomes evident, he or she is unprepared to manage it. If parents know their teens are participating in a good program with solid coaches, however, they can rest assured that their children will get a fair shake and develop a realistic sense of their skills and abilities.

A Closer Look: Sarah, the Cross-Country Star

Like Alex, Sarah, the 17-year-old cross-country runner, feels shame and humiliation long after her disappointment in sports. After losing the second race of her junior year to the new freshman runner, Sarah sits at the dinner table with a glum look on her face. Now that she has lost to the freshman for a second time, her mood and outlook have worsened. Just as Sarah begins to clear the plates from the dinner table, her mother asks, "Hey, how'd it go with the meet today? You haven't mentioned a thing about it."

"I don't want to talk about it, Mom. I lost to that freshman again. I'm better than she is. I hate cross-country. It's such a dumb sport."

Trying to contain her own frustration at this criticism of her own long-time favorite sport, Sarah's mother responds, "Well, honey, sometimes you get beat, and you just have to work harder. I remember when I was in high school, and I lost a meet to a younger kid on the team. I was really angry, but it made me work that much harder. The next meet, I caught her. You can do the same."

"I don't want to work that much harder," Sarah shrieks. "You just don't understand!" Sarah heads to the den to read. Her father rolls his eyes at his wife. Not an athlete himself, he can't fathom the importance of sports to his wife and daughter. Conversations like the one that has just transpired aren't unusual, and it seems that Sarah ends up feeling worse afterward.

To ease the tension, Sarah's father says to her mother, "You know, sometimes you just have to listen to her. She's upset, honey, and she doesn't want you to push her. She pushes herself enough as it is. She's worried about getting into Duke the way that you were too, and she's burning herself out. I think you need to back off a bit."

Later in the evening, Sarah's mother decides to talk with Sarah about running. Knocking on her daughter's bedroom door, she anxiously awaits Sarah's response.

"Go away! I don't want to talk to anyone."

Sarah's mother is not sure what to do.

Know Your Child

Why is Sarah tanking in her meets? Is the freshman just a better runner? Or is something going on beyond what Sarah's telling her parents? To figure this out, we need to consider the challenges of being a 17-year-old young woman in sports. Changing from a girl into a young woman raises a host of issues. Some changes are welcome, but others are at times embarrassing, making the girl feel uncomfortable about her body. For some female athletes, particularly runners, gymnasts, and swimmers, these changes can make it more difficult to compete. Female swimmers may develop wider hips in their adolescent years, which create more water resistance and consequently slow them down. The development of breasts, possible increase in body weight, and onset of hormonal surges make it hard for some female athletes to match the performance they could achieve when their bodies were more slender. The freshman who beat Sarah has still not matured in this way. She is thin, with narrow hips. Though Sarah has more strength, the freshman is much lighter, making it easier, in some ways, to compete.

Some athletes in Sarah's position may resist these natural body changes by starving themselves and exercising excessively, making themselves vulnerable to eating disorders and injury. Parents need to be sensitive to the changes in adolescent girls' bodies and how girls adjust to

> For some female athletes, particularly runners, gymnasts, and swimmers, changes in their bodies can make it more difficult to compete.

them. Accepting and welcoming these changes is important to their development. Playing sports can ease this process by building physical self-confidence, but it also might produce excessive self-criticism. If Sarah can recognize that her muscular build is a strength, she will both improve her physical self-image and capitalize on her strength by using it in competition.

Parents don't want to consider the possibility that they occasionally lose sight of what's best for their children.

Most running coaches emphasize that success lies in training properly. Rest, water intake, and varied workouts all play a role. On the other hand, stress, whether internal or external, can hinder performance. If Sarah is feeling both pressure from her mother to excel and fear that the freshman will continue to beat her, she will be susceptible to performing below her ability. Stress soaks up energy, makes the body tense, and may even disturb sleep. By contrast, the freshman runner feels none of this; she's just the new kid on the block, with no expectations or worries. Sarah, as an upperclassman, is expected to achieve at high levels. Pressure to win and overtrain may be a factor in Sarah's performance decline.

Parents, whether athletic or not, sometimes forget how stressful high school sports can be. Practices can run into the dinner hour, and teens are expected to return home, do several hours of homework, and then reprise the performance the next day. College applications and SATs are just around the corner, another source of pressure for Sarah. A disappointment in sports tips Sarah's emotional scale from its typical intensity to a sense of being overwhelmed. Taking time to gain support from others is what she needs to regain balance and confidence.

Know Yourself

Even to the inexperienced eye, Sarah has obvious talent for her sport; she has a shot at running for a college team. And Sarah is both blessed and cursed to have a high-achieving mother. Clearly, the drive for achievement has been a source of contention in the household. Sarah's parents need to consider how they affect their daughter's performance.

It is striking how frequently parents lose sight of the impact they have on their children. In our clinical work, young athletes often tell us that their parents don't pressure them to win, but they later inform us that those same parents get very disappointed if they lose. It's as if both parties don't want to admit that pressure exists. Our children don't want to make us look bad, nor do they want to anger us by confronting us about how much we push. Perhaps driven by pride and fear, we as parents don't want to consider the possibility that we occasionally lose sight of what's best for our children. This leads to a silent standoff; the family behavior remains the same as the problem worsens.

Sarah has big shoes to fill. She feels she must live up to the example of her mother, a serious jock. A former collegiate runner at Duke, Sarah's mother incorporates competitiveness and discipline in running her pediatrics practice. She continues to stay fit, and Sarah's friends admire her, seeing her as a model of beauty, capable motherhood, and professional success. Sarah views her mother as perfect; she doesn't sense that her mother struggled too as a young woman. She feels pressured by her mother's success, and Sarah's mother is not fully aware of the effect she has on her daughter.

Our children tune in to us. They remember things we say, especially the foul language that slips out at the dinner table. But more important, they remember the comments we make about how they look, act, and perform. Comments that Sarah's mother makes about her daughter's performance have great power. They make Sarah feel even more frustrated and self-critical. Adolescents like Sarah now have the intellectual capacity to understand and remember these comments, but they are still quite fragile in their sense of self. We need to remind ourselves that though our children may look and act like adults at times, they are still adolescents, not thick skinned like adults. Because an adolescent is still a kid in some ways, parents need to soften their comments and reduce the pressure they might unwittingly put on their kids. Adolescents will likely enjoy their sport and perform at their ability level if they feel less stress.

Yet the success of Sarah's mother is not necessarily detrimental to her daughter. In fact, successful parents can provide wonderful role models for their children. By seeing her mother as a woman who can achieve in the world, Sarah can begin to believe in her ability to do the same. But Sarah does not yet understand that her mother is not perfect or that she achieved her position in life through hard work and many ups and downs. Although Sarah's mother tries to remind her daughter of her own struggles, the message does not sink in. As parents, we know our adolescents can be stubborn or slow to grasp what is clearly stated to them. Sarah's mother may have to tell Sarah frequently of her own difficulties and imperfections if Sarah is to understand that failure is a normal part of life. Such reminders may need to come thick and fast before our children truly hear them and take them in.

Sarah's father plays a more subtle yet crucial role. He provides helpful feedback to his wife. Though he is also ambitious, he is more laid back about sports. He can see how Sarah feels pressured and finds a way to communicate this effectively to his wife. Sarah's mother, after time and self-examination, realizes that she sees herself in her daughter. She wants Sarah to do well so badly that it can be hard for her to remember that they are two different people, with different personalities, temperaments, and goals. Recognizing that her own ambition may contribute to Sarah's performance decline, the mother wisely pulls back and plans to soften her words to her daughter. This turns out to be an effective approach, allowing Sarah to feel less defensive. She now feels free to consult her mother as a resource as she recovers from her setback in running.

How much should parents worry when adolescents drop from the height of great achievement to a trend of low self-confidence and poor performance? Will this difficulty ultimately undermine athletic performance and result in burnout? The answer depends on the issue causing the problem and who the athlete is. In high school, most athletes experience some setbacks or failures. How they handle these trials will influence how they manage future adversities in sports and other contexts. Sarah's parents have an opportunity to support Sarah as she struggles through her junior year. They can remain staunchly at her side as she comes to realize that competition entails many highs and lows. Truly great athletes know how to bounce back from failure, make adjustments to their game or training, and then try again. Therefore, failures like the one Sarah is experiencing present meaningful opportunities for learning. If parents can take this perspective, they can keep their own anxiety in check and focus on helping their child become a stronger, more versatile athlete, competitor, and human being.

Know Your Child's Sports Environment

What is the atmosphere of Sarah's cross-country team? How does the coach respond to Sarah's loss? Some cross-country coaches interpret poor performances like Sarah's as evidence of a flaw in training and will use the setback as an opportunity to reevaluate. If Sarah's parents consider her coach's perspective, it will help them provide appropriate support for their daughter. For example, telling Sarah to work harder when her coach is encouraging her to rest will cause more harm than good. Being knowledgeable about Sarah's team, and, in this instance, her coach, can prevent a young athlete from getting a confusing mixed message.

Sometimes older teens rely more on their coaches and communicate less with their parents. This is a natural part of becoming independent, but it can be difficult for parents to manage. But if parents respect and have faith in a coach, they can feel comfortable encouraging their teens to seek the coach's help in resolving problems. Although some of us parents with a history of high-level athletic experience may believe that they are more knowledgeable and experienced than our kids' coaches, they must nonetheless pass the baton to the coach. Adolescents need to learn from other adults so that they can later tackle the challenges of leaving home. As parents, we should see our new position not as a demotion but rather a gracious step aside to let our children grow and become independent young adults.

> Though our children may look and act like adults at times, they are still adolescents.

Though Sarah possesses greater maturity than Alex the soccer player, she still struggles with confidence. Success boosts her self-image, but failure knocks her down. She is still coming to recognize and accept her strengths and weaknesses. Her impulse to quit running, though understandable, signifies a somewhat immature response to frustration. Sarah will eventually learn from her failure and address her difficulties in running with emotional stability. Leaning on the teaching and support of her coach will help her grow to greater maturity and independence.

A Closer Look: David, the Lacrosse Player

In contrast to Sarah and Alex, David is not a highly driven athlete. His years of playing lacrosse have been fun, but he recognizes that he lacks the passion and talent to compete at the highest levels. David knows that his father will likely not support a decision to quit lacrosse; however, he feels he really needs a change. At dinner one night, David garners enough courage to raise the issue with his parents.

"Dad, I know you love it that I play lacrosse, but I just don't like it anymore. I'm not going to get any playing time, and I'd rather do something that I'm really into. There's this awesome play, and the theater teacher asked me to try out for the lead. I think I'm going to go for it."

David's father drops his fork on the plate and shouts, "Are you kiddin' me? After all these years, you're going to quit lacrosse?" Silence follows as David tries to contain his frustration. David's parents make eye contact while their son clears his dishes from the dinner table. They can't find the words to express how they feel.

After this blowup, David and his father don't speak for over a week. David's mother is stuck in the middle. She's beginning to think that her son is making the best choice, but she doesn't want to alienate her husband by agreeing with her son.

Clearly, David's father is passionate about his son's lacrosse. Yet it's not clear that playing is in David's best interest. Like many parents, David's father asks himself, "Is my son just doing this to spite us? Is he just being rebellious?" Part of the problem is that David's parents are not in agreement. It's challenging for parents to continue to work together even when they don't agree.

> Truly great athletes know how to bounce back from failure.

KNOW YOUR CHILD

Painful as it may be, many older high school athletes must face the fact that they will play for the team, sit on the bench, get cut, or move on. Although some parents never had to "ride the pines" during a high school game, many of us had the painful, frustrating, and at times humiliating experience of sitting on the bench in uniform and watching the game without ever participating. It really sucks! If the situation persists over the course of one or more seasons, athletes have to ask themselves, "Is this really worth it?"

David finds himself in this position. Since his sophomore year in high school, he has been five feet, eight inches tall. He understands that his body will not grow much more, even if he lifts weights and attends extra practice sessions. Though he has decent stick skills in lacrosse, David recognizes that he lacks the speed, size, and talent of the other players. He was the backup JV goalie in his junior year, but that wasn't much fun. He rarely played, and most of his friends were either on the varsity team or playing a different sport. Going into his senior year, he realizes he has little chance of receiving playing time. The coach has been frank about this. Most important, David's desire is not with lacrosse. Though several of his good friends play on the team, the divide between the "starters" and the "bench players" is strongly pronounced. He can see the writing on the wall.

When the opportunity arises to play the lead in the school play, David is truly excited. It's a chance for him to shine in a new and fascinating activity. He's always been interested in theater but never tried it because it conflicted with sports. David is not dropping a sport because he is depressed or angry; he isn't tempted to try risky behaviors. He's a good student who has never gotten into trouble and is now attempting to take charge of his life. His decision to pursue acting instead of lacrosse is somewhat like taking on a new job. It represents a healthy challenge that involves both excitement and uncertainty.

David's choice may also reflect a measure of rebellion against his parents, particularly his father, yet this is not necessarily unhealthy. Older adolescents need to stand up to their parents. In less than six months, David will be heading off to college. He will have complete control of his decisions there — he can pick his classes, friends, and activities with limited input from his parents. It's no surprise that he is beginning to make his own choices now.

Know Yourself

For David's parents to work through this family crisis, they must become aware of their own biases and the influence of their own experiences. David's father is a former lacrosse player who has lost touch with the game. Because he has not attended many of David's games or spoken with the parents of other players, he's not aware of the present talent level on the team. He doesn't know what it's like for David to practice every day and feel left out, disregarded by his coaches. His memories of playing lacrosse in his senior year of high school are some of his fondest. He recalls the great friendships he made and how being a part of the team helped him feel confident as a young man. Thinking that David might not have the same wonderful experience makes him sick inside, a feeling worsened by the guilt he experiences for remaining uninvolved in his son's athletic activities. Now, faced with these strong feelings, he is unprepared to support David's decision to quit.

It can be difficult for parents to realize how our past experiences influence our reactions to our kids. Some self-questioning can help raise our awareness: "Why am I reacting so strongly? What's the big deal if my kid does acting instead of playing lacrosse? What am I really worried about here?" Even parents who don't think of themselves as the introspective type can benefit from struggling to answer such questions, especially when our children are about to leave home, a time when feelings can intensify. We might have regrets about the things we should have done, and even though our kids often drive us crazy, we are sad to see them go. For David's father, complicated feelings make it difficult for him to understand the purpose and importance of his son's decision.

David's father also lacks awareness of the danger of imposing lacrosse on his son. For athletes to perform at their best, they must love the sport. Without passion, the hard work involved in the game does not seem worthwhile, and the joy of relaxed and energized focus does not kick in. David needs to discover where his own passions lie. The pressure from his father and the unrest between his parents about lacrosse could cloud David's vision of what is best for him.

The standoff between David and his father makes life difficult for David's mother. What is she to do with these two stubborn males? She might let her son know that she supports his decision and explain that his father is just being stubborn because he used to enjoy playing lacrosse. However, she will also need to address these issues with her husband. She might gently try to draw him into a discussion: "Honey, is it really a terrible thing that David is trying theater? What's so bad about this decision if he really loves it? Why are you so angry over this?" Even if a discussion does not immediately follow, David's father can mull over the questions when he's alone. Eventually, he may be able to discuss David's decision with less intensity of emotion. Even if David's father never becomes fully comfortable with the decision, he can agree to support his son in it. This period marks a time of stress in David's relationship with his parents. The challenge for them is to stay engaged in their son's life, whatever his decisions may be.

They need to continue to be available and interested because it is not uncommon for young adults to return to their parents for support and advice.

Once young adults demonstrate that they can live on their own, they may seek out the wisdom and experience from their parents with less resistance and defensiveness.

Older adolescents often need to stand up to their parents.

Know Your Child's Sports Environment

David's parents are well aware that his school community greatly emphasizes sports. Choosing drama over athletics does have some consequences. The jocks are the cool kids at school. Among most students, actors are considered a little bizarre, out of touch with the school spirit. David has to both manage the tension of displeasing his father and be strong enough to go against the grain. Choosing to act is a courageous step on his part; he is making strides toward becoming an independent thinker.

Interestingly, in David's freshman year of college, he resumes playing lacrosse at the club level. By quitting lacrosse before playing became too painful, he preserved his enjoyment of the game. He returns to lacrosse on his own terms, not because his parents or his school wants him to play, but because he does. As a college freshman, he brings passion, joy, and a sense of ownership to the game, which helps him play at a higher level than he ever imagined he could. In essence, quitting lacrosse ultimately made David a better athlete. At the same time, he took one broad step toward adulthood. As parents, one of our long-term goals for our adolescents in addition to the development of independence is for them to maintain a positive relationship with being physically active. If we force sports on our adolescents, the risk is that they will hate playing and stop being physically active. This is why it is important for us as parents to keep our eye on the big picture. We need to let them choose their passions, even if they aren't the ones we wanted for them. Although it is cliché, sometimes losing the battle is winning the war.

Useful Tips

- It's natural for our adolescents to pull away from us. This will be hard for the entire family but important for our kids' growth.

- Still, teens want us to attend their games and be there for them when they need help and support.
- Coaches and teachers can play a crucial role in helping adolescents become stronger and more independent. It's wise for parents to let this happen. We can be proactive by helping our kids find great coaches to play for.
- The brains and bodies of our adolescents are developing at a frantic rate. This process will not be complete until young adulthood. Just because they may look and act like adults does not mean adolescents are adults.
- Physical growth and mental maturity are unpredictable. Talent in a young adolescent does not guarantee talent and success during young adulthood. Some teens are late bloomers. Keeping them engaged in sports with reasonable expectations is the best formula to promote their athletic development.
- To play at the higher levels demanded in high school, kids really have to love their sport. If they play primarily for parents or for others, they will experience less enjoyment and perform worse.
- Quitting a sport isn't always a cop-out. Sometimes it means that adolescents are coming to terms with their strengths and weaknesses or seeking the right sport. Explore how they feel before assuming that they are being lazy or acting on an unhealthy impulse.
- Few adolescents will get a sports scholarship or play for a Division I program. Intense pressure to achieve this goal will likely have a negative impact on an adolescent's athletic performance.
- If our teens are naturally talented, it's wise for parents to remember that teens play their best when they feel supported by parents, feel relaxed, and enjoy their sport.
- Adolescents may take different paths in sports than their parents did. This is not a problem. As long as they are engaged in sports of some kind, it is likely that they will remain physically active throughout adulthood.

5

HIGHER LEARNING AND
HIGHER STAKES (AGE 19 AND UP)
College Sports and Sports for Life

THE START OF YOUNG ADULTHOOD is complex. Leaving home inspires both excitement and fear about entering a whole new world, where young adults are expected to be simultaneously devoted to school, sports, and social life. This move away from home typically marks the entrance into adulthood.

For perhaps the first time, these young people can independently choose what they do with their time and energy. They face easy access to drugs and alcohol and the option to develop intimate relationships. They can stay out partying until 3:00 A.M. and attend morning practice at 6:00 A.M. Generally, as long as they "show up," coaches, professors, and dorm monitors are little concerned about other choices that college students are making.

> Helping kids understand that they are worthy people whether they play sports or not may be parents' most important task.

Young adults who participate in college athletics are among the elite. Less than 5 percent make it there. Those kids typically confront major change; after being the "big fish in a little pond," they find themselves a "little fish in a big pond." The student who earns a college scholarship was probably the dominant player on the high school team; now, at college, he or she may sit on the bench for at least the first year. Their teammates will likely be excellent athletes and often good students as well. College athletes must adjust to competing against better athletes and are also expected to work harder.

To thrive in this competitive arena, college kids must literally become obsessed with improving as athletes. They often are required to achieve demanding goals in physical conditioning, from adding massive amounts of muscle to achieving extremely low levels of body fat. They may be required to practice four to five hours a day, miss classes, and choose from a limited selection of courses to accommodate practice and competition schedules. Many coaches require extra "optional" weight-lifting sessions, individual training sessions, and videotape viewing to analyze skills or strategize against opponents. This level of commitment to a sport may appear unbalanced to parents, and sometimes even to the athletes themselves. Yet college athletes must totally invest themselves in their sports training to have success. Kids who earned an athletic scholarship often experience the highest expectations from coaches. Since they are "on the money," coaches often believe that scholarship athletes owe the team total commitment. Yet this focus on improving in sports can serve kids well in many ways. They can make the winning shot to help their team win a championship. They can enjoy living in lean, strong bodies. Their peers often admire them, and some will go on to professional, Olympic, or national teams.

But ironically, the intensive training required for collegiate and elite sports puts young adult bodies at greater risk of injury. Often, varsity athletic schedules require that our kids practice twice a day, six days a week. They are expected to stretch themselves to the limit in terms of fitness, strength, and skill refinement. The excessive demands on their bodies, paired with highly structured, exhausting schedules and intense pressure to win, can lead to burnout or physical breakdown and injury. For example, one in ten participants on college women's soccer teams will tear an ACL (anterior cruciate ligament) each season. Also, overidentifying as an athlete can make kids believe that they don't matter as human beings unless they succeed in sports. Helping them understand that they are worthy people whether they play sports and succeed or not may be parents' most important task at this time. Young adults need empathy from us. We need to do our best to understand their new, highly demanding lives and help them feel good about themselves and thrive in their college careers.

Consider Cindy, a sophomore and Division I scholarship swimmer. She was an excellent high school swimmer, and everyone in her small hometown, especially her dad, expected that she would be a star college swimmer. Cindy progressed well until the start of her sophomore year, when her world started to crumble. Her times have dramatically increased, which is putting her scholarship in jeopardy. Cindy's mom is quite sick, and her dad's business of twenty-five years is on the brink of collapse. Cindy has not told anyone at school about her family problems. Her coach yells at her during practice: "Cindy, you are just going through the motions! Where is your drive? You are wasting my time! If you don't get it going, we can find someone else to fill your scholarship spot!"

Cindy's parents are struggling with how to help her. She is having trouble in the pool, and they don't like how the coach is treating their little girl. How can they best support Cindy, who is geographically distant and dealing with people and challenges that are unfamiliar to them?

Kenny, a lean, muscle-dense, superconfident young man, has been playing football since he started in Pop Warner football. He has been recognized as one of the best players on every team he has joined. Though he started as a "walk-on" at college, at the start of his sophomore year he was awarded a partial scholarship. Football has been a tradition in Kenny's family; both his dad and grandfather were great players, and Kenny's accomplishments have been a source of pride for his family. Imagine their shock when Kenny calls home to say that he has been suspended from the team because he tested positive for marijuana use. He now must attend mandatory counseling sessions, and if he tests positive again, he will be permanently removed from the team.

Consider Molly, a player on the U.S. National Soccer Team. A top collegiate soccer player, she now is in the middle of her first season on the U.S. team. Molly has again injured her left knee. She tore her ACL for the third time, underwent surgery two months ago, and is currently rehabilitating her knee, which is not responding in the way she or her doctors had hoped it would. She is in a lot of pain, and her range of motion is still limited. She is struggling with whether or not to retire from the sport.

Molly's mom feels torn about how to counsel her daughter. She feels proud of Molly's accomplishments and believes that if Molly gets back on the field, she will have a good chance of making the next Olympic team. Yet another injury could affect Molly's long-term health. Also, Molly's identity is totally tied up in being a soccer player. Her mother wonders what might happen to Molly's self-esteem and confidence if she quits.

ESSENTIAL SKILLS FOR YOUNG ADULTS AGE 19 AND UP

Confidence

At the beginning of adulthood, our kids learn to evaluate aspects of the world around them and themselves as well. We as parents naturally hope that our young adults will be confident and successful. And in collegiate sports, confidence is essential. In high-level competition, the difference between the top athlete and the one who struggles is often the level of self-confidence. Our young adults must develop a belief in their ability to perform; the confident athlete has learned how to maintain that belief when competition gets stiff. Setting achievable daily goals that support long-term sports goals helps athletes build confidence every day. In addition, making use of input from coaches and other knowledgeable people can sustain this effort. Confident young adults can also employ positive self-talk — messages that they say to themselves — to maintain an empowering mental focus.

Confidence plays a part in all aspects of life. If Molly chooses to retire from soccer less than two years away from the formation of the next Olympic team, she will need confidence in herself to thrive in a role other than that of athlete. Kenny will need to draw on his own inner confidence to shake his marijuana habit. We as parents can greatly help our children as they face similar challenges by voicing our belief in them.

Interests

Young adults want to explore new experiences. They are bombarded with new ideas and opportunities, yet they must find a sense of balance. Their interests include developing close, intimate relationships; participating in, or observing from a close perch, the use of drugs and alcohol; experimenting with body piercing, tattooing, or styles of clothing that might puzzle their parents; and different academic and recreational pursuits. Whatever their interests, young adults feel a deep craving to fit in and be cool. And of course, sports remain an intense interest for those still involved in athletic competition at this age. This interest can lead them to try performance-enhancement drugs or restrictive or excessive eating patterns to meet the weight requirements of a sport.

Young adults need meaningful relationships.

Kenny has gotten caught up in the cool crowd and is paying the price by failing a drug test. Athletes like him are lucky if they have parents who know how to offer thoughtful support as they sort out the problems and challenges of being an independent adult. We as parents can provide a soft place for our young adult children to land and remain a source of wisdom and guidance as our children choose among interests that may benefit or harm them.

Relationships

Young adults need meaningful relationships. Key friendships that develop at this phase can last a lifetime. We as parents can encourage our children to appreciate and maintain room for these important relationships. Young adult athletes are often valued mainly for their ability to perform, which can make it hard to learn that sports performance does not define a person. If young adults overidentify with their sport, they can lose perspective and deify it. Developing meaningful relationships is not always easy in high-level athletics. Athletes can become almost exclusively self-focused — that is, selfish. Individual sports, such as tennis or track, can pose a particular challenge. In these sports, your "teammates" can be your biggest competitors, making it hard to develop close friendships. Young adults who are excessively competitive — those who value winning above all else — may jeopardize the formation of relationships. Parents can help their children keep sports in perspective by reminding them that they are first and foremost precious human beings — regardless of how they place in a race or other competition.

Judgment

Young adults are expected to have a clear sense of right and wrong and the confidence to choose what is right. However, Shields and Bredemeier's research[1] in the realm of competitive sports and moral development indicates that involvement in highly competitive sports can almost corrupt athletes. They are often taught that the umpire calls what is right and wrong, and their task often is to get away with whatever they can — and not get caught. This view matches how kids think when they are less than 5 years old — they'll do whatever they can to get what they want at that level of maturity.

The demand to win, paired with the need to be excessively self-focused, can train young adults to care little for others. This reduction in empathy, paired with training that relegates the judgment of right and wrong to referees, can cause young athletes to avoid taking responsibility for their actions both on and off the playing field. Healthy young adults, by contrast, have enough respect for themselves — including the long-term health of their bodies — and others to make choices based on what's right rather than what they can get away with. Unfortunately Kenny did not take this path. He decided to join in the partying with his teammates and figured that as long as he didn't get caught, his pot smoking didn't hurt anyone.

As parents, we can help our young adult children best by modeling and discussing good choices. Though the kids may not show it, they deeply care about what their parents say and think. We need to help them differentiate between getting away with something and taking the right action.

Emotional Control

By early adulthood, habits of emotional control are beginning to firm up. From the time our kids were in diapers, we have been trying to help them learn to control their emotions — from temper tantrums to crying fits. In early adulthood, our children continue to need our help in refining their ability to control their emotions. This can be a volatile time in life — it may include falling in love or becoming passionately identified with a sport. Romantic breakups can be devastating. Losing a competition can be incredibly embarrassing. Choosing a college major can cause angst for months. Deciding where to live can cause great excitement to collide with intense dread. Young adults must learn to master their emotions as they experience worries, dread, fears, and overwhelming joy. They must rein themselves in enough to focus when necessary. And in sports, controlling and channeling emotions is critical if they want to perform well consistently. During competition, feelings may oscillate from high-energy enthusiasm to chaotic disappointment or anger. Good emotional control helps the high-level college or elite-level athlete attain strong character and improve in both practice and competition.

> Healthy young adults have enough respect for themselves — including the long-term health of their bodies — to make choices based on what's right rather than what they can get away with.

Cindy's parents can help her with emotional control. They can talk openly with her about the stressors in their lives—Cindy's mom's battle with cancer and her dad's business problems. Her parents can model to Cindy the importance of being honest about difficulties while at the same time maintaining perspective. Taking the pressure off Cindy—helping her realize that she will be fine with or without swimming—could relieve stress and help her simply focus on her sport.

Sports-Related Skills

In this stage of athletic development, young adults are at their peak in terms of ability to play their sport. Often, they focus on fine-tuning technique; the core physical skills have long since been developed and become virtually automatic. One major area of continued development is the honing of mental skills, which includes handling competitive pressure and retaining love and passion for the experience of the sport itself.

A CLOSER LOOK: CINDY, THE SCHOLARSHIP SWIMMER

Cindy's dad is overwhelmed with the dramatic changes taking place at home. His wife was just diagnosed with cancer, and his business of twenty-five years is about to close down. He can no longer compete with the big chain stores. The effect of this news on Cindy has been weighing on his mind. But when he and his wife called Cindy to tell her what was going on, she seemed fine—concerned for her parents yet able to take events in stride. She told them that she would focus on her studies and swimming—they could count on her. But it hasn't turned out that way.

> Good emotional control helps the high-level college athlete attain strong character and improve in both practice and competition.

Over the past few months, Cindy has begun failing in many parts of her life. Her grades are terrible, and her swimming performance has gone downhill. The meets are the worst; Cindy feels as if they don't matter compared with what is happening at home—and she feels powerless to do anything about it.

In a recent meet Cindy again missed her speed goal. In fact, she is 3.5 seconds slower in the 100-meter butterfly than she was last season. Her coach is totally exasperated. In fact, he is close to asking Cindy to sit out the season. Cindy knows that if she doesn't pick up some speed, she could lose her scholarship. The pressure from her coach, a tough course load, and the fact that her mom is sick and her parents may be on the brink of financial disaster are more than she can bear. Cindy dreads calling home to report on her swimming; it's just one more downer for her parents. As she makes the call, her stomach begins to turn, and she feels nauseated and nervous, just as she does at every practice. It seems that the harder she tries, the worse she does at everything.

"Oh, hi, honey," her mother says. "It is so great to hear from you! How did your race go?"

Cindy replies, "Not so well . . ."

By Cindy's tone, her mother knows that it has been another bad week for Cindy. "Sweetheart, you know that your dad and I love you, no matter how you do in swimming. We just want you to be happy and do well in school."

Cindy begins to cry. "It's all too much. I miss you guys; I'm so worried about you and dad. Swimming used to be so important to me, but now I just don't care. My teammates are mad at me because they think that I am not helping the team win. I am still trying hard, but I'm not making my times. I hate it. Maybe I should just come home for a while."

The pressures on this family are intense, and swimming at this level when a scholarship is on the line adds to the stress. How can Cindy's mom help Cindy keep family concerns from dominating her thoughts so that she can manage her own pressures and enjoy her college experience?

Know Your Child

Cindy's chronic state of worry and dread is a major challenge for her. As she worries about her mom's health, her dad's business, and the need to go faster in the water, she is losing sleep and swimming poorly. During practices and races, her mind is never focused on the swimming itself; instead, it swarms with worry. Her body is in a chronic state of "bracing" — she literally fights against her muscles as she swims. Worry and anxiety can make muscles chronically tight, and tightened muscles create additional resistance as Cindy is practicing and competing. Though talented athletically, this young woman is fighting against herself with every stroke.

Given her lack of success, Cindy might appear to be going through the motions; it looks as if she isn't motivated to push herself. But in high-level sport, when young adults demonstrate a lack of effort, it is usually due to fear of letting down themselves, their parents, their coach, or their teammates. Fear disables them mentally and physically or discourages them from even trying. When such highly competitive athletes appear unmotivated, it may be a sign of burnout or a loss of self-confidence. Cindy's coach thinks that she is simply not trying hard enough; because he has no idea of what is happening with her family, he misreads Cindy's efforts. In fact, she is trying too hard and literally fighting against herself.

Recently, after practice on the way to the dining hall, Cindy finally talked with her best friend on the team: "Jen, everything totally sucks right now. The coach is always screaming at me. I'm dead slow in the water. I don't know what the hell is going on. I hate going to practice. I'm getting so bored. How can you stand it? The workouts are so repetitive. I hate it that Helen was in front of me all practice. I hate everything so much right now. My mom is really sick; I just want to move home. I'd love to quit, but I'm on the money." Though Cindy felt better for a moment after getting this off her chest, she soon felt embarrassed and wished that she hadn't confided in Jen. Cindy likes others to see her as strong. She's a "pleaser"; she is the first person in the family to attend college and wants to be a source of pride for her parents. In addition, since she is on scholarship, she knows that the only way she can stay at school is to do well in swimming. It's hard enough to live up to these demands under the best of circumstances, but now that Cindy's mom is sick, the expectations that Cindy puts on herself are unbearable. Cindy needs to feel empathy and unconditional love from her parents and to know that she matters to them whether or not she does well in school or maintains her scholarship.

Know Yourself

Cindy's parents would benefit from considering their own sports experience, which shapes how they assess Cindy's. Neither Cindy's mom nor dad attended college. In high school Cindy's dad was a wrestler, and her mom was not involved in sports. Her mom struggles to decide whether she really wants her little girl to be working so hard as an athlete; she doesn't grasp the intense demands of college sports. Nonetheless, Cindy's mom was ecstatic about the swimming scholarship because the family couldn't afford to send Cindy to a top school without incurring a huge debt. The scholarship was

Cindy's "ticket," yet her mom has doubts as to whether swimming is right for her girl.

Though Cindy's dad identifies himself as an athlete and is truly happy about Cindy's swimming, neither parent really understands what it takes to juggle a college academic load and a varsity sport. Unless they ask Cindy to talk about her experiences, they will have no real sense of the stresses and challenges that she is facing and will not be able to truly support her. They could ask her questions like these:

> "Honey, I don't know what it is like to be in your situation. Can you tell me about your daily training?"
>
> "Can you tell me what is great about what you are doing? What is really hard about it?"
>
> "Help me understand how you feel about swimming, school, and living on campus."

Discussing topics like these could help Cindy feel supported and understood, which might relieve some of the pressure that she is feeling. Young people at this age tend to act as if they don't need support from their parents, but in fact they will listen carefully to what their parents have to say.

In addition, Cindy's parents need to be honest about what they are dealing with, such as her mom's cancer treatment and her dad's business closing. Providing this type of information shows that they are treating Cindy like the young adult that she is.

On a different note, Cindy's parents have become so accustomed to seeing Cindy excel in swimming that they are unprepared to respond to her current lack of success — not an unusual outcome for someone adapting to swimming at a higher level. In this situation, some parents may demand that their children continue to excel; others, like Cindy's parents, may feel uncomfortable about the higher level of commitment their college-age children are expected to make. Both types of parents may unwittingly place pressure on their children. Cindy's parents are somewhat naive about Cindy's college experience. They've always simply expected that she would dominate and are at a loss to help her in her slump.

Cindy's parents could help her by encouraging her to think back on why she began to swim competitively in the first place. Visualizing times when she swam with joy and passion, even creating cue words to remind her of these times, could be very helpful. Her parents might also urge her to focus on one day at a time. Cindy is thinking too far ahead, as many athletes do. They are so worried about trying to win a championship in six months that they lose sight of what will get them there. Instead of worrying about how to keep her scholarship, Cindy should home in on the small daily steps covered in practice — improving her technique, simply feeling the water. These daily goals should be slightly challenging yet achievable, to ensure that success will follow effort. In our research with elite and Olympic oarsmen, we found that the very best of the group — those who won gold medals internationally — tend to use the one-practice-at-a-time approach. When one multiple-gold-medal winner was asked about the expectation of winning another medal, she laughed and said, "It is all that I can do to focus on one practice or event at a time. This takes all of me. And then I spend the time until the next practice or race mentally and physically recovering." Becoming a champion is cumulative — it is a summation of what the athlete does each day.

A lack of effort is usually due to fear of letting down parents, coaches, or teammates.

When the desire to win — to be successful — dominates the thoughts of young adult athletes, it can create performance anxiety or a sense that all the practice and preparation are mere drudgery. A way to help Cindy overcome this thinking pattern is to encourage her to focus only on swimming itself, NOT how she will do. Cindy needs permission from her parents to use swimming as an outlet, a place where she can put aside her worries and be regenerated.

Know Your Child's Sports Environment

College student athletes have brutal schedules. From early in the morning until late evening, they attend classes, go to meals, participate in often two practices a day, attend study halls, and work out during off-seasons. During season, most sports include dozens of competitions, which require time on the road. In addition, these young people are expected to be involved in team social activities, help entertain recruits, and then meet their basic need for sleep — often in loud, jam-packed dorms.

Young adults in college sports also must fight against certain biases.

Other students may resent it when they are required to miss some classes because of competition scheduling, and some professors automatically have lower expectations of athletes' intellectual ability. These kids are stretched in many directions and often feel exhausted. On top of this, these college students are expected to win. Coaches' jobs depend on winning seasons. This environment can make sports less enjoyable. Athletes can find themselves worried or dreading practice or training. In college sports their performance has high stakes: signing bonuses, scholarship money, and other related opportunities. College Division I sports are very demanding. Cindy's parents need to know about this environment so that they can be a source of unconditional support and encouragement to her.

Cindy continues to swim both because of her scholarship and because swimming has become a part of her, yet the pressures of high-level competition, the demands of school, and troubles at home have drained Cindy's passion for her sport. She is on the brink of burnout and needs to get some perspective. If she can accept that she is doing the best she can and focus on one task at a time, she may be able to manage the remarkable juggling act that the college sports environment requires of athletes.

A Closer Look: Kenny—Drugs or Sports?

Kenny has been playing football since he was 10 years old. But at college, he has been sitting on the bench for the first six games of his sophomore season. It wasn't so bad during freshman year; he rode the bench just like all the other freshman players. But this year sitting out during games has been awful. Kenny's dad has attended every high school and college game that Kenny has been dressed for. When Kenny plays well and the team wins, his dad is totally exuberant and excitedly points out to Kenny all of his impressive moves, in great detail. But when Kenny loses or doesn't play, his dad just sits back in dark silence. Kenny went to college only to play football, and he dreams of becoming a pro player. He has been back at school for only two months and is totally miserable. As the third running back in practice, he is bored and easily distracted.

Kenny is fast friends with some of the guys who also rode the bench during freshman year. They were superfun to hang out with. They were also big partiers. At first Kenny didn't join in with doing drugs, but eventually he began to experiment and before long he was smoking a lot of pot.

Because he doesn't drink much, he justified his smoking as not much of a problem.

This fall has been embarrassing and frustrating on the field for Kenny. But hanging out with the guys and getting high have been a nice, relaxing way to end the day. Lately, Kenny has been smoking every day and sometimes two or three times a day. He's been having the most fun that he's ever had — it didn't seem to matter that he was riding the bench anymore. Then he got called in for the drug test and tested positive for marijuana use. He never thought he'd get tested since he hadn't been playing. The athletic director called his parents about the drug test results. He told them of the university's "one chance" policy. If Kenny fails another test, he will be thrown off the team permanently.

Kenny has had a hard time talking to his dad for his whole life. He calls home, praying that his mom will answer. Then his dad says, "Hello?"

Kenny hesitates and then says, "Dad, I know that you know about the drug test. I just smoked one time. Just don't say anything. I won't do it again. I promise . . . can I talk to Mom?"

Kenny's parents are facing a situation that they never expected. They have never talked or thought about how to deal with the issue of their son's drug use. They knew that he was frustrated by sitting on the bench but expected that things would turn around for him this season. His dad is furious, wondering how Kenny could blow his golden opportunity to play in college. His mom wants to do what is best for her son.

Know Your Child

Kenny has always been concerned with his father's assessment of his ability to play football. Like most young adults of his age, he wants his parents to be proud of him. In some of our research with thousands of athletes, we've found that boys in their late teens consider their father the most influential person in their sports life, with the exception of their coach. What Dad thinks matters a lot. Kenny has always wanted to live up to his father's expectations and become a professional player, but this intense need to please his dad has impeded Kenny's development. Kenny is so worried about his dad's opinion that he was overcome with humiliation during his freshman year on the bench, and he had no skills to cope with this emotional turmoil. The easy answer was drugs. He saw his bench mates having a good time, and he figured that he needed some fun too. He was simply too miserable, thinking about how bad the next game would be. His dad would just sit and watch in dark, disappointed silence when Kenny didn't play. Kenny is an emotionally sensitive person, and pot helps dull the strong feelings that make him uncomfortable. If Kenny believed that his dad thought he mattered with or without football, Kenny would be better able to tolerate time on the bench.

Also, for Kenny, "failing" in sports has been devastating, partly because he has overidentified with the role of athlete. This identity developed because he was treated as a star and gifted athlete in youth and high school sports. He never had to endure being picked last for a competitive game in elementary school. He was never cut from a team. And Kenny, like many other star athletes, never had to sit on the bench or play as a substitute for another better-skilled athlete. Thus, he missed one of the important life lessons that sports typically offer: how to fail and recover. He will have to learn this now.

Kenny will have to choose between drug use and football; likewise, he will eventually have to face the ugly feelings stirred up by having to ride the bench. Kenny's parents can help by talking with him about these feelings. They can also help Kenny focus on what he can control and let go of the rest.

Know Yourself

Kenny's parents know that drugs and alcohol are a powerful component of college life. Yet when they heard that their child was involved in abusing drugs, they were caught completely off guard. Kenny's mother wonders how to deal with her son and her husband. She knows that her husband almost breathes through Kenny's football.

Kenny's father had been struggling for years with the fact that his son tries painfully hard to please him. Kenny's father is motivated to see his children succeed, but not at the cost of their happiness. He thought that simply playing would be enough to make Kenny happy, since football was his own biggest joy when he was young. His dad knows that Kenny needs his support right now but does not know how to give it. He is shocked and disappointed that Kenny

> Worry, the biggest drain of energy, tends to get our young adults to focus on the wrong thing on the field.

would risk so much for a few joints. Football is a tradition in their house. Respecting the game is a big deal for Kenny's dad, and Kenny simply disrespected it.

Kenny's dad could write Kenny a letter, saying how he feels yet also offering a few statements of support: "Son, I am disappointed in the fact that you are using marijuana. I know that this fall has been really hard for you. Regardless of what happens, I want you to know that I'm proud of what you've done in sports. It is normal to sit on the bench some, even as a sophomore. I want you to get some help with kicking that drug habit. Go tell the coach that you are sorry and you will commit to playing clean. Work hard and be thankful for this situation. You will eventually play if you keep a good attitude and listen to what your coach has to say. I need you to promise me that you will stop using marijuana today."

Kenny's mother doesn't care much for football but tolerates it because her husband is so passionate about it. She was a cross-country runner in high school and college. She understands the pressures of sports, yet she thinks that if Kenny is unhappy, he should just quit. But at the same time, she feels that the most important thing is supporting her son. She can accept it if he wants to keep playing, as long as he can feel satisfied about it. She can provide comfort for Kenny because the two have always had a close relationship.

Kenny's mom could talk with him about her disappointment with the drug use but spend more time trying to understand what led him to it. She knows that being surrounded with other top players has been hard. Yet she could talk with him about the positive aspects of his situation: He now has an opportunity to play with some of the best players in the country. He has a chance to become an even better ball player. Talking truthfully and honestly about Kenny's situation is the best thing that his parents can do for him. Through empathy they can help Kenny get through this difficult time.

Know Your Child's Sports Environment

Making the transition to top-level college sports was particularly hard for Kenny, having been a star athlete as a child. He had heard that at college some people were "red-shirted" their first year, meaning that they sat out the year and then played from year two through year four of college. Yet Kenny somehow thought that he'd be one of the best freshmen — that he would surprise the coaches and play his first season — but he was not in fact one of the chosen few. His coach's job depended on the win-loss record, and he was not going to take a chance with such a green player. Coaches are pushed to make decisions that will beef up the win record almost at any cost, for short-term benefit. Therefore Kenny's first and second seasons on the team saw him stranded on the bench.

Kenny attends a Division I school; such colleges tend to be extremely demanding of a young adult's time and often are dominated by a "win at any cost" mentality, though this depends somewhat on the coach's style and expectations. If Kenny's parents had done some research into the pros and cons on joining this particular team, they could have headed off some of Kenny's frustrations. They could have predicted Kenny's likely playing time as a freshman and even as a sophomore — the coach would have provided this information. His parents could also have requested to talk with an athlete graduated from the program. After going through the four- or five-year cycle, graduates have perspective and can articulate the pros and cons of a given program.

Also, Kenny is negotiating more factors than sitting on the bench and getting tangled up in the wrong crowd. He moved from a small town into a big university system, which meant change in almost every corner of his life. He now lives on campus with a huge number of other young adults of his age, eating different food, getting used to different sleep patterns. In addition, as a varsity college athlete, he was immediately put on a rigid schedule, booked from early morning workouts to late evening study halls. He fulfills additional requirements that most college students don't deal with, such as team meals, travel, study hall, mentoring and tutoring support, and extra weight-training and fitness sessions, to name a few. And, he faced the temptation of abusing drugs and alcohol, a typical feature of college social life. Kenny was unprepared for this avalanche of change to his lifestyle. His parents can help him understand how he got off track and encourage him to put his time and energy into improving his fitness, strength, and skills. They need to remain a constant force in Kenny's life. Phone calls, e-mails, and occasional visits will remind him of their unconditional love and support.

A Closer Look: Molly, the Potential Olympic Athlete

A member of the U.S. National Soccer Team, Molly has just gone through her third knee surgery. At 21 years of age, she has been playing soccer for the past 16 years. Her mom has always been very enthusiastic about her playing. Her mom never had a chance to compete as an athlete and loves it that her daughter has had many successes in soccer. From the start, it has been just Molly and her mom. Molly is an only child, and her dad left them when she was 6 months old. Beginning in ninth grade she was the top scorer for her varsity team. Ever since she can remember, people have expected that she would be the star player, and she always has been. Molly has withstood pressure well and has performed consistently. In fact, she doesn't really feel any pressure; she just loves soccer and competing. She and her mom talk on the telephone two or three times a week because Molly lives with her team on the opposite side of the country.

With the Olympics just two years away, Molly feels immense pressure to keep training to make the U.S. Olympic Soccer Team. Yet she has been thinking a lot about quitting lately. She feels in her soul that she needs to stop, to retire, but she worries about how her mom will respond. Molly has been experiencing a lot of sadness lately. She thinks that facing the awful uphill battle to recover from injury for the third time and return to competition is the problem. Molly knows that her mom in many ways lives through Molly's soccer. It is hard for Molly to tell her mom that she thinks it is time to stop playing.

"Hey, how is the rehab going?" Molly's mom asks over the telephone. "The doctor said you'd be back on the field in six weeks."

"I'm not 100 percent back to it yet. I just don't know . . ." Molly's voice trails off.

"What's the matter? Is the rehab really painful again?"

"No, no. That's not it. In fact, I'm recovering pretty well this time. I'm just not sure if . . ."

"If what? Is that team doctor giving you a hard time again? He is just so impatient."

"No, Mom. That's not it. I just don't seem to have the drive anymore. I'm just not as into it as I used to be. It is a really strange feeling . . ."

"Oh, you'll get it back. This is normal. You've gone through this before."

Molly gets control of her emotions and says, "Mom, it's really hard to say this out loud. I think this last injury is a sign that I need to move on. I'm tired of being in pain. I really don't think that I want to play anymore. I just don't love it anymore. It doesn't feel worth it."

"Molly, just two more years. This is who you are!"

"Oh, Mom, don't make this harder than it already is."

Molly's mother cannot imagine that Molly would want to retire. She wonders how to support Molly but at the same time prevent a potentially rash decision that her daughter might regret for the rest of her life.

Know Your Child

Molly by nature is very upbeat and yet seriously committed to training and play. Soccer has been her life. She has loved being an athlete and making close friends through her sport. Though from the start she was able to dominate, what she really cared about was enjoyment. The drain of enduring three bouts of injury has been hard on Molly. Nursing herself back from injury has robbed her of the fun of just playing. Currently, she has to be careful about how she runs; she can't even practice cutting and turning yet. And even though she knows that she healed up fully twice before, she has become aware of the vulnerability of her body and sometimes is too cautious. She can't recapture the free, effortless play that she used to experience. And she wonders if she will ever feel that again.

When Molly talks to her best friend, she admits, "I've really been down lately. Climbing back out of an injury hole again just doesn't feel worth it. I know that the Olympics are just two years away, but I can't imagine having to fight this knee thing for that long. I just feel like I'm done." Though usually spunky, Molly is in a downward spiral. Her hesitation about continuing to play is affected by a group of factors, one of which is her dark mood. Coping with depressive emotions is not unusual for an athlete recovering from injury. Molly will need to sort through her values, goals, and emotions to determine whether she is truly ready to retire or is simply having a difficult time working through this third injury. She'll have to decide if she's willing to risk long-term damage to her knee, work through depressive emotions, and endure another round of tedious physical-recovery sessions in exchange for the possibility of regaining her free, dominant playing style and, of course, the opportunity to represent her country in the Olympics.

Even when they are burned out and have lost their passion to compete, many young adults continue participating in their sport.

As Molly has discovered, the young adult's level of commitment to a sport can swing dramatically, from total obsession with it on one day to the compulsion to immediately drop out of it on another. Often, after young adults have lived with an intense focus on a sport for years, there comes a time when they are simply ready to stop. Molly may have arrived at the point where she can no longer tolerate the extreme ups and downs of high-level soccer, particularly while coping with injury. Because Molly has been training three to five hours a day for a few years now, she — like many other elite athletes — is living on the edge physically, close to injury or mental burnout. And Molly has fallen off the edge a few times, as represented by her chronic knee injury.

Yet with some good rehabilitation and perspective taking, Molly may find that she wants to try for the next Olympic team after all. She might spend some time thinking about how a full recovery would make her feel, in case her current physical condition is blocking her from considering all possibilities. She could focus on her love of play — how she thought and felt when she was playing at her best. This may change her view of things.

Know Yourself

Molly's mother is so invested in Molly's soccer that she may unknowingly pressure the girl to continue playing for the wrong reasons — to simply meet her mother's needs. Molly's mother had a hard time raising Molly alone. She sacrificed her own dreams of being an artist, in exchange for getting a "normal" job to provide financially for Molly. Though at the time she was happy to do anything to support her child, her life now is a little empty with her daughter living across the country. Molly's mom gets great joy from following Molly's sports career; the thought of giving up the chance to play on the Olympic team seems unconscionable to her. It makes her mother wonder why she sacrificed so much for Molly if she is willing to throw it away just because of her injury. Her mom thinks, "She's recovered before; she can do it again."

In fact, Molly's mom should reflect on how her own agenda may get in the way of what is best for her daughter. If her mother could take a step back, she might be able to help Molly sort out whether she is afraid of not fully recovering and not making the Olympic team or whether she truly is ready to stop. They have always enjoyed a close relationship. Molly's mother needs to realize how her opinion can sway Molly.

Also, Molly's mom could urge Molly to see both her trainer and her doctor to make sure that she can overcome the injury. Her mom could in addition make sure that Molly has thought about how her decision would affect her future, over both the short and long terms. She can provide emotional support for Molly as she works through depressive feelings related to recovery from surgery. Molly is at risk for making an emotional decision without considering its long-term implications. Molly's mother could help by giving her daughter permission to make the best decision for herself, regardless of what others think — including Molly's mother. Molly may not be willing to honor her own desires if she believes they would disappoint her mother.

> The young adult's level of commitment to a sport can swing dramatically, from total obsession with it on one day to the compulsion to immediately drop out of it on another.

Know Your Child's Sports Environment

Molly's level of sports participation requires 100 percent commitment. Molly knows that to make the Olympic team, she will have to push herself physically and emotionally to the edge, daily. Though she is highly talented, if she is not at the top of her game, another talented player could easily bump her off the team. Most players at her level are very similar in skill, talent, and physical conditioning. Even though she is well liked and trusted by the coaches and teammates, she still is easily replaceable. Molly is aware that younger, fully healthy players are vying for her spot. Even if she recovers well, she may never be able to play the same way again.

Molly also knows that if she keeps playing, she will travel extensively for both training and competition. She used to love this but now wishes that she could turn down the intensity. Molly also notices that many of her friends have started graduate school, secured great-paying jobs, or started a family. Though she loves the game of soccer, she has begun yearning to live a "normal" or "real" life. She is afraid that if she puts this off for another two years, she could permanently lose out on dreams like these.

On elite teams, athletes must constantly confront the tradeoffs required by the highest levels of competition. Many "normal" pursuits are put on hold; friends lead lives that contrast sharply with a tight athletic focus. Each athlete must decide whether this realm offers an experience that he or she passionately desires — if so, then it is worth the tradeoffs. It is also possible that pulling away may be the better decision.

Useful Tips

- Help your children maintain perspective, treat them as if they still matter regardless of their sports performance, and at once encourage them to pursue their sports goals. Celebrate with them in the wins and successes, but consistently tell them, through word and action, that your support and love will remain constant whether they continue playing or not.
- Young adult athletes are pressured to perform by parents, coaches, teammates, and often the media. Talk with them about what they are experiencing, and consistently remind them that doing the best they can each day is enough and is worthy of great respect.
- It is essential that young adults simultaneously invest themselves fully in sports and accept the possibility and reality of failure. We need to teach our children to accept disappointments so they can be free to embrace opportunities.
- Our children need to be able to rely on us consistently. It is best that parents keep their own wants and needs out of the picture when supporting their children in athletic pursuits.
- When only the win is valued, the young adult can be set up to overemphasize winning. When only success is focused on, the supportive, loving parent may unwittingly add destructive pressure to the many demands their child is already facing.
- Emphasize the factors over which young adults have control on the field — in the face of success or failure. This habit can give them a sense of empowerment and confidence.

PART TWO

PITFALLS AND
POSSIBILITIES IN SPORTS

6

SHOULD WE PUSH OUR CHILDREN?
HOW MUCH?

It's 4:30 P.M. Sam's parents are racing to pick him up at school. Still sweaty from hockey practice, Sam, a 15-year-old sophomore in high school, jumps in the car as his parents speed off to get him to his select team practice, where he will play until 6:45 P.M. If he doesn't make it to practice on time, his coach will bench him for the upcoming weekend tournament. He needs to start on his travel team if he is to ever have a chance of being recruited to play in college. On the ride home after that practice, Sam's father reviews the strengths and weaknesses of his performance and begins to discuss strategies for the weekend tournament. Sam has a test in math the next day. He needs to score well if he expects to get into honors precalculus next year.

Imagine being in Sam's shoes. He might be inspired by his investment in high-powered sports and academics, but it's possible that he may be overloaded. As parents of children like Sam, we are confronted with choices about how much to encourage and in some cases push them to excel to reach their potential. The challenge is to know when and how to push, and when to lighten up.

We're living in an increasingly competitive and overscheduled sports culture. Our children are experiencing stresses and pressures that many of us never felt in childhood. In sports, our kids practice more often and longer, play on demanding travel teams, and are expected to win at every age and level. As parents, we want our kids to be happy. We can see how this craziness detracts from our kids' enjoyment of playing. Yet we also worry that if we don't put them in the proper situations and fail to encourage them enough, they won't become capable achievers.

Research has shown that when children feel supported and encouraged by their parents, they perform better and experience greater joy when they play. But when parents push their kids too hard, children enjoy their sport less, and their performance declines.[1] In our national research on youth soccer kids (ages 7–14) and their parents, we learned that up to 27 percent of the boys and girls playing soccer reported that it was either their mother or father who most wanted them to play. Further, those children whose parents most wanted them to play were most concerned about their parents yelling at them during games. In contrast, kids who most wanted to play reported greater importance to having fun and learning skills. Parents who most wanted their children to play were more likely to care about their child's performance and want the coach to be more involved with the team winning games. Perhaps the most telling finding is that parents who most want their children to play also want them to get as much playing time as possible, whereas their children don't care about playing time.

Finding a balance in challenging and supporting our children in athletics requires diligence and sensitivity, and any approach must evolve over time as our kids grow up. As parents we have to do our homework and learn about our children, keep our own personal agendas in check, and discover what actually helps them have fun and thrive in sports. This is much easier said than done.

We often hear parents say to their kids as they drop them off at the field or gym, "Have fun out there!" However, we know as parents ourselves that expectations are often more complex than this casual send-off implies. Behind closed doors, many parents debate what they think their children should accomplish in sports. In one instance, a mother says to her husband, "I think Betsy could be a great ice hockey player if she just practiced more often." In a different circumstance, a father says to his wife, "We can't expect Tommy to make the team when he is so clumsy and uncoordinated. No one in our family is a jock." It is difficult to predict how these contrasting parental expectations will affect Betsy and Tommy.

Our children are experiencing stresses and pressures that many of us never felt in childhood.

The expression "You're damned if you do, and you're damned if you don't" articulates the dilemma many parents experience in regard to pushing their children. Kids can face problems if expectations run too high *or* too low. For example, an athlete like Betsy might feel overly pressured to improve. Going to practice begins to feel like a chore. When she plays, Betsy feels a pressure to please her parents by playing well, and as a result her performance declines. On the other hand, parents who have limited expectations can do a disservice to their children in a different way. Tommy might interpret his father's lack of pushing as meaning that, "Dad doesn't really think I can do it, so why should I try? I'll never be good at anything."

Parents need to emphasize values such as effort, attitude, and skill development more heavily than outcomes, such as winning or scoring goals. If children sense that their parents believe in their ability and encourage their effort to enjoy themselves and work hard, they are likely to have a better, more successful experience. If Tommy's father provides positive motivation, his son might think, "If Dad thinks I can do it, I must be able to. All I have to do is try hard. Dad will be happy because I am trying hard. That's all I have to do." Belief in Tommy's ability can translate into a foundation for confidence. This is one of the greatest gifts we as parents can give to our children.

In our clinical work with athletes and their parents and even coaches, we often reiterate a central tenet in sport psychology: prioritizing the process of playing a sport, such as paying attention to details in the moment, succeeds better than focusing on the outcome. Countless stories from our clinical work and research support this idea. When working with the parents of a 7-year-old softball player who struggled at the plate, we encouraged them to tell her to focus on watching the ball and keeping her back foot down when she swings. Their daughter had become so focused on getting a hit that she forgot to attend to the fundamentals of swinging the bat. She was also making herself anxious before each swing: "Oh, God. Just let me get a hit." No athlete performs well under these circumstances. Once she focused on watching the ball, waiting for the pitch, and swinging with her back foot down, she was able to hit the ball more consistently. Most important, playing softball became fun for her.

Of course, outcomes should not be entirely disregarded. They offer a means to measure progress and inspire us to work harder and be wiser in order to achieve our goals. However, improvement and excellence are achieved by focusing on controllable aspects of performance. Parents who encourage their child to embrace values, such as effort, courage, and fun, and offer specific tips that empower him or her to engage in the game, such as watching the ball, reduce the pressure on their child: "Okay, all I have to do is try hard, focus, and have fun. I can do that."

Most of us perform at our best when we're not under pressure, but there are some who thrive when the heat is on — these folks are the exception not the norm. Imagine how difficult it would be to work if the boss was constantly looking over your shoulder, reminding you of the importance of success and the dire consequences of failure, including embarrassment and humiliation. You'd be miserable and paralyzed. Kids can have a similar experience if pushed too hard.

Imagine an adult parent playing golf. When she shanks her shot, does she say to herself, "Nice swing, kiddo. You'll get them the next time. Isn't golf fun? Wow, it's beautiful out here on the course. Love being with my friends. Life is great!"

More often than not, she says, "Damn it! I can't believe I did this again. Did everyone see how bad my swing was? This is going to be a painful day if I don't get my act together."

These negative thoughts usually hinder performance, according to sport psychologists. Exceptions to the rule exist, but generally speaking, most players are discouraged by negative thoughts and images. The same is true for our children. If not phrased positively, criticisms can be interpreted as negative aspects of our child's sense of self regardless of age.

If we know pressuring doesn't help most people, including children, why do we continue to do it? Parents who drive their children too hard are often influenced by their own anxiety, which can take on many forms. One common fear is that a child will be robbed of opportunities unless he or she works to maximum capacity. Parents can also pressure each other about their kids' path to success:

"Did you sign up Johnny for tryouts yet?"

"No. Why? Is it important?"

"Of course it is. If he doesn't make this team, he'll never play for the high school team. That's what we're hearing from some of the coaches and parents."

"Really? How long are these tryouts?"

"It's not too bad — three-hour practices for the first week, and then they make cuts at the end of the second week."

"Are you serious?"

"Of course. That's just the way it is."

Tryouts are just the beginning. Driven to create optimal opportunities for their children, parents devote significant energy, time, and money to kids' sports. They get up early to drive their children to indoor soccer practice. They buy expensive hockey equipment so their son won't be at a disadvantage during tryouts. They sacrifice their own leisure time to attend games, sometimes traveling long distances. Frankly, this effort is exhausting. Many of us can see there is a problem. We feel like saying, "Hey! This is nuts. It's just a kids' game. We're not in the pros here." But we do worry that our children will be at a disadvantage if they don't play for this travel team or that elite team or attend five practices per week. If they quit, would they lose friends? Would they be bored? Thus parents keep investing in the sport, and a game designed for the joy and benefit of children and adolescents begins to have increasing importance for adults, and their words show it:

"Their team had better win. We've spent so much time and money
    this season."
"She should get that scholarship. We've given her every possible
    advantage. The personal coach, the camps . . . it had better pay off."
"Are you kidding me, ref? How come you didn't start Teddy? He's
    your best player!"

Another factor that causes parents to place pressure on their children is the living out of unfulfilled fantasies. Researchers in youth sports note that parents can become dependent on the successes and achievements of their children.[2] This is why the second step in the three-step approach — know yourself — is particularly difficult to accomplish. A father pushes his son to become a college hockey player because he failed to do so twenty-five years earlier. A mother pushes her daughter to train harder in track because she never had the opportunity to be an athlete when she was younger. In cases like these, we as parents are typically unaware of the impact we have on our children. Then — seemingly without reason — a child begins to perform poorly, becomes injured, or just decides to quit.

Rather than blame someone else ("His coach never plays him, and that's why he quit." "The coach isn't training him properly."), we as parents need to examine our own behavior and role and then adjust them. Even better, we could take a hard look at our parenting style before problems surface. This is without a doubt a difficult challenge. It requires a review of our own successes and failures in sports and other areas.

Most of us don't want to go back to those places. We don't want to acknowledge that events from the past still affect us. But our children stir up uncomfortable feelings because they return us to times when we felt hurt or disappointed as children. In the arena of our children's sports it seems that our vulnerabilities come back to haunt us, making it easy to overreact in a public place or, later, at home with our kids. Becoming aware of these complicated feelings and their origins will help keep our behavior in check and remind us that sports are for our children, not for us. The earlier we start, the better the outcome for our kids.

Still, we know that there are times when our children do in fact need a little push — a challenge to take on more, to work harder or take a risk that they are ready for. How do we push our children appropriately? Each child poses unique challenges. The following section offers ideas for dealing with kids of various levels of athletic skill and motivation. The first challenge for many young parents occurs when their child does not want to participate in sports. In this situation, parents wonder if they should push anyway. At the same time, they worry about pushing their kids too much or not enough.

ANTHONY, THE NONATHLETE

Anthony's parents are alarmed to learn from his third-grade teacher that Anthony has no friends at school. At 8 years of age, he is the shortest boy in the class. He often eats lunch alone, hunched over his peanut butter and jelly sandwich. When the recess bell rings and all the children run outside, Anthony stays in and reads a book. He loves to read and enjoys talking about books, but most of his peers don't respond to him. Anthony seems happiest when he's at home, reading or talking to his parents.

Concerned that their son is becoming isolated and possibly depressed, the parents try to encourage Anthony to play touch football with the neighborhood boys. "No, I'm fine. I don't feel like playing," he says, returning his glance to his book. Anthony has shown difficulty with hand-eye coordination and doesn't seem to enjoy sports. He can't really catch or throw a ball. Even when his father throws him a fluffy orange Nerf ball, it bounces awkwardly out of Anthony's hands and onto the floor; Anthony's reaction reflects lack of interest rather than disappointment. His parents worry that he avoids physical activity because he is afraid to fail in front of his peers. Anthony's father, a former high school baseball player, is beside himself with sadness and frustration at his failure to understand his son and get him interested in physical activity. Anthony's mother, who is less interested in athletics, is concerned that her son is hesitant to join any sort of group activity.

Then an opportunity arises for Anthony to play on the town Little League team. His parents wonder whether they should sign him up, even though he says that he doesn't want to play. They worry that his lack of physical activity and friendships will worsen with time. What if Anthony later complains, "Mom, how come you didn't push me to play? I would have enjoyed just being on a team and learning to throw so kids wouldn't make fun of me." The prospect of making the wrong move can be paralyzing to parents.

First, parents need to know their child. The three-step approach can help in this situation. Anthony may not be ready for baseball. Forcing him to perform a sport in which he has limited ability may embarrass him in front of his peers and further alienate him. On the other hand, not playing a sport raises the possibility that Anthony will miss the experiences of trying something new and meeting different kids. These dilemmas are enough to make parents pull their hair out. They feel the stakes are high no matter what they do.

Perhaps Anthony could try an individual sport, such as swimming, that requires less coordination. This knowledge implies that Anthony's parents have really done their homework in terms of the three-step approach. The first step is to know their child. Anthony is likely to feel overwhelmed if he is forced into a dreaded sport. Choosing a sport like swimming suggests that his parents are tuned in to what will work for him. Once Anthony builds his confidence in the pool, he may be ready to try a team sport again the next season. This avoids exposing him to humiliating athletic situations at a young age, which can undermine the development of a lifelong appreciation of physical activity.

Because Anthony also needs an opportunity to make friends in sports, his parents will need to be resourceful in finding the right team activity when Anthony is ready for one.

We know from talking to hundreds of parents that finding an activity that is appealing to kids like Anthony takes more time and patience than expected. Anthony's mother tries to make a handful of suggestions, but Anthony is hardly cooperative.

"What do you think about swimming or gymnastics?"

"No, I hate the pool, and I can't do gymnastics," he replies defiantly as he pulls his book over his face. When parents like Anthony's face this level of resistance, they may consider providing a list of activities from which he can choose:

"Look, Anthony, you have a choice. You can select any one of the following sports. We'll be fine with whatever you choose, we promise, but you have to pick one." As parents in situations like this one, we often need to be firm, even though it's painful. We worry that our children will hate us and the sport we're forcing them to do, making them feel worse and us responsible for the mess. Anthony's parents know that their son will continue to stay home and read books by himself if allowed to do so. He needs a push to break this pattern.

His mother decides to call the local YMCA and review all the different activities available. Anthony's parents review these with him and tell him that he is to choose his favorite activity. The choices are swimming, gymnastics, basketball, yoga, and karate. After much deliberation and arguing, Anthony chooses karate. Though the first few weeks of practice may involve protests and temper tantrums, a child like Anthony will begin to experience small improvements in skill. He says to his father proudly, "I can kick my foot way above my shoulder. Watch this, Dad." While he still had some difficulty with his peers, he is at least engaged with them for a few days a week. In the months that follow, Anthony's parents see that he is carrying himself with greater confidence, and his relationships with other kids start to improve. The push his parents undertook is beginning to pay off. Though Anthony will never overtly thank his parents, his improvement in mood will provide more than adequate feedback. They'll know they acted in his best interest.

Had Anthony absolutely resisted all athletic activities, a consultation with the school counselor would be an appropriate next step. Sometimes parents sense that a child is becoming depressed or socially isolated and needs special attention. Resistance to sports may indicate a problem that parents can act on at an early stage, avoiding more complex difficulties later.

SANDY, THE TALENTED ATHLETE

As children get older, they take more responsibility for their decisions, and parents often struggle to step back enough to give a child room, but not so much that the child is stranded without support and guidance. This type of situation is exemplified by Sandy, a naturally athletic 15-year-old high school sophomore who is trying to decide whether to try out for the varsity basketball team. At five feet, seven inches, Sandy is an agile, lean athlete with long legs and strong hands. Her parents frequently get to watch her tear down a rebound, dribble the length of the court,

Kids can face problems if expectations run too high *or* too low.

and make an easy layup. Her bright blue eyes sparkle as she chats with friends during warmups — her conversations are marked by laughter and joy. Sandy has always played sports with ease and agility. Last summer she picked up a tennis racket and was beating her experienced tennis-playing peers within months. And although Sandy is a natural talent and a leader, she struggles to push herself to higher levels.

Prior to tryouts, she says to her parents, "I think I want to play junior varsity again this year. None of my friends will be playing varsity. Plus, I don't think those older girls are very nice. I'd hate it." She claims that most of her friends feel more comfortable at the JV level, but in fact many of them may never advance; Sandy's talent makes her the one capable of moving up. The varsity coach is begging Sandy to try out for the team. The coach explains to Sandy's parents that Sandy won't be challenged at the junior varsity level and that an extra year on varsity will help prepare her for college basketball, maybe even a scholarship. Sandy's parents have always respected the choices their daughter has made in sports and have never challenged her. Her father, though, leans toward encouraging her to try out for varsity. Her mother worries that she'll miss her friends but at the same time she fears that Sandy is holding herself back. Both parents notice that she passes up easy shots and holds herself back when she could be taking over the game. When they encourage her to shoot more often, she just rolls her eyes and says, "Okay, I'll think about that." After games in which she was the leading scorer, Sandy tells her parents that her friends are colder toward her, something she dreads. She'd rather be a team player who scores below her potential than the star who gets the cold shoulder.

Given Sandy's dilemma, should her parents push her anyway? If they encourage her to go out for the varsity team, Sandy may get to find out how good a player she can be, build her confidence, and make new friends. On the other hand, this may affect the close relationships she has with friends on the JV team. They may become jealous and resent her success. Sandy could be unjustly criticized, or worse, ignored by her peers.

Using the three-step approach may provide a window into the dynamics of this dilemma. Getting to know Sandy and her environment could raise interesting questions. What particular pressures does Sandy deal with because she is a girl? How much trust can be placed in the coach to have Sandy's best interests in mind? What role should Sandy play in making this decision?

Five to ten years ago, parents might have been warned not to push girls in Sandy's position because of the risk of alienating Sandy from her peers. However, with the tremendous development of women's sports over the past decade, particularly the Women's World Cup and U.S. Olympic Soccer, Women's Olympic Softball, and women's tennis, girls have stronger role models in sports and are evolving into strong, competitive women. Furthermore, girls are learning that they can be good competitors *and* fine team players — their excellence can attract, rather than alienate, friends. Girls like Sandy have permission to be powerful and successful, increasing their self-confidence and ability to achieve.

However, girls and women are still influenced by other messages prevalent in our society. Being strong and successful in sports does not fit traditional ideals of femininity. Mary Pipher addresses how adolescent girls are affected by these ideals in her book *Reviving Ophelia*.[3] She notes that it's okay for girls to be tomboys until they reach early adolescence, when the rules change abruptly. At that time, girls get the message that they must start to defer to others. Boys are supposed to be the strong leaders, and girls should by contrast be more nurturing and supportive of others. Although this view lacks the power it once had, girls are still told that being a jock will make them unattractive to boys. Many girls hold themselves back on the court or athletic field, avoid discussions of their athletic ability, and almost apologize for their success. Others, however, refuse to accept the chauvinistic view and embrace their strengths.

> Parents can become dependent on the successes and achievements of their children.

Many girls and young women find themselves stuck between these two ideals. In some instances, this may help girls empathize with and support one another in the struggle of defining themselves. In other circumstances, girls may be at odds with one another, and their exchanges can get nasty:

"She's such a little prissy daddy's girl."
"That girl's an Amazon. Look at her clothes. . . . Hello? Has she ever heard of makeup?"

Sandy's parents consider these dynamics as part of step one of the three-step process. As they focus on knowing their daughter, they find that she is less concerned about her identity as an athletic girl but worries about maintaining strong bonds with her friends. She also struggles to acknowledge and embrace her own impressive strength as an athlete. Often a coach can be instrumental in helping girls work through this issue. But as Sandy's parents get to know Sandy's sports environment, they're not sure that they trust the coach's judgment.

Overzealous coaches can make the parents' job more confusing. Parents may want to believe that their children are as talented as coaches might suggest, but they fear setting their kids up for failure. On the other hand, parents may be the ones who overestimate their children's talent, and the coach has to bring them down to earth about realistic expectations. Neither situation is easy for parents to manage.

In Sandy's case, the varsity basketball coach uses the prospect of college basketball to convince Sandy's parents that playing at a more competitive level is in Sandy's best interest. For some parents, the mention of college sports has instant appeal, but not for Sandy's parents. They simply want her to attend a good college and make the most of her ability. Therefore, they look for more information by speaking with a few parents who have daughters on the varsity team and ask them about the coach's style. They learn that the coach is intense, but most of the girls enjoy playing on the team. Encouraged by these conversations, although still a bit cautious, Sandy's parents begin to hope that she will at least try out for the team.

Sandy's parents decide to have a talk with her. Her father says, "You know, Sandy, whatever you do is entirely your choice, and we'll support your decision. But why don't you just give it a try. See if you like the girls and the coach. After tryouts are over, then make your decision." Sandy's mother adds, "Honey, we think you are a wonderful athlete and would benefit from a challenging experience like this. If you don't like it, then you can play junior varsity for another year and try again next year."

Sandy's reaction is initially negative. She storms off to her room, slams the door, and screams, "You just don't get it!" Her parents look at each other with pained expressions, worrying that they pushed too hard. But the next day at breakfast, Sandy reports that she will at least try.

Sandy's parents are wise not to demand that she try out for the team. They simply state their feelings and their belief in her and also explain why they think the experience would be good for her. Their encouragement is rooted in the values of effort and courage. They remind Sandy that she still has control over her decision. At the same time, they encourage her to challenge herself, a message that will be important to her in late adolescence and early adulthood. By taking the time to understand Sandy's dilemma with her friends and her sports environment, Sandy's parents are better able to support her in an effective way. They encourage her without pushing too much.

RORY, THE ELITE TENNIS PLAYER

Similar to Sandy, Rory is an excellent athlete. At 17 years of age, he has matured into a talented tennis player. On the court, Rory has astounding quickness, complemented by graceful ground strokes. Often exhausting his opponents through outlasting them, Rory is like a human backboard. He can return any serve. His hero is Arthur Ashe, the first African American to win a major tournament in professional tennis. Rory admired Ashe's ability to keep his cool under pressure and overcome prejudice to achieve his goals. Rory's father, a self-made businessman who started a successful computer company, has been centrally involved in coaching and training his son since the boy was 6 years old. Rory's father is particularly proud that his son is now playing competitively at the junior national level; by contrast, he always had to work after school when growing up and didn't have the opportunity to play organized sports.

Problems begin to occur, however, when Rory loses a few matches in a row. His father plays down the situation and says to Rory, "Hey, as long as you work hard and are having fun, the outcome doesn't matter." When asked if he puts pressure on his son, Rory's father denies it. But Rory notices how his father always tells parents of other players, and anyone else who will listen, how talented his son is and how he expects him to go far in the sport. After the lost matches, his father is quiet and seems depressed.

Rory's father is behaving in a manner typical of many parents of talented athletes. We want our kids to do well, and we are disappointed when they fail. The challenge is to consider how our reaction is being perceived by our kids. In this situation, Rory's father is so well intentioned that he doesn't suspect that he could be part of the problem. Such unspoken, even subconscious, parental expectations constitute one of the most common forms of pressure that young athletes feel.

In private, Rory admits to his mother, after much questioning, that he doesn't want to disappoint his dad. His father has devoted so much time and energy to his tennis that the prospect of continuing this losing streak feels overwhelming. Rory insists that his mother promise not to mention this fact to his father. In a bind, Rory's mother agrees to keep this secret but recognizes that tension is building between her husband and son.

Based on the three-step approach, the first question Rory's mother needs to ask is "Does my son still love to play?" If Rory does love playing, then she must begin to address the second step, knowing herself and helping her husband to recognize how he is pressuring Rory. If Rory does not love playing anymore, then his mother may need to prepare herself and her husband for the possibility that their son may want to quit. If Rory has an ongoing passion for tennis, then he'll have the desire and ability to work through rough spots; but if the passion dies, he will lack the fortitude to bounce back from his recent losing streak. (Parents may think that we overemphasize the importance of fun and the love of sports. Discipline, talent, coaching, and intelligence might appear to be more important. But when top professional athletes are playing at peak levels, they almost without exception report having fun. Michael Jordan emphasizes that the most important skill for young players to develop is a love for the game.)

It is clear to Rory's mother that her son does love the game of tennis, but his ability to compete at this higher level is in question. She can see how discouraged he becomes before matches — it's as if he loses before he begins. Elite athletes who are overwhelmed with pressure and negative thinking are at a great disadvantage during competition. They end up beating themselves, regardless of their talent. Rory's father might be able to help his son face up to the stress, if he could recognize the subtle difference between encouraging and pressuring his son. Also, Rory is so good at masking his fear and dread that his father is unable to detect them. Rory instead tells his dad that he is tired and in a mild slump. But while playing in his next tournament, Rory recognizes that he's dealing with more than a slump. When hitting his second serve, he grows fearful that his father will be disappointed if he double-faults. He actually visualizes the double fault: he throws the ball up in the air and sees an image of his father's disgruntled face when his second serve hits the tape and drops to the ground. He hears the words *double fault* in his head, and an awful feeling of humiliation comes over him. Over the course of the match, this mental image makes him tense his muscles and hit the ball long or into the net more than usual. He loses to a weaker opponent for the second straight tournament.

Concerned that something is wrong, Rory's father decides to show more support and attends some of Rory's practices. But the father fails to notice that Rory feels crowded by his presence; his increased involvement is adding to his son's troubles.

Although she does not want to divulge the feelings her son has confided to her, Rory's mother feels that she needs to take action to defuse the tension about Rory's performance. One evening, after another disappointing loss, she raises her concerns with her husband over coffee while Rory is upstairs doing his homework.

"You know, I'm wondering whether Rory is feeling pressure from us. He used to have so much fun playing. Now it's getting so serious. Do you think we should back off?"

Initially, Rory's father disregards her comment. "Are you kidding? He needs our support."

"Yeah, I know he needs our support, but maybe the best way we can help him relax is by relaxing a bit ourselves. Face it. You've been taking more time off from work and putting it into his tennis. Do you think it's possible that this makes Rory feel pressured?"

We know from our clinical and personal experiences that conversations between parents about the potential negative influences they may be having on their child can be extremely sensitive. It's easy for one spouse to unintentionally offend the other, causing resentment. Parents may be surprised by the strength of their feelings. Rory's mother is an effective communicator, though; she does not directly accuse her husband of pressuring their son. She includes the possibility that she may be contributing to the pressure and uses questions rather than accusations to start the discussion. This allows her husband to contemplate her comments objectively without getting defensive. She is suggesting possible ways to help Rory without breaking her promise to her son.

Eventually Rory's parents agree that some backing off is in order. They will continue to attend his matches, but his father decides not to watch practices anymore. Following matches, he makes fewer comments. On occasion, he'll ask, "How are you feeling out there?" He'll offer more compliments: "Wow, that was a great match to watch!" Although the losing streak continues for a while, Rory starts to share more about his struggles. He discusses how the increased competitiveness makes tennis less enjoyable than before, and this admission seems to give him some relief.

In a poignant father-son conversation, his dad says, "Look, we just want you to be happy."

"Really? Sometimes I feel that I'm playing tennis to make you happy." Shocked that these words escaped him, Rory waits for his father to yell. Instead, there is silence. Rory's father drops his head and slowly returns his gaze to his son.

> Being strong and successful in sports does not fit traditional ideals of femininity.

"You know what, you're absolutely right. This is your game. It's not mine to play. You have to do what is going to make you happiest. While I would love for you to play as long as you are able, if you are not playing for yourself, that takes the fun and drive out of playing."

Parents may find a comment like this incredibly difficult to make, particularly when they have a talented child like Rory, but such statements can greatly reduce the pressure on the athlete. It frees Rory to decide for himself if he really wants to play. His father is not the only source of pressure he feels; tennis at this level is very competitive and exhausting at times. Now that his father is more supportive, Rory decides that he can handle the other pressures that come with playing. When Rory's father takes a step back, he helps his son take a step forward.

THE PARENTAL PRESSURE GAUGE

One thing is absolutely clear. It is hard for us as parents to monitor how much we push our children. How can we tell if we are pushing too much or not enough? The Parental Pressure Gauge is designed to guide parents as they assess how their behavior affects the performance of their children. The age and athletic experience of each child will influence his or her response to parental pressure. Some young athletes may like to be pushed or challenged to play harder; others may just want a pat on the back for encouragement. Some may need more positive comments than others do. Some may be able to handle more pressure from a coach than from a parent. Some may respond to encouragement from Mom rather than Dad. The Parental Pressure Gauge can help parents determine any changes needed to improve the experience and performance of their children.

The Parental Pressure Gauge

HOW PARENTAL PRESSURE AFFECTS PERFORMANCE AND PERSONAL GROWTH			
PRESSURE RPMs = REVOLUTIONS OF PRESSURE PER MINUTE			
			Parental blindness, *overheated*, pressure meltdown
		Blind pressure, *heated*	
	Healthy expectation, *slightly revved*		
No pressure			
5 RPMs, no pressure	25 RPMs, healthy expectation	50 RPMs, borderline "blind pressure"	80 RPMs, overload

Interpreting the Parental Pressure Gauge

At 5 RPMs — practically no parental pressure exists, only encouragement. This is particularly appropriate for children age 6 and under. Cheering and limited discussion about outcomes of performance are characteristic of this approach. Fun and joy are paramount.

At 25 RPMs — parents do far more encouraging than critiquing. They expect their children to try new activities, give their best effort, and conduct themselves appropriately while playing, but this is promoted in a positive, inspiring manner. Discussions of performance are acceptable, but enjoyment and effort are emphasized far more than winning. Winning is important, but playing hard and having fun take precedence. This level, reflecting mostly encouragement and very limited pushing or pressure, is appropriate for any age level.

At 50 RPMs — parents have stepped away from encouragement and healthy pushing and are engaged in pressuring behavior. This change is rarely recognizable to parents and difficult for the child to articulate. This type of pressure can undermine performance and decrease playing enjoyment by making the young athlete fearful of displeasing the parents.

At 80 RPMs — parents have lost control while watching or discussing their child's performance. Parents may yell, scream, or even become violent. This type of pressure damages the child's experience in sports and his or her relationship with parents. It also teaches children that the way to resolve conflicts is through violence and unmanaged aggression.

The Myth of Zero Pressure

The idea that there is a sports situation characterized by no pressure at all is a myth. Children experience some form of pressure, either from parents or the environment. In addition, children learn to put pressure on themselves by watching parents and other adults. They see us pressure ourselves in athletic and professional endeavors and consequently follow suit. Sometimes children experience pressure through competing with their peers. A young boy trying to gain the acceptance of his peer group may strive to win the race or the game. An adolescent girl wants to be the best player in her grade, so she spends extra time shooting foul shots on weekends. In other circumstances, children experience pressure through focusing on a single critical comment that a parent made in passing, yet it stuck. A father says to his daughter on one Saturday afternoon that she is lazy on the soccer field. Unbeknownst to him, she frequently worries that he thinks she never tries hard enough, though he was referring to a single Saturday game. It's wise to note that kids can magnify what we say to them, and this puts pressure on them.

As we mention elsewhere, even what we *don't* say can be taken the wrong way: Youth sport researchers report that children under the age of 8 struggle to interpret facial expressions accurately. When a parent makes a sad face, they may interpret it as angry. If a parent has a neutral face, they may read that the parent is disappointed.[4] So our children may come to the wrong conclusion as they struggle to understand our underlying emotions, and may feel pressure that we don't intend to convey.

We all pressure our children at one point or another. How can we make sure that it's the right amount? First, we can follow step two of the three-step approach; by coming to understand ourselves, we can avoid unwittingly pressuring our kids to meet our own needs. Second, we can keep in mind that children, regardless of their age, are better able to have fun and develop skills if they play in a low-pressure environment. This is particularly true for kids who are 12 and under. Anthony, the 8-year-old boy with limited athletic ability, would have performed poorly in a pressured situation. His parents needed patience, encouragement, and creativity to help him feel engaged in sports. Parents with children like Anthony are wise to keep their RPMs in the 5 to 15 range, strong enough to get him involved and yet supportive enough to make him feel comfortable. This approach provides Anthony with the opportunity to develop the confidence and joy of using his body while also benefiting from the social experience of being in a group.

> As parents we are prone to overestimating the talent of our children.

Of course, many of us as parents will have children who are not athletic. In these situations it is still our responsibility to help them build comfort with their bodies and establish healthy exercise habits. They don't need to be varsity players or get college scholarships. They just need to feel the joy of physical activity enough to make it a part of their lives. Developing a comfort with their bodies through physical activity helps our children establish a healthier self-image. It is our belief that teaching our children to enjoy using their bodies also creates a foundation for them to develop healthy exercise patterns that will persist well into their adult lives.

Healthy Expectation: 25 RPMs

Adults and children alike feel compelled to improve their skills, prove themselves to their peers, and strive to win. We cannot prevent our children from experiencing competition; at the right time and in the right situation it can be a positive experience. But how can parents support natural competition and avoid extreme competition? Those with healthy expectations emphasize fun but also recognize that effort, skill development, and dedication matter. When these values and parental practices are in place, we observe happier and more balanced parents and players.

Sandy, the naturally talented 15-year-old basketball player, is a good example of an athlete who benefits from 25 RPMs of parental encouragement. Uncertain of her abilities and concerned about the loss of her peer group should she join the more demanding and competitive varsity team,

Sandy needs guidance and encouragement from her parents. They push her to explore her athletic potential while acknowledging the importance of her friendships. Sandy is likely to experience that her parents believe in her ability but also care about how much she values her friendships.

Sandy is not forced to try out for the varsity basketball team. She is encouraged to try. This form of pushing is the right balance for Sandy. For other children her age, it may not work as well. Another adolescent might find such a parenting approach insensitive or overly pushy, which may result in quitting the sport entirely. Perhaps with an overly sensitive child a parent might say, "Wow, you are such a wonderful player, and I could see how you would do well on the varsity, but you have to be comfortable with that decision, and we'll support you either way."

Exceeding 25 RPMs: Warm to Hot

It can be hard to discern when parental pressure exceeds 25 RPMs. It may appear that parents are doing all the right things: emphasizing fun and never criticizing their children or yelling at games. But a message is communicated through facial expressions or what is left unsaid.

The term *blind parental pressure* reflects this insidious pressure, which can surprise both children and parents. It can appear through casual statements that nonetheless imply a mixed message. For example, a father drops off his son

When top professional athletes are playing at peak levels, they almost without exception report having fun.

for a basketball game and says, "Hey, have fun." Then, after the game, he says, "Did you win? Did you score? How come you didn't score more?" Parents may be blind to this pressure, but kids feel it.

Even in the most innocent attempts to encourage our children, the pressure can accumulate insidiously and take its toll. The story of Rory, the elite tennis player, and his father best illustrates this type of pressure. Here we see how the pressure revs up from 25 RPMs of encouragement toward 50 RPMs of a subtle but increasingly problematic form of pressure. Rory's father is blind to the increasing pressure he is placing on his son, exceeding the 50-RPM range. The unfortunate result is that Rory's performance in tennis declines and his future playing is in jeopardy. When we are unable to recognize our parental pressure blind spots, the performance and joy of the game for our children can be adversely affected, and we are left confused as to the cause.

For many of us parents with high-achieving athletes, this can be a common occurrence. We want to encourage our children to believe in themselves. At the same time, we also need to monitor our growing investment in their success. When Rory's mother confronts her husband about his pressuring style with their son, he wisely steps back. Making adjustments like this is challenging for parents like Rory's father, particularly because they feel they are so supportive and devoted to what is best for their child. Having a trusted ally like a spouse or close friend is a necessary safeguard for most of us, as it is often difficult to anticipate or recognize these subtle forms of pressure.

> At the right time and in the right situation, competition can be a positive and important experience.

Of course, parents aren't the only source of performance pressure. The Parental Pressure Gauge might be used to estimate the amount and type of stress kids receive from other sources, particularly elite and all-star teams, which can also reach the 50-RPM range. For example, Mr. O'Brien's daughter, 11-year-old Kelly, just made an elite, all-star soccer team. As he says, "The coaches on this team are really tough. They push the girls, but they are not cruel or degrading." Though he is impressed with the positive features of this team, Mr. O'Brien might want to consider Kelly's age and developmental readiness for competition at this level; the "really tough" coaching style and highly competitive program might be too much for her.

It is difficult to evaluate the subtle risks and benefits of playing elite sports. The excitement and sense of pride in seeing one's child excel in sports is a powerful experience for parents. Special opportunities also may be on offer; for example, Kelly has been asked to travel with the team to Russia for two weeks in the summer. Yet she is only 11 years old and misses activities that she has given up to play at the elite level. Upon reflection, Kelly's father realizes that perhaps she needs some time off from soccer to achieve better balance in her life. Monitoring the level of intensity in competition and giving kids much-needed breaks set the foundation for longer participation and better performance.

Burning Down the House: From 50 to 80 RPMs

For most athletes, parental pressure at 80 RPMs burns down the athlete and the rest of the household. Some kids respond to this positively (for example, when getting psyched before a high school football game), but this rarely is the case. In the end most kids suffer, and the parents suffer as well. Performance declines and parents become even more enraged, in a downward spiral. We use the term *overheating* because we believe the athletes get worked so hard mentally that they can't concentrate, have fun, and let the joy of the game drive them to play to their potential.

The well-known author Pat Conroy often writes about his incredibly demanding, abusive father, who pressured him to win and demeaned him even when he played well at basketball. In Conroy's book *My Losing Season*,[5] he describes his father sitting in the stands and looking disgusted although Conroy is playing one of the best games in his life. The way his father yells from the sidelines reflects the RPMs shooting up from 50 toward the 80 range. After the game, this father goes on yelling and tells Conroy that he is soft and will never be able to match the level of play that the father had achieved in college. This is parental pressure of the worst kind. It was damaging to Conroy's basketball game, though at times it motivated him to prove his father wrong, and it significantly hurt his sense of self.

> In our culture, we've become so accustomed to outcomes that we don't even know how to ask about the experience.

Long-term parental pressure is unacceptable behavior; however, all of us have the occasional bad moment when we say or do something we regret. These moments strike at some core vulnerability within us, and the inability to contain the feeling is overpowering. But rather than condemn ourselves for losing control, we can explore our reaction. Did we want to protect our child from failure or humiliation — perhaps because through similar experiences we know what it's like? Understanding the cause of a high-RPM reaction can be the first step in avoiding future outbursts.

To help parents determine the level of pressure they place on their child athlete, we've provided this survey. There is no scoring profile for this questionnaire; rather its main purpose is to lay a foundation for discussion about the issue of pressure in sports. We hope that discussing each question will guide parents to explore their own past experiences in sports and bring attention to potential problems. It can also help parents come to agreement about how to approach the issue of pressure in their child's sports experiences. It might also be wise to seek the counsel of a trusted sports figure such as a great coach or a counselor.

> Accurate praise is the building block of self-confidence.

The Parental Pressure Gauge Survey

1. How often do you and your spouse discuss the impact of your behavior on your child's experience in sports?
   A. Sometimes
   B. Never
   C. Right before each season
   D. At least a few times per week
   E. Almost every day

2. How would you describe yourself as an athlete when you were your child's age?
   A. Great
   B. Good
   C. Average
   D. Below average
   E. Poor

3. How would you describe your sports experiences as a child?
   A. Awesome
   B. Usually good
   C. Okay
   D. Often not so good
   E. Negative

4. If your 3-year-old does not want to jump into the pool after multiple attempts to teach him or her to swim, you are most likely to
   A. Give up for the day
   B. Try to talk the child into it
   C. Try other games

D. Have your spouse take care of it

E. None of the above

5. If you pick up your child after a game, how often do you ask about the outcome?

   A. All of the time

   B. Some of the time

   C. Wait until my child raises it

   D. Rarely

   E. Never

6. Which item below best describes your behavior during your child's games?

   A. I ignore the game because it makes me too nervous to watch.

   B. I cheer for my child and team.

   C. I cheer but sometimes complain to the ref.

   D. I cheer our team and sometimes boo the other team.

   E. I have a hard time controlling myself.

7. Rank in order the values you emphasize in your child's sports experience.

   A. Respect for self, others, and game

   B. Loyalty to team and coach

   C. Cooperation with team and coach

   D. Achievement

   E. Dedication and effort

   F. Fun

8. Which of the following makes you most nervous when your child plays?

   A. I think my child might get hurt.

   B. I think my child is going to feel bad after the game.

   C. I think my child is not getting enough playing time.

   D. I think my child is not improving in skill.

   E. I think my child is likely to lose.

9. All children experience some type of pressure from their parents to perform well. Which of the following best describes the pressure you bring to bear?

    A. I yell a lot at games.

    B. I ask my child a lot about practice and preparation.

    C. I talk a lot about winning and losing.

    D. I encourage my child to work harder.

    E. I'm not aware of pressuring my child at all.

10. After a poor performance, what are you most likely to say to your child?

    A. Good try. You'll get 'em next time.

    B. What the heck happened?

    C. I think you did great.

    D. Do you want to talk about it?

    E. I say nothing at all.

11. To what extent do you think your child is performing below his or her level?

    A. Not at all

    B. A little bit

    C. A moderate amount

    D. A lot

    E. I don't think about it.

12. Do you think sports will help your child get into college?

    A. No

    B. Possibly

    C. Yes

    D. The coaches say so.

    E. The coaches say no, but I think so.

13. Do you think your child has a chance to play at the professional level someday?

    A. Yes

    B. No

    C. The coaches say no, but I think so.

    D. Possibly

    E. The coaches say it's possible.

14. Up to what level did you play sports?

    A. Not at all

    B. Just recreational

C. Sports was not a good experience, so I never played.
D. Junior high school
E. Senior high school
F. College
G. Club sports
H. Professional

15. In what areas did your parents pressure you when you were growing up?
    A. Academics
    B. Social life
    C. Sports
    D. Family obligations
    E. None

16. If you checked A, B, C, or D above, how intense overall was this pressure?
    A. Very minor
    B. Mostly minor, but I recall a few tough times.
    C. Moderate
    D. Sometimes too much
    E. All the time

17. From which area did you derive the most pleasure while growing up?
    A. Doing well in school
    B. Friendships
    C. Music, dance, or art
    D. Sports
    E. Growing up was mostly not fun.

18. Who was most responsible for getting you to choose this area of strong interest?
    A. My mom
    B. My sister or brother
    C. My father
    D. A grandparent
    E. Me
    F. Other _____

7

WHEN THE APPLE FALLS FAR
FROM THE TREE:

What to Do When Kids' Athletic Abilities and Interests Differ from Our Own

AT TIMES MOTHER NATURE will play tricks on us. Our kid enters the world and acts in ways completely foreign to us. Sometimes we wonder whether the staff at the hospital switched our child with another. He or she simply doesn't act or behave the way we do.

What happens when the apple falls far from the tree? Sometimes complications arise when the athletic inclinations and experiences of children differ from those of the parents. This can cause disappointment or pain. Some of us hope our children will excel beyond what we achieved in sports. In these situations, our children often feel pressured. How can parents anticipate such problems so that they provide the best possible sports experience for their children?

NELLIE, THE TALENTED HOCKEY PLAYER

Mr. and Mrs. Wooster, a young married couple ensconced in academia, are bewildered to discover that their 12-year-old daughter, Nellie, is becoming an outstanding hockey player. Nellie is one of the best skaters her coach has ever seen. She can change directions on a dime, and she has great vision on the ice. While proud of her accomplishments, the Woosters feel rather lost when attending her games because of their limited experience as athletes. Both of the Woosters grew up in New York City. They attended huge public schools that required little physical education, and only the supertalented athletes played for school teams. Their parents were European immigrants who emphasized education as a means to assimilate into the country; sports were never valued. Seeing Nellie so interested in sports is quite a shock. They make some effort to learn more about hockey, but they worry that Nellie is not devoted enough to her studies. Her 5:00 A.M. practices and weekend tournaments are interfering with her study time. The Woosters are concerned that Nellie's sports will distract her from being a good student.

In such families, problems can emerge when parents emphasize one thing but the child prefers another. This can lead to standoffs: parents may become more stubborn, and the child may rebel. No one wins. When Nellie's parents tell her that she must miss her hockey game over the weekend to prepare for a math test, Nellie refuses to study. She sits in her room listening to music and staring at the wall. When test time comes, she's unprepared, performs poorly, and feels bad about herself. The good intentions of Nellie's parents have backfired. Nellie misses the opportunity to play her favorite sport and feels even worse as she falls further behind in school.

What are we to do as parents in these situations? We want our children to be prepared for the future. We try to help them balance a variety of interests. When we feel they are running amuck, we rack our brains to come up with fair rules and consequences. But sometimes, the limits we set make us into unpopular villains. In times like these, nothing feels right or effective. Often, we are left to wonder whether we could have handled the situation differently.

Was there a more effective way for Nellie's parents to respond? Perhaps they could have said, "Look, Nellie, we know that you really want to play hockey this weekend, but you also have a huge math test coming up on Monday. If we can work out a schedule by which you study a few hours on Saturday and Sunday mornings, we'll let you play."

Such compromises allow everyone to get at least part of what they want. Nellie's parents acknowledge how much she loves hockey and offer a means through which she can compete. At the same time, they communicate the importance of schoolwork and use hockey as an incentive for Nellie to take her studies more seriously. Inherent in

Almost 100 percent of children want their parents to attend their games.

this interaction is the message that Nellie must be prepared to work for the things she loves and that both sports and academics are important. Also, by allowing Nellie to decide, her parents can't be seen as "the bad guys" or parents who always say no.

Furthermore, the Woosters can make efforts to understand Nellie's love of hockey. By doing this, they will begin to appreciate the confidence she is gaining from making friends and building competencies in hockey. They will learn about the utter joy their daughter feels in playing the game. Asking questions about hockey is a good place to start: "How did the game go out there? Was it hard playing against that team? I saw you made some really nice passes." These questions will show Nellie that her parents are interested in what she does — that they care. Our kids need to feel that we respect and value what is most important to them, even if we don't share the same passion. It allows our children to feel supported in their efforts to define themselves, a crucial goal in adolescence.

Also, the Woosters might talk to some of the coaches and parents about hockey to find ways to become more involved as fans. Parents shouldn't underestimate the importance of attending kids' competitions. In a national youth sports soccer survey we conducted several years ago, we found that almost 100 percent of children want their parents to attend their games. Kids want their parents to take notice of their accomplishments; it can give them a boost in self-worth. Nellie might say to herself, "My parents value what I do and who I am."

> Problems occur when we cannot differentiate our children's performance from how we feel about ourselves.

DARREN AND HIS NONATHLETIC FATHER

Darren, an 8-year-old baseball player, is one of the best players on his Little League baseball team, the Tigers. When Darren strolls up to the plate or the pitching mound, most parents from the opposing team will ask if he's 11 years old, as Darren stands several inches taller than most of his peers. Though Darren's good eye-hand coordination and physical strength make him one of the team's star hitters, he is a slow runner, which makes him self-conscious. He worries that he'll never be able to run the bases quickly enough when he reaches junior high school. If his lack of speed becomes enough of a liability to the team, he may lose the admiration of his buddies and, worst of all, face harsh criticism from his father.

Darren's father is his biggest fan and greatest critic. Brutally teased as a young boy for being the last one picked for a team in every game he can remember, Darren's father is excited about the success his son is having in playing baseball. He often thinks to himself, "Finally, someone in this family can enjoy playing sports without feeling horribly anxious and self-conscious." Celebrating this wonderful talent in his son, Darren's father cheers wildly at games, attends many of his son's practices, and brags openly to his friends about Darren's prowess: "Did you see that hit? That was a major league homer!" However, on car rides home, Darren's father often suggests ways for his son to perform better.

"You know, I think you're taking your eye off the ball. When you swing, your head is way too high." Completely unaware of the fact that he is putting pressure on Darren, Darren's father is surprised and becomes agitated when Darren's pitching and hitting start to decline.

After Darren strikes out in one game, his father yells, "Come on, Darren. I expect better from you! Where's that home-run swing?" Darren drops his head and kicks the dirt as he heads back to the dugout. His father feels encouraged by his son's reaction. He thinks it's a sign that his son wants to win, but Darren actually wants his father to keep quiet when he's playing. Darren fails to get a hit the entire game.

His father raises the subject at the dinner table that night. In an impatient, irritated voice, he asks his son, "What's gotten into you? You used to hit so well against that team. Seems like you're just not trying out there."

Unable to share how he really feels, Darren keeps his head down at the dinner table and excuses himself early to go to his room. As the sound of Darren's footsteps fades, Darren's father grimaces as his wife gives him a disapproving glance.

Darren's poor performances and his father's angry reactions worsen, and the whole family feels it. Darren begins to hate playing baseball but wants to please his father. Darren's father wants to heal his own emotional wounds through the success of his son. Darren's mother wants to protect her son from discouragement yet also help her husband develop a healthier parenting style.

In our experience with parents like Darren's father, we have been almost completely unsuccessful in helping when we say, "Hey, it doesn't matter if your son does well. It only matters if he's having fun." Typically, we get a vacant stare and an obligatory "Thanks for your input, Doc. We'll give you a call if we need you." More often than not, we need to focus on helping the child perform better because that is where the parent is focused. So, we might say something like "We think you have a fabulous son who is a talented player. One thing we noticed is that he seems stressed out when he's up at the plate. He seems worried about screwing up. So, we all have to work together to help him relax more. Do you notice when he seems stressed or worried about failing? If so, when did this start? Any idea why he gets so worried?" In this manner, we show Darren's father that we want the same thing that he does, namely, to help his son be a better player. Once we've done this, we have more wiggle room to address the more challenging issues.

Darren's father needs to see how his past disappointments in sports are influencing his behavior, but this is a difficult process. He may need time and space to address these painful, often humiliating feelings. Darren's mother might consider making gentle suggestions that draw on her own experience to assist in this process; for example, she might say, "Sometimes seeing Darren struggle in sports reminds me of how hard it was for me to get cut from the ninth-grade basketball team. I know that still bothers me today. Do you ever get feelings like that?" Sharing her difficult experiences may reduce her husband's defensiveness and encourage him to express similar feelings. Eventually he may be able to make even more substantial changes in how he thinks and acts with regard to his son's athletics.

For parents, no matter how hard we try, discussions about our negative roles in the sports experiences of our child don't go over well. In some instances, we become angered when our spouse or partner tries to discuss these issues with us. While the three-step approach requires that we take time to know ourselves, some of us are not ready to consider our unresolved painful feelings. When confronted about our attitudes and behavior, we will at times pull away from our spouse or become even more focused on our child's performance. There is no one right way to handle these interactions, and much of how we talk to each other in situations like these depends on the nature of the marital relationship and how we communicate. If the communication lines remain open, problems can be talked through in most instances. If we make no attempt to talk to our spouse openly about the problem, our child's performance will continue to worsen, increasing the risk that they will burn out and quit.

For parents of younger athletes, it is crucial to recognize that the physical ability and talent of our children may fluctuate greatly over time. Some of Darren's friends who are uncoordinated at 8 years old may become high school stars. This is particularly important for Darren's father to consider. Will he be prepared should his son become an average player? Will he be happy with the fact that his son just enjoys being on the team? Darren already feels pressure to perform well for his father; imagine how difficult it will be when he can't hit big home runs anymore. Anticipating his father's disappointment may tempt him to quit, since Darren is not free to enjoy himself. As parents we want to avoid placing our children in this dilemma because the possibility of quitting may rob the child of the benefits sports offer.

The desire to be involved in Darren's sports experience can be more positive if Darren's dad helps his son set realistic goals prior to the beginning of the season. These goals should be based on aspects of the game that an athlete can control, such as effort, dedication, and skill development. Such goals can lay the foundation for fun, the monitoring of progress, and joy in sharing these experiences with parents. The measuring stick is not home runs or shutout innings, but achievements that reflect sound values and long-term planning. Meeting such goals will help children like Darren feel good about themselves without worrying that they may disappoint their parents.

HOLLY AND HER ATHLETIC MOTHER AND SISTER

In some families, one child may be just like the parents, but another may be totally different. These distinctions can create tension among both kids and parents. Parents may be drawn to the interests of the child who is similar to them, perhaps leaving another child to feel left out. Parents don't intend to hurt their children or love them differently, but at times, one child may feel that a brother or sister is favored.

Such is the case for Holly Bernstein, a 15-year-old girl. Even though her sister, Tina, is 2 years younger, Holly can't match Tina's athletic talent. Though Holly has always experienced moderate success in sports, Tina is a natural. She excels in every sport she plays, much like the girls' mother. Over the past few weeks, their mother is having problems in her relationship with Holly. They are arguing more frequently, particularly over basketball. Mrs. Bernstein is concerned that Holly has decided to quit basketball after years of playing at the youth and junior high levels. At the same time, Holly's grades are beginning to decline, an unusual change, given how good a student she is. Mrs. Bernstein wants to improve her relationship with Holly, but she is unable to see that Holly realizes that she will never be as athletically talented as her mother and sister. This awareness is making her feel alienated and unworthy.

Holly has always tried to achieve the level of athletic prominence that her mother did, but Holly always fell short. In her early years playing basketball, Holly played for her mother's youth basketball team. Everyone respected Mrs. Bernstein, a former high school All-American and college basketball star. Holly's mother, and for that matter, most of her teammates, expected Holly to be a great player as well. Yet it became apparent after a few months that she was just average. Tall for her age, she often played center. Although she was not a big scorer, her long arms

> The eldest child in a family commonly receives the most anxious attention and pressure from parents.

and big hands helped her become a good rebounder and defensive player. Despite doing footwork drills before and after practice for weeks, her rate of improvement was minor. Discouraged by her lack of progress, she felt she could never meet her mother's expectations.

Hopeful that Holly would develop as a player over time, Mrs. Bernstein often challenged her to do better, thus creating tension between them. During practice, Mrs. Bernstein would bellow, "Come on, Holly, where's that footwork?" Although Holly liked having her mother involved, she couldn't relax and play. She'd occasionally trip, lose her balance, or even worse, travel when she received the ball. Every mistake made her feel more self-conscious, even if her mother didn't notice.

Then Tina starts to play for her mother's team, and almost immediately, she becomes a star. Often heading off to practice early, Tina and her mother spend an increasing amount of time together. This leaves Holly alone frequently because her father is still at work when she comes home after school. Dinnertime conversations often focus on Tina's progress and amazing skills: "You should have seen that pass Tina made. If I didn't know her age, I would have thought she was a high school player." Trying to stay positive, Holly wants to be happy for her sister, but worries that she is becoming invisible to her mother. When Holly's grades worsen over the following months, her parents recognize that a problem exists.

What should Mrs. Bernstein do? Should she encourage Holly to play basketball again so they have more in common? Should she act less excited about Tina's basketball skills to protect Holly from feeling bad? Would this be fair to Tina? Coaches face similar challenges when they are assigned a team of individuals with a variety of talents and weaknesses. They must find a way for all of them to work together so that the group can function effectively as a whole. This is also true of parenting, particularly when skill diversity exists in the family.

To do this, parents must try to be fair about how they communicate their love for their kids. In this case, Mrs. Bernstein is understandably excited about Tina's interest in and passion for basketball. Downplaying her excitement would be an injustice to Tina. Although Tina is naturally talented, she will need her mother's encouragement and support as she develops as an athlete. But Holly needs encouragement from her mother as well. As an adolescent girl, she needs help, particularly from her mother, in forming a sense of identity as she approaches adulthood. Part of this will entail discovering what she can do well — a potential source of joy for both daughter and mother.

Perhaps Holly can pursue other sports. If she tries swimming or volleyball, Mrs. Bernstein can take her place as a fan instead of a tough coach who knows the sport of basketball inside out. Perhaps she and her husband can also find other avenues for reminding Holly she is valued and loved. This assurance will buoy her up as she progresses through the social, athletic, and academic challenges of high school.

Possibly Holly might have developed into a more successful basketball player if her mother had been less critical. The eldest child in a family commonly receives the most anxious attention and pressure from parents, who may fear overmuch that this child will get hurt or perform without distinction in school and sports. Holly's parents might consider this family dynamic as they help their older daughter both excel and enjoy herself.

Taking the time to consider the three-step approach would be useful for Mrs. Bernstein. By understanding that Holly feels pressure to perform well but lacks the physical skills of her sister, Mrs. Bernstein may decide to ease up on her daughter. Also, recognizing her own bias toward excellence in sports, Mrs. Bernstein can become more sensitive to how she might be favoring Tina to the detriment of Holly. To no surprise, these steps are quite difficult to take.

In reality, Mrs. Bernstein's vision of herself and her daughter are clouded. Having had a wonderfully positive and important experience as a high school basketball player, Mrs. Bernstein has such high expectations for Holly that she pushes her too hard. It's hard for her to see the value in backing off. We know from our work with some families that high

> Fortunately, there is room for mistakes in raising children. By seeing our flaws and the mistakes we make, kids begin to solve problems with less assistance.

expectations for the oldest child can lead to impressive achievements; however, in this situation, the intensity is too high, and Holly's talent, while decent, does not lead to great performances. Tina has the benefit of being the younger sibling who exceeds her mother's expectations. This is an easier position to be in. Most important, these parents can strive to give equal attention to both their daughters.

It is a tall order to lovingly parent children through thick and thin — even children who differ greatly from their parents. Fortunately, there is room for mistakes in raising children. In fact, as Donald Winnicott, a famous British psychoanalyst, noted, children can grow from parents' unintended missteps, which he calls "empathic failures."[1] By seeing our flaws and the mistakes we make, our kids begin to solve problems with less assistance from us. They rely on their own abilities, and this helps establish independence. For example, a young adolescent may realize that though his father is devoted to his athletic performance, he lacks the expertise to continue coaching him. Though this may disappoint both father and son, it is an important step in the boy's transition to adulthood. The father's support continues, but the son is ready to move forward by working with another coach.

As parents, one of the biggest challenges is to continually remind ourselves that our children are individuals separate from us, with their own unique traits and talents. We can take pleasure in valuing them for who they are.

8

BOYS AND GIRLS

Similarities and Differences in Sports

ONE CROSS-COUNTRY COACH says, "I can really ride the boys in practice. I can raise my voice if necessary, but if I do the same thing with the girls' squad, they take it personally and sometimes give up." Another coach commented at a girls' basketball game, "Gee, girls just play much better team ball. They are unselfish. My boys' team has such a hard time playing together. They're just interested in their individual performance."

GENDER DIFFERENCES: NATURE VERSUS NURTURE

When you compare large groups of boys and girls in athletics, some general differences can be found. For example, boys tend to be more aggressive than girls — yet there are exceptions. Some girls are extremely intent on competition and in contrast, some boys are gentle and docile. On the whole, however, girls tend to be more in tune with one another emotionally; they demonstrate higher levels of empathy. When this trait is employed well, girls can be very helpful to one another on the athletic field. Yet girls also tend to be crueler to one another emotionally. Boys largely do not develop strong emotional bonds; they rely less on this type of connection to feel good about themselves or to perform well.

> Girls tend to develop a chronic, highly critical, typically negative assessment of themselves.

Though our world is changing, sports are still promoted more heavily to boys. In fact, more boys participate in high school sports compared to girls, and more boys take part in youth sports than girls do (63 percent versus 37 percent, respectively).[1]

Boys' love of rough-and-tumble play combined with the cultural ideal that boys should be athletic and strong makes it easier for them to participate in sports. They do not struggle with issues that girls in sports must deal with, such as whether their growing muscles are attractive, whether they should beat a boy in a sprinting race, or whether they should try hard and perspire or keep their makeup looking nice. Being an athlete can conflict with societal ideas about what girls should do and be.

Generalizing about the differences between boys and girls and using these ideas as a basis for parenting would be unwise. Getting to know the unique traits of a particular child — girl or boy — and assessing the child's strengths and weaknesses will provide more helpful information. In sports, much overlap exists in what boys and girls need from coaches, parents, and the athletic experience itself. Differences occur in how boys and girls, and young men and women, approach sports.

Confidence

In general, our preadolescent boys and girls largely get involved in sports to have fun. These kids don't tend to worry about their ability to excel because they are happily caught up in moving their bodies and being with their friends. Confidence becomes an issue when parents, coaches, or an older sibling begins to promote the attitude that only winning counts. This teaches children that only when they win do they matter as human beings. Unfortunately this attitude is now striking our children at earlier phases in their development. When our kids get the message that sports involvement requires trying to beat out friends and determine whether your parents or coach will find you worthy of attention, trouble hits.

Girls are far more at risk for eating disorders, or disordered eating, than boys are.

This idea seems to affect our boys and girls a little differently. Our girls tend to develop a chronic, highly critical, typically negative assessment of themselves. They might think, "I'll never be as good as she is," "I'm just not going to be able to make it around the track that fast," "I'll never be as fast as, as strong as, as good as . . ." — girls fill in the blank with the name of almost anyone standing nearby. This negative thinking can wreak havoc on confidence. Being perfectionistic and harsh to themselves is common, even among highly competitive girls. These internal struggles can make girls sometimes appear not to try hard enough on the field. Chronic negative self-assessment can cause them to lose motivation to compete, simply because they can't meet their own unrealistic performance expectations. They tend to set the mark so high that a sense of hopelessness overwhelms them, and they believe that their efforts simply will not pay off. These thoughts can sap the fun out of sports. Filled with dread, these girls worry about upcoming competitions, perhaps unable to sleep at night.

Coaches and parents can help build girls' confidence by choosing their words carefully when they comment on girls' athletic performance. Both message and tone are important. Specific feedback about skills that need improvement, paired with words of encouragement, can go a long way. Generally, the kinder the tone, the better girls can handle the information. They need to feel respected, and a gentle approach can communicate respect. When our girls feel understood, it frees them up to do their best in sports while feeling more enjoyment and fulfillment in the process.

Both boys and girls struggle to believe in themselves, yet girls have a harder time of it. They tend to blame themselves for their failures or shortcomings. In contrast, boys tend to blame outside factors — their coach or others — for their difficulties. When boys lose confidence, instead of taking responsibility for what they can change or do, they tend to hold others responsible: "The coach hates me." "The coach doesn't know who can cut it when it really matters." Or in frustration they may proclaim, "I don't like this stupid sport anyway!" We can help our sons see that they indeed have some control over their athletic efforts and can regain confidence by trying hard.

Sports-Related Skills

In terms of athletic ability, boys and girls start out *very* similarly. Babies and young toddlers are often distinguished by the color of their clothing, not their physical size or shape. Yet the biochemical changes and how people treat them begin to influence how young children act and think from the start. We hear parents saying to their baby boys, "Oh, what a strong little man you are," and to their girls, "Oh, what a sweet, gentle creature you are!" Whether based on nature or nurture, boys are more physical and aggressive in their play even at ages 1, 2, and 3. However, when boys and girls enter school, their ability to run, jump, and demonstrate signs of physical strength and coordination run parallel, and this similarity continues throughout the preadolescent years. At adolescence, boys tend to become relatively bigger, faster, and stronger. How well our boys and girls develop their sports skills depends on how they are coached, their level of interest in and commitment to their sport — which is strongly influenced by what we as parents value — and individual differences in terms of talent. Huge variations in natural skills and abilities exist among people; much of our children's ability to excel in a specific sport has to do with such individual differences, not gender. Certainly, in some areas boys outperform girls because of boys' physical strength and size. And at times girls, because they tend to internalize mistakes — meaning they blame themselves for what goes wrong and take responsibility for it — learn some sports skills more quickly.

Attitude Toward and Treatment of the Physical Body

Perhaps because of the different expectations of boys and girls in our culture, significant differences in concerns about the body show up in sports. As girls enter adolescence, they tend to focus on their weight and body shape, and this concern affects many women throughout their lives. Girls are far more at risk for eating disorders, or disordered eating (meaning they have only certain symptoms of an eating disorder), than boys are. And female athletes are even more at risk than their nonathletic counterparts. Our girls in sports face a difficult predicament, particularly those participating in sports that require strength. Girls typically want to remain attractive by mainstream standards. When their sport requires power and strength, girls can become conflicted about whether to train hard and "bulk up" or maintain relatively slim arms, legs, and torsos.

Recently, a full-scholarship collegiate triple jumper reflected on what it's like to be a female athlete. She shared this information with her sport psychologist: "Oh, we have to be really careful that our thighs don't get too big. I really do like working out hard in the weight room — but I really don't like doing squats and exercises like that. When the trainer isn't looking, I just stop doing my sets. Having really big thighs just doesn't look good!" It is striking that this athlete, at five feet, six inches, and weighing 120 pounds, is afraid of developing bigger legs — especially since more strength in her legs potentially would allow her to jump farther. She has been training as a triple jumper for almost eight years, on full scholarship, and still is very concerned about her looks. She is willing to sacrifice performance in exchange for being "more attractive."

By virtue of being an athlete, girls become more aware of their bodies—both how they feel moving within their own skin and how they are assessed socially based on looks. They know that leanness often confers enhanced performance. Boys are naturally leaner than girls, but when puberty and adolescence hit, girls gain fat in their legs, hips, and breasts. It can be hard for young girl athletes to watch their male counterparts remain lean yet easily gain muscle mass. Girls may come to dangerous conclusions about how to deal with this challenge for themselves.

Generally, a girl wants to get leaner and boys more muscular.

Many high school and college girls starve or undernourish their bodies to get or stay lean, which jeopardizes both their sports performance and their health. Girls at this age are at risk for clinical and subclinical eating disorders, meaning they might meet some, but not all, the criteria that psychologists use to diagnose an eating disorder. This problem is more acute for girls in sports such as figure skating, dance, and gymnastics that emphasize leanness for aesthetic reasons. For them weight concerns can begin as early as age 5. Compared to male athletes, female athletes are at much greater risk for developing disordered eating patterns, which include undereating, fasting, and using laxatives and excessive exercising to burn calories and keep themselves as lean as possible. And athletes, both male and female, are at a greater risk for eating disorders than nonathletes are. The main contributors to the development of disordered eating patterns include the athlete's personality, coach, parents, and demands of the sport.[2]

Male athletes of all sizes and shapes can also face issues related to lean body mass. The expectations for male athletes can be equally difficult to achieve. Recently Joe—a college scholarship basketball player who stands six feet, eight inches tall—talked about his struggle with his body: "It is really hard to be one of the fat ones on the team. I'm 14 percent body fat. The coach and trainer give me a really hard time. I have to do extra workouts to try to burn off the fat. I want 'six-pack abs' too. I just don't look like the other guys. It's embarrassing! How would you like to be in the chub club?" Joe is actually a lean, powerful-looking young man. Yet his sport requires that he achieve almost unreasonably low levels of body fat. Though the subject is somewhat taboo, our boys also have high expectations of how lean they should be, and some have a difficult time striving toward the ideal.

Other boys tend to be concerned about lack of muscle mass. Wanting to "get big," they are tempted by and at risk for using performance-enhancing drugs. A current study in Massachusetts indicated that approximately 3 percent of high school boys reported using steroids at least once.[3] Some boys are naturally bigger, thicker, and stronger, yet many are overeating or tempted to use drugs to help them achieve a size unnatural for their bodies, both for aesthetic reasons and for sports performance. Recently a college football player revealed how he got into a Division I football program: "The only way I could have made it, earned a college scholarship, was to use 'roids.' I just wasn't big enough. Now I'm one of the biggest guys on my team. It was worth it. I'd be nobody right now if I hadn't used. I'd be on the streets or in jail. I have no regrets."

Not only illegal substances are used in the attempt to bulk up. Health food stores offer shelves of legal products of questionable long-term impact, including creatine and protein powders, that boys and girls use to recover more quickly between workouts, put on more muscle mass, and achieve "six-pack abs." Researchers have not yet fully investigated the potential negative side effects of these substances on children and adolescents. However, there is some concern that adults' overuse of protein supplements can lead to kidney damage, among other problems. Among children and adolescents, these products may present similar or even more dangerous risk. Yet using legal substances for increasing muscle mass and reducing body fat is widely accepted. One college hockey player recently said, "Hey, we'd never use steroids — it would make us too bulky and we wouldn't be able to play our best. But we have no problem with creatine. In fact, our trainer encourages us to use it. We just know that we shouldn't use it all the time. It's best just to use it for a few weeks and then let your body recover." Use of these supplements is one more result of the intense pressure on our children to achieve an unrealistic ideal body size and shape.

As further evidence of athletics-related abuse of the human body, wrestlers will dehydrate and starve themselves to lose ten to fifteen pounds in a few days, offensive linemen will gorge themselves with food to put on that last twenty pounds, and gymnasts and figure skaters fast excessively or take diet pills to keep themselves lean. We need to talk with our kids about issues related to body shape and size: "I notice that your coach has you lifting weights a few times a week — how do you feel about that?" Or we could ask our boys, "It seems there is a lot of pressure on you to put a lot of weight on [or off] — how do you feel about that? Would you like some information about how to make the change healthfully?" We need to make sure that coaches or the pressures of the sport don't make kids modify their bodies in a manner or at a speed that is not healthy. We can't turn a blind eye to what the coach or the sports culture demands. Instead, we can help kids make sensible choices that will help them compete yet keep them healthy.

Good information and parental monitoring can help avoid such problems. For example, both our girls and boys need nutrition information in order to make good food choices. Also, a little sensitivity to kids' concern for their body image is also in order. For example, if weigh-ins are considered critical to a sport, the coach could have a sports medicine staff person administer them and make sure the weights remain unposted. We as parents might also direct kids to sports that suit their physical build, so they won't be tempted to modify their bodies to meet the demands of a sport and the expectations of their coaches. Use of steroids and supplements and the general pressures on our young athletes to develop high-performing bodies is addressed in greater detail in Chapter 14.

Styles of Social Interaction and Friendship

Anyone who has spent time in the hallways of a junior high school knows that differences exist in how girls and boys function socially. For example, boys tend to be more aggressive, whereas girls are more easily influenced. A summary of studies regarding such gender differences was published many years ago by Dr. Eleanor Maccoby, and her findings retain significance to this day. Both boys and girls from age 3 to at least age 11 strongly prefer playing with members of their own sex. Boys are particularly resistant to being influenced by girls in their play. Boys tend to play in larger groups, and their play is rougher and takes up more space. Boys more often play in streets, and girls more often play at home or at a friend's home. Girls tend to form close intimate friendships with one or two girls, and sharing of personal feelings marks these friendships. Boys' friendships are more oriented to mutual interests or activities.[4]

In terms of speech patterns, boys and girls display some interesting differences. Boys are more likely to interrupt; to issue commands, threats, or boasts; and to refuse to comply with another child's commands, especially if the child is a girl. Boys are more likely to verbally dominate an interaction by heckling or using humor or name calling. Girls, on the other hand, are more likely to express agreement with what someone has just said and politely give another person the chance to speak. For boys, speech is a way to establish turf and express individual dominance; for girls, it is a way to make social connection and build relationships. By middle childhood, boys and girls tend to develop the interaction styles that characterize their gender; generally, boys exhibit the friendly rivalry, joking, and competitive play that their fathers or other older male role models may exhibit. Girls manifest the greater intimacy and sharing of emotions that may have been demonstrated by their mothers or by other older females.[5] Of course, these are broad generalizations. Interaction styles vary widely, depending on the individual and the context.

How boys and girls relate and function in the social realm is also visible in sports. Boys tend to be more outcome- or task-oriented, whereas girls, though they too care about success, tend to primarily focus on relationships with teammates and coaches and on fitness. Because boys tend to be interested in achieving success, they can participate in and enjoy sports whether they like their coach or not. They can be successful on a team, whether they like their teammates or not. However, if given the option, male athletes prefer to engage in the close friendships that sports can inspire. A Division I hockey player slated to make an NHL team reflected, "Friendship and competitiveness are the most important things to me. The guys on my team are like my family. I really value being able to get through the hard times, when we aren't getting along. Of course, winning also really matters to me." But male athletes can stay focused on the goal of winning whether they get along with others or not. Even if they strongly dislike certain teammates, they'll play well together as long as they all help achieve success. Furthermore, boys can treat one another harshly on the field or court, but when the game is over, they can often drop the grudge on the field. This is rarely the case with girls.

The expectations related to sports can mar children's good judgment.

Girls tend to be much more relational in nature. If our girls are not getting along with a teammate or a coach, their performance tends to decline dramatically. In one instance two girls on a soccer team would not pass the ball to each other because they were fighting over a boyfriend. Yet when girls support one another or when they have a best friend on a team, they will do almost anything for one another. Jessie, a high school soccer goalie, said, "I hate it when I think my teammates are down on how I'm playing. In the last game I did really badly as a goalkeeper because I thought my best friend was mad at me. After the game she told me that she wasn't mad at me; she was just bummed that we were losing. I did really well in practice the next day, once I knew that things were cool between us."

Girls and young women tend to rely heavily on one another for inspiration, motivation, and feeling valued. This certainly can work to the advantage of girls in sports; they can often empower one another to do extraordinary things beyond their own or others' expectations. However, not getting along can be a major block to top-level performance.

Judgment

Boys and girls can greatly diverge in the area of judgment. Whether because of biochemical differences or socialization, our girls tend to make decisions based on empathy, whereas our boys make decisions based on what seems fair. Our girls tend to tune in to what others feel; this information can be used to help or to hurt. Our girls, particularly when younger, make decisions based on what they *feel* is right rather than what they *think* is right. In contrast, our boys are more likely to make decisions based on what they think is fair or just. Often they will not consider how an action will make a friend or teammate feel; what seems right or fair is more important to them.

Younger children — below the age of 4 or 5 — of both genders will tend to make decisions based on what they want or what's best for them. As older children and preadolescents, boys and girls move to making decisions based on what is best for their own group — perhaps their friends or team. Problems certainly can arise here — we need to encourage our kids — particularly boys — to have empathy for teammates and competitors and consider how they may feel when getting taunted or beaten. Girls may need help in thinking about what is fair for all — not just what they want for their best friend, but for the whole team, league, or sport itself. Both boys and girls need to cultivate empathy and a sense of justice in order to exercise good judgment.

Our boys' and girls' judgment can be affected by the "win at any cost" attitude prevalent in sports today. Whether they are wired to demonstrate higher levels of empathy or justice, all can be lost when kids are pressured to win no matter what. As a high school tennis player revealed, "My mom is all about winning. If I win, she looks so happy and bubbly. But if I lose, she won't talk to me for hours. She pouts. My dad will talk about the cost of my tennis. He'll say something like 'Why am I spending all of this money on lessons if you go out there and lose?'" The pressure to win can come from parents, the coach, teammates, or the media. It can lead our children, boys or girls, to make decisions that they know are wrong. For example, tennis players may be tempted to call balls out when they are in, ice hockey players may be tempted to take cheap shots when the referee isn't looking, and swimmers may be tempted to cheat on times when necessary. Kids also may be tempted to damage their bodies through excessive exercise, overeating, drug use, or starvation. The expectations related to sports can mar our children's good judgment. We as parents can resist these negative influences so that the positive aspects of sports can help shape kids' decision-making skills.

GIRLS' TEAMS

Jillian and Kerry are eighth-graders in a public city junior and senior high school. Their school is a magnet school, a competitive academic school that draws children from different neighborhoods. Because of limited resources and a low player pool due to economic realities (many kids work after school), the junior high students are frequently included on varsity sport teams. Jillian begs her friend Kerry to try out for the soccer team and Kerry obliges, provided that Jillian reciprocates by going out for ice hockey. They agree to the deal.

The catch for Jillian is that she has not skated competitively in a hockey game in over four years. But a deal is a deal, especially with a close friend. For girls, spending time with a best friend at this age takes precedence over just about anything. So while Jillian struggles to stay on her feet on the ice, Kerry shines, an outstanding talent who plays at a level beyond her years. Yet despite Jillian's skating incompetence, the girls on the team consistently support her. On one level, Jillian's presence helps defend their program from budget cuts, since greater player participation strengthens the team's position with the school administration. But Jillian and her parents can tell that she is genuinely accepted by her teammates, who make every effort to help her improve. And given that she is tight with Kerry, she holds special status — Kerry is a star player.

Also, the coaches strongly support Jillian. Because she helps fill out the squad (there were no cuts), Jillian sees spot duty as a member of the third line. The coaches find ways to give her limited ice time without jeopardizing the team's performance. Jillian accepts her role and strives to improve. Her teammates shepherd her as caring older sisters. Because these girls clearly value qualities other than athletic prowess alone, particularly friendship, Jillian experiences the chance to risk trying something new. Her parents know that in no way would they have been able to rekindle her interest in ice hockey if the idea had come from them. They are thrilled that she demonstrates the willingness and courage to take on this challenge. Eventually, Kerry and Jillian's team make the semifinals of the division playoffs and have a very successful season. Jillian improves to a moderate degree and plans to attend a summer hockey camp to get ready for next year's hockey season. The girls plan on playing softball together in the spring. Such a wonderful example of caring seems rare in male sports.

But what about the pitfalls of girls' athletics? What special challenges do female athletes face that might undermine both outstanding performance and the quality of the sports experience?

One can witness wonderful examples of caring among girls that are rare in male sports.

Grace, a sophomore in high school, is a better-than-average swimmer for the YMCA USA swim team. She loves being part of the team and looks forward to the early morning swims at the "Y" because she gets to joke and talk with teammates and coaches. Grace is one of the fastest 400-meter freestyle swimmers on the team. The coaches take pride in her speed and hope that she will earn an athletic scholarship in swimming. Grace's mother sees things a little differently. Each time she watches Grace compete, she can see her daughter's face turn red and the tears welling up just prior to the start of a race. Though Grace moves fast through the water, usually in first place, her mom finds it hard to see her daughter suffer emotionally.

Based on her mother's suggestion, Grace goes to a few sessions with a sport psychologist. It turns out that she feels a lot of pressure to perform and is not having much fun, especially in the 500-meter freestyle race—a situation very typical for girls of this age. Grace reflects, "Everyone is expecting so much from me. I don't want to let my team down. I know that I need to get a certain time to help the team win the whole event—and sometimes I'm not sure that I can go fast enough. Plus, it really hurts when I'm going so fast!" In discussion of how she would like to feel in the water—after the starting gun goes off and before she touches the final wall at the finish—it becomes clear that Grace worries about the outcome of a race. Through use of visualization and cue words, Grace's enjoyment of racing radically improves as does her speed. She begins achieving personal bests in every event. Grace's mother is relieved; she loves to see her little girl enjoy swimming once again.

However, a major disadvantage accompanies Grace's accomplishment: "My friends on the team treat me differently now. Some of them are mad at me and won't even talk to me. Now that I'm beating some of the better girls, they really don't like me. I'm not sure that going so fast is worth it. It used to be so much fun to go to practice; now I don't like it. Some of the older girls are so mean to me. They try to make me look bad, especially in front of the other swimmers and the coach." It is hard for Grace to get the cold shoulder from her friends and see the jealousy in their eyes. Grace doesn't want to hurt anyone and wants her friends back.

Her experience is not unusual. Sometimes girls are afraid to outdo their friends for fear of hurting their friendships. Sometimes our girls struggle to choose between doing what is best for themselves and what their group of friends or teammates want. It can jostle the social hierarchy when a young girl unexpectedly outperforms her teammates. It would be helpful to Grace if her parents directly talk with her about what has happened. They might discuss why it might be hard for her teammates to accept Grace's new status on the team. If she can be steadily kind to them yet also swim well, she might ultimately inspire them through her hard work as a swimmer and her faithfulness as a friend. Parents can provide significant support in situations like this as long as they do so gently and sensitively.

Cliques result from girls' need for one or two very close friends. Girls' teams that are subdivided into small special friendship groups are common. Cliques can turn ugly when their members are purposely rude to outsiders. Being left out of a clique in sports can be painful for both boys and girls, but especially so for girls. They can become distracted by feeling that they don't matter; such girls may stop trying hard, and then their performance plummets. Parents could urge coaches to try to separate cliques. This could be accomplished by integrating groups in terms of placement on the field, purposely grouping athletes in a way that breaks up cliques, and giving off-field tasks to mixed groupings. Parents can discuss with their children how cliques develop and why they shouldn't take them personally.

BOYS' TEAMS

Austin watches his son Tom's teen-league baseball game with interest yet also a sense of detachment. He likes to sit by himself, away from other fans, and take in the game. Occasionally he shouts words of encouragement to his son or a reminder here and there. But at this point, he trusts Tom's skills and prefers to back off and let him learn from other coaches. Tom is new to the teen league as a 13-year-old but he had been one of the better players in the A League, and his dad is confident that he'll fit in and play well.

Suddenly an incident on the field makes Austin furious. His son is playing second base when the pitcher on his own team, the oldest and best player, motions Tom over to confer just before the first batter of the inning. Then, unnoticed by everybody but Austin, the pitcher discreetly spits on Tom's uniform. The pitcher smirks. Tom flashes a brief look of disgust and runs back to second base to start the inning.

"What the hell was that all about!" yells Austin to no one in particular. He feels anger surging up in his gut. "How dare that little bastard spit on my kid!" he mutters loud enough for the other fans in the stands to hear him. Between innings Austin slides behind the chain-link fence and says to his son, "You have my permission to punch anyone who does that to you again. Do you understand? Don't let anyone ever do that to you again!"

Tom nods silently. He feels embarrassed by what his teammate Shawn has done and is glad it went mostly unnoticed. Though none too happy about it, Tom thinks it was a stupid way for Shawn to goof on him. The spit was not too much more than wet sunflower seeds, and Shawn was smiling when he did it. Tom generally feels good about being on this team, and if he had to guess, he'd say his teammates respect him as a good player. Shawn is African American and Tom isn't, but that doesn't seem to be a big deal to anyone, and besides, they had gotten along together at the boys and girls club on the travel hoop team two years ago. Tom is a little worried that his father might lose it after the game. He's a great dad and generally keeps his cool, but today he looks pissed.

Clearly, competition can trump relationship for boys. The wild horse of aggressiveness often accompanies young males in sports. While boys try to find their place in the social hierarchy, their competitive spirit can lighten into playful fun or escalate into unpleasantness and even violence. Adults can mistakenly attribute various ulterior motives and devious intentions to the actions of young male athletes, but boys simply engage in a lot of rough, "I'm going to put you in your place" verbal and physical aggression. Their behavior is not unlike bear cubs wrestling to test their own strength. That's not to suggest that this roughhousing is routinely benign. Any parent that has set foot in a Squirt or Pee Wee hockey locker room or observes unsupervised Pop Warner football players wrestling during delays before or after practices or games understands that horseplay can lead to physical and emotional injury. Male aggressiveness, be it verbal or physical, does need to be monitored and checked by good coaching and good parenting. Still, caution must also be taken not to crush boys' natural desire to play hard.

Austin, who happens to be an official in the league, speaks with Tom's coach after the game, after his anger has cooled a bit. Together they approach Shawn and quietly but firmly reprimand him for his behavior: "That's not how we do things in this league. It's disrespectful to your teammates, the game, and yourself. Don't let it happen again." Shawn nods yes, in a manner that suggests he gets the message, and that's where the matter ends. Both Austin and the coach don't think it necessary to let Shawn's parents know about the incident. Once cooler heads prevail, it becomes clear that Shawn is not a malicious, domineering kid. He just committed a stupid goof that required a reprimand. Shawn does not engage in that behavior again during the season.

> While boys try to find their place in the social hierarchy, their competitive spirit can lighten into playful fun or escalate into unpleasantness and even violence.

In addition to setting limits on aggressive behavior toward their own teammates, boys need help controlling aggression toward opponents and officials. In many sports, a fine line runs between what constitutes acceptable and penalty behavior. Brush-back pitches in baseball, hard picks in basketball, sliding tackles in soccer, and "message" hits in contact sports such as football, lacrosse, hockey, and rugby are examples of controlled aggression that dances along the line between fair and dirty play. Whereas it is not unusual to observe girls in team sports, even contact sports, apologizing for knocking over an opponent, this is rarely the case in boys' sports. Parents and coaches give multiple subtle messages to boys about acceptable levels of aggressive play — and they need to make sure that the messages fit their values. This is an area in which fathers and male coaches, perhaps with unresolved issues from their own past, might have a blind spot.

Jack is a 15-year-old hockey player who has been catching hell from his bantam league coach for not being willing to hit as much as the coach would like. He is a gifted play maker; "more of a Gretzky than a Messier" is how his father would describe him. Jack is certainly not frightened of contact, since he plays both lacrosse and football, but Jack prefers the speed and passing aspects of the game. The coach has nothing against speed and passing, but he's convinced that Jack is "soft" and will play to his full scoring potential only by getting a lot more physical. Unbeknownst to Jack's parents, this coach has been badgering Jack to change his style of play and has occasionally sent designated teammates to rough him up in the corners at practice in order to goad him into a tougher stance. The coach has muttered a few choice words for Jack under his breath, rudely questioning his manhood: "You [so and so], I'm not playing you until you grow a pair!"

Finally this situation gets to Jack; he blows up in practice, drops his gloves, and beats the heck out of a teammate in utter frustration. The coach feigns concern, for the sake of the few parents observing practice, but secretly he is pleased and says to Jack, under his breath, "That's more like it." This type of encounter occurs more than parents realize. Although sadistic coaches exist on both male and female teams, they are more frequently tolerated on boys' and men's teams. The details of coaches' abusive behavior typically aren't revealed until well after the season is over because coaches can intimidate through fear and bullying. Unfortunately, fear and anger are powerful motivating tools and can result in wins, at least over the short term. Parents and young athletes have to be careful not to be seduced by the "wins justify the means" philosophy. Developing a winning team through sadistic manipulation is not good coaching. It's emotional abuse, and especially heinous when dealing with young athletes. Championship victories never make it right.

COEDUCATIONAL TEAMS

Working with teams that include both boys and girls can pose other challenges. Because boys on average are more autonomous and girls are more relational in nature, it can be difficult for a coach to navigate working with them. It may be even harder for parents to know how to guide their children who participate in coeducational teams.

Frank, a high school diving coach, is confronting his ignorance about coaching girls. His diving team is small — three girls and four boys. Practice consists of a short warmup and stretching period followed by an hour of diving practice. Divers line up and take turns working on their front, back, inward, twist, and reverse dives; then they move to more difficult dives: one-and-one-half flips; back, inward, and reverse one-and-one-halfs; and twisting somersaults. Talent level varies among the boys and girls, but they all are motivated, good kids.

The role of the diving coach is to evaluate each dive. The great coaches know how to say the right things in the right way, so the diver can both feel encouraged to continue the effort and motivated to correct errors. When Frank coaches the boys, he can be pretty direct with them. If he feels that a boy isn't focused, he says, "Come on, David, where is your effort? Try it again." The tone sometimes can sound impatient. Though the boys like it when Frank makes positive comments, they seem able to understand his sometimes harsh tone — they trust that Frank cares about them. Frank says, "In fact, I think they like it that I am observing them so closely and challenging them to be better, even if I am a little tough."

In contrast, when he applies the same tactics to high school girls, Frank gets an entirely different reaction. If he says, "Hey, Lila, you really need to work on your hurdle. You're not getting any height off the board," Lila lowers her head and slowly walks away. Not only do the girls respond poorly to his suggestions, but sometimes they get upset and even cry. After a day or two of failure, Frank completely reevaluates how he coaches his team. Many questions run through his head: How could the boys and girls respond so differently? Am I a mean coach?

Through watching his colleague Jen coach her girls' softball team,

Frank learns what he is missing. Jen emphasizes how being a team is fun. She spends time developing the relationships of the girls. She challenges them, even raising her voice at times, but she pays close attention to how the group is feeling; if they are not happy, she attends to the problem. When the team does well, she celebrates with them. At the end of practice, she always says something positive about how the team is doing.

Jen is also a spectacular coach with boys. She is tough in a different way with them, but she still manages to find the right balance between fun and challenge. Her girls stay on task longer and require less pushing; they seem to consistently push themselves and need only a positive environment in order to thrive. In contrast, Jen uses a little tougher tone with the boys because they need more of a push to do their best — the girls already seem wired to do so.

Boys can typically handle a harsh or curt tone from their coach or peers, yet boys seem to need more attention. They need to know that their coach values them in some way. If the coach is extremely demanding in tone and manner, some boys will in fact struggle with this. But it is much harder for a girl than a boy to handle a tough, aggressive coach.

If not distracted by hurt feelings or pressure to please others, girls in general tend to be willing to push themselves hard; they so much want to please others and do well for their teammates. Their ability to focus and try hard seems to outdo the boys, and perhaps because of this, girls have a hard time when they get stern feedback from coaches — the girls are already trying their best, and it seems as if the coach is not recognizing this fact. This can make girls think that they aren't being valued, respected, or understood.

INDIVIDUAL DIFFERENCES

Brent is in his sophomore year in high school. A 220-pound football player, he is known as one of the most talented players to have played for the Hawks football team. Everyone knows that Brent will be a scholarship player. Plus he is an A student. He seems to have everything. And to top it off, he is a really nice person. Yet only his mother knows how much he is suffering privately. Confidentially he tells his mom, "Mom, I hate how the coach screams at me. When he is yelling, all I can see are the veins popping out of his neck and his red face. It is getting so bad that I can't even think straight when he is yelling. It makes me hesitate to go back the next day. I don't know why he always has to be so harsh. It is awful. I love to play, but not for him!"

Brent's mom empathizes with her son, but she is also confused. Everyone says that boys are tough and can handle anything. Why can't her son take the heat? Why is it so hard for him? It would be helpful for Brent's mother to realize that Brent may not be like the average boy, though he looks the part of handsome superstar athlete who can handle anything; he is in fact quite sensitive. Brent's mother could help Brent by being an emotional support — listening to how he feels and encouraging him to focus on the intent of the coach, not the tone of the message: "Oh, the coach is trying to help me. He is paying attention to me because he thinks that I can do better. This is just his way of trying to make me better." Self-talk like this could help him to be more able to deal with the coach. (This approach could also help girls struggling with a tough coach.)

In contrast, Mary is a top-notch hurdler for a Division I college team who loves it when coaches yell at her; it sparks her motivation. She almost laughs when she hears about the "harsh" men's coaches; she says, "I wish I had a coach like that! They are so motivating. I'd show them what I was made of if they treated me like that! Those guys are lucky. My coach is way too soft. She is too easy on people and doesn't tell us exactly how to improve. I'd way rather have a coach who will tell it like it is!" Mary is an unusual girl, but often one or two girls on a team will have a similar attitude. Mary has a ready explanation for it: "Hey, I have four older brothers. What do you expect?" Knowing that Mary can be motivated by a tough coach and that her sports environment is not challenging enough, her parents might help her look for other sources of challenge so that she can do her best in college hurdling. For example, she could hire an intense, tough coach for a session every few weeks.

Overall, a range of differences and similarities characterize girls and boys as they play sports, and considering their general tendencies hand in hand with individual traits will help parents nurture both boys and girls in the complex world of athletics.

9

RAGE AND EXPLOSIONS

Learning to Practice Emotional Control in Sports

HOW CAN WE TELL our children to control their emotions when they regularly observe adults letting their temper fly at competitions in youth, high school, and professional sports? In July 2000, two fathers of youth hockey players fought over a hockey scrimmage, and one father killed the other — one son was left without a dad. What lessons are our children learning from such incidents? It would be short-sighted to think that our children remain unaffected by such behavior.

Violence in sports is most pervasive at the professional level. Emotional control is not highly valued by the media; in fact, when professional athletes fight, TV ratings soar. Adults make money, but our children and the integrity of sports suffer. Ron Artest of the Indiana Pacers offered a prime example of how adults can put others in danger by losing self-control in fall 2004. In a game against the defending NBA champions, the Detroit Pistons, Ron Artest fouled Ben Wallace on his way to making a layup. Wallace, upset by this flagrant foul, aggressively pushed Artest back. Artest regained control of himself and avoided further physical aggression. However, moments later, when Artest was lying down on the score table, a fan threw a cup of ice and hit him in the head. The moments that followed were horrific. Artest jumped up and attacked the person he thought was the culprit, throwing punches and wrestling him. Fans and other players got involved until the entire arena was transformed into a violent melee, which was televised. Food, punches, and profanities flew throughout the arena. After this episode, some of our younger therapy clients said that they thought the incident was funny and entertaining. Others said they love to watch fighting. Is it any wonder that children imitate the stars and lose control themselves?

In fall 2003, we attended game three of the Yankees–Red Sox play-off series. It was a beautiful Saturday. Fathers attended with their sons to watch as Roger Clemens and Pedro Martinez — two of the game's greatest pitchers from the best teams in baseball — faced one final duel before Clemens retired from the Yankees.

What could be better than this? The answer is that a lot could be better. With millions of fans watching, professional baseball players — living legends and heroes to youth — behaved like hoodlums. They fired fastballs at players' heads. The Yankees' bench coach, Don

> Convincing our kids that emotional control is better for their performance and for their personal growth is a challenging job.

Zimmer, attacked Pedro Martinez, ace pitcher of the Red Sox, because Martinez had hit one of the Yankee players with a pitch. Images of this fight and other impulsive behaviors that evening became lasting memories for observant children. Those not present got to view the episode on television over and over again, seemingly for weeks, as children's role models demonstrated that impulsive, violent behavior is acceptable when facing frustration.

Scenarios like these in professional sports make it even more challenging for parents to convince their kids that emotional control is better for performance and personal growth. It's difficult for children to find fault in the behavior of their heroes, especially because no consequences seem to follow their actions. Big-name professional athletes are celebrated regardless of their behavior. Pedro Martinez and Don Zimmer were fined, but it didn't change their position in the series. Neither one was kicked out of the game or suspended for part of the series; they both continued to coach and play. In the basketball meltdown mentioned earlier, players from the Pistons and Pacers were suspended and fined, but Jermaine O'Neil, who violently punched a fan, got his suspension reduced so he could play during a televised holiday game. The message sent to our children was that it doesn't matter if players lose control — all that matters is that they win, so professional leagues can provide entertainment and make money. Though the NBA tried to take a firm stance about inappropriate behavior, this reaction constitutes only a small step toward the change needed in sports culture.

It is worth pointing out to our children that Roger Clemens, the Yankees' pitcher in the game we cited in the Yankees–Red Sox series, kept his emotions under control throughout that game and went on to win. (This is hard for many adamant Red Sox fans to admit—we are members of this group—although at last winning the World Series has eased our pain.) Clemens demonstrated better character and self-control than did Martinez, his opponent. While members of the two teams were arguing, Clemens made sure he kept his arm warm during the delay. He stayed away from the conflict, and when the game began again, he struck out Manny Ramirez, one of the best hitters in baseball. Disappointingly, few news stories celebrated how well Clemens had kept his cool in the heat of battle. Instead, the focus was on Zimmer, the 70-year-old man willing to attack Pedro Martinez to protect and fight for his own team. He was given an army helmet and feted by the media and fans, though the real hero was Clemens.

Though episodes like these are worrisome enough, evidence suggests that violence and impulsivity in sports are getting worse, and the media are increasing coverage of such events. Unfortunately, this undermines the wonderful efforts to promote good sportsmanship made by many sports programs across the country. We as parents have to manage what our kids hear, see, and experience in the context of sports, talking openly about fights that occur during professional matches. We can discuss who the real winners are when tempers flare. Most important, we need to be mindful of our own behavior and actions.

PARENTS' GUIDE TO EMOTIONAL CONTROL

Some of us simply lose control when watching our children play sports. When we watch them perform in a public place such as an athletic field, many emotions come into play. We can feel exposed and vulnerable to the judgments of others: Do they think our kids are good players? What will they think of us as parents if our children lose control and get angry? Will people blame us for our kids' behavior and think we are bad parents? Do other kids fear our child? Sitting in the stands or on the sidelines with so many feelings brewing inside us, we feel helpless—mere spectators. These feelings, which may include guilt and a sense of responsibility, can overwhelm a parent. If our child assaults another player or gets decked by an opponent, it's easy to get enraged, tense, and fearful. Control can slip.

One positive approach is to recognize that the problem probably can't be entirely resolved at the moment — but parents can consider ways to prevent similar events from happening in the future. The following four steps can help parents maintain control in the heat of the moment.

Step One: Pause
The first reaction should be no reaction. Take a deep breath and regain composure before saying or doing anything. Though it's incredibly difficult to watch a referee make a horrible call or an opposing player foul our child, it's important to buy some time before taking action. It is possible to miss something that happened or fail to understand it. A calm, emotionally neutral pause for thought is likely to help bring about an effective, just response to the situation.

Step Two: Name Your Feelings
Before saying anything, imagine what you might say if no one could hear you and you faced no consequences for your words. For example, when seeing their child lose control on the field and punch another player, parents might wish they could say, "Goddamn it! You really did it this time. You embarrassed me. I'm so pissed at you!" Giving words to feelings does not mean that those words have to be spoken, but thinking them provides the opportunity to honor feelings and genuine immediate responses to a situation without exacerbating it.

Step Three: Communicate Calmly but Firmly
Typically, yelling and losing control do not help kids calm down. How can we as parents transform angry feelings into a reasonable and effective response? Instead of screaming at our child, the ref, or a player from the opposing team, we might say something like this: "What happened to you out there? That behavior did not seem like something you'd do. I know the referee made a terrible call, but that doesn't mean you can punch your opponent."

Furthermore, the mom or dad can take this opportunity to reinforce the limits of acceptable behavior: "You need to take a break right now. You're not going back into the game until you calm down and explain yourself." Statements like this show that we are angry while also expressing concern and articulating the consequences of the behavior. Requiring this break serves a constructive purpose: it helps ensure the safety of the child and other players while giving the child an opportunity to reflect on what just happened.

Step Four: When in Doubt, Consult

When strong emotions bubble up, we as parents know that the first thing out of our mouth isn't likely to be helpful. In these situations, don't hesitate to consult spouses, colleagues, or friends before taking action. Sometimes a parent or coach feels so furious, he or she can't think of how to respond effectively. In such events, it is both honest and productive to say, "I'm so angry at what just happened that I don't know what to say. Go sit on the bench for a minute. Let's talk about it when we both have calmed down." These statements model to kids that it is okay to be angry and that sometimes it is better to wait before taking action.

Yet certain occasions demand a quick response. In an unusually dangerous situation, such as an unmanageable brawl, parents should not hesitate to call school security or dial 911. Don't delay taking action in an emergency.

Our efforts to maintain self-control are crucial because our children will struggle tremendously in sports if we are unable to model appropriate behavior or fail to teach them when they go off track. We and other respected adults such as coaches and teachers need to guide our kids, who will inevitably test the limits of self-control. The professional sports culture and the media are formidable adversaries in this task. We must be prepared and willing to do the hard work for our kids. Even if our children are the most talented athletes, they may still struggle to keep their emotions and behavior under control. We have to be ready to work with them and their coaches to nip negative behavior in the bud before it becomes a chronic or even dangerous pattern.

> When we watch our children perform in a public place such as an athletic field, many emotions come into play.

ZACK, THE SOCCER GOALIE

With a minute and a half left in the game and the score tied 1–1, Zack, a 16-year-old soccer goalie, explodes out of the goalie's box on a corner kick and levels the attacking striker, who was attempting to head the ball. At six feet, one inch in height and 175 pounds in weight and a sophomore in high school, Zack does not try to knock the ball out; rather he is trying to knock the player out. Frustrated because the referee made what he thought was a bad call on the previous play, Zack directs his aggression at his opponent and nearly breaks that player's nose. Zack gets a yellow card, a formal warning that his next infraction will lead to expulsion from the game. The opposing team is awarded an indirect kick inside the box and scores the winning goal. Furious at himself, Zack kicks the goal post and fractures his ankle.

Perhaps the best athlete on the team, Zack has sabotaged his and the team's success through poor emotional control. His behavior has jeopardized his physical safety and the emotional stability of the team. Crying on the sideline after being helped off the field, Zack hysterically apologizes to his coach: "Coach, I'm so sorry I did this. I'm such a screwup!"

Zack's parents are horrified to watch their son punch another player and then fracture his own ankle. First, they worry about his health. Is he seriously injured? Has he hurt another player? They also feel responsible for his behavior, wondering whether a stricter approach as parents could have prevented this unfortunate incident. In sum, Zack's conduct is an embarrassment to his parents, the team, the coaching staff, and the school.

Many extremely talented athletes have learned lessons about self-control from parents who also served as coaches. Professional golf legend Jack Nicklaus wrote in *Sports Illustrated* about an important lesson he learned from his father about controlling his emotions in sports:

> I've always thought you learn how to win by winning, but Dad taught me that losing provides lasting lessons as well. I remember being 11 years old and playing with him. . . . We were on the 15th hole and I had an eight-iron to the green. I hit it about 130 yards into the sand, and I heaved the club darn near into the same bunker. Dad just said, "O.K., go pick up your club, we're going to the clubhouse. That's the last time I'll see you do that or you'll never go to the golf course again," . . . I had to learn how to behave as a young golfer, how to control my emotions and not let poor shots or other players affect me. . . . My concentration and tight rein over my emotions let me perform under pressure and wall off distractions that might've bothered another guy.[1]

It's remarkable that Nicklaus's father did not respond to this incident with anger. He was stern, and he established significant consequences should his son behave similarly in the future. He got a clear message across to his immature yet enormously talented son. He also modeled self-control for Jack, showing that one can remain calm even when a situation warrants a strong emotional response. Imagine how different Nicklaus's experience would have been if his father had screamed at him; the power of the message might have been lost. The long-term effects of the example of Nicklaus's dad are impressive. For Nicklaus, gaining emotional control helped him become a better competitor. In later tournaments when the stakes were much higher, Nicklaus was able to compete effectively under pressure, even when his emotions were running high. His father's lesson helped Nicklaus become a better kid and a greatly improved player.

Some believe, however, that emotional explosiveness can lead to great performance in athletics. In contact sports such as football and hockey, this may be true. But rarely is it the case that athletes play well without exercising some form of self-control. Athletes need to tense their muscles to get them to perform, but they also need grace and control to complete their task adequately. Whether they are swinging a golf club or tennis racket or shooting a basketball, soccer ball, or lacrosse ball, they need to harness their body, mind, and emotions. For example, a major league pitcher uses a lot of force to throw a fastball at ninety-five miles per hour. This action requires an explosion of energy starting in the legs, shifting through the hips, and catapulting through the shoulders, arms, hands, and fingers. Yet this energy must be channeled in a disciplined way for the ball to soar and then hit the catcher's mitt ninety feet away. Nervousness or anger in response to a misfortunate play or bad call is understandable, but if it takes on a life of its own, performance suffers. The pitcher will miss the target or simply throw the wrong pitch. Often, veteran athletes talk about how rookies become true superstars only when they learn to manage failures and setbacks and thus stay focused in the face of adversity.

> Without patience and a willingness to continue to provide explanations, setting firm limits can be meaningless and even destructive.

John McEnroe, a tremendous tennis player in the 1980s and 1990s, addressed this issue in his book *You Cannot Be Serious.*[2] Many observers thought that McEnroe used emotional outbursts to increase concentration and motivation, but in the book he shares that the opposite was true. He admits that he lost control because he was terrified of failure. He hated being a brat on the tennis court and wondered how many more tournaments he would have won if someone had taught him self-control. But he was so talented that no one dared challenge the behavior of the number one player in the world. That might have hurt TV ratings and the pockets of big business. Thus short-term gain was embraced, sacrificing the potential long-term gain to McEnroe and the game of tennis.

Returning to Zack's story — his coach decides to confront the boy in a manner similar to that of Nicklaus's father: "Zack, if I ever see you do something like that in a game again, I will pull you out immediately and suspend you from the team. I just want you to know that. But I have to tell you that I'm a bit confused. Every time we try to help you control yourself, you seem to understand, but then something clicks in your head and you lose it. What happens to you out there?"

Setting limits is not enough for Zack's coach. He takes the additional step of trying to understand what is motivating Zack's behavior. Zack himself can't explain it, though he hazards a few guesses: "I don't know. I was just so pissed about that previous play. I just lost it. I can't control myself. I don't know what to do."

In further discussion, Zack states that he had felt that everyone was turning against him: The referee was trying to distract him by making a bad call, and the opposing team was pressuring him. Some opponents verbally harassed Zack when he made a save, and fans from the sidelines heckled him. He tried to ignore their remarks and laugh them off, but eventually he reached the breaking point and couldn't take it anymore. He felt angry, scared, disappointed, isolated, and ridiculed.

Establishing firm rules about emotional control *before* the beginning of the season can help prevent problems from occurring.

He speaks with honesty to his coach: "Once I begin to lose control, when I feel that I have to stand up for myself and fight, there is no going back." Zack feels that his character is being tested, and he is right. But such a test is not primarily physical — it has to do with emotions.

As we try to understand why our children lose control, we need to consider genetic heritage, the environment in which children are raised, and the environment in which they play. Sometimes biochemical, physiological, or cognitive problems fuel the disturbing behavior. Impulse control problems or attention deficit disorder with hyperactivity may run in the family. If such a diagnosis is confirmed, we as parents may want to consult with the family doctor and specialists about treatments such as counseling, medication, or both. Learning disabilities can also be a source of frustration for some of our athletic children; they may have a hard time understanding the coach's advice or processing the information in a complicated play or strategy. They may feel overwhelmed and as a result perform poorly and lose control of emotions and behavior. One or two episodes of inappropriate aggression on the athletic field don't typically signal a physiological problem. But a persistent pattern of poor self-control should lead parents to explore these possible sources of the problem.

Other difficulties can cause emotional outbursts and inappropriate behavior in sports. A child may be reacting to a family crisis, such as the recent death of a family member, parents' marital problems, or substance abuse within the family, to name just a few examples. Our child might be emotionally exhausted by these problems, burdened by emotions that are hard to express and manage. Acting out in sports might be a child's way of showing that something is wrong. Kids may also mimic behavior they observe at home, such as loud arguments. Addressing the family problem may help reduce the likelihood that such children will continue to experience behavioral problems in sports. This is not easy: parents must attend to step two of the three-step approach — they must examine themselves. There is no easy route to quick results; professional help may be needed.

Also, the team environment may affect our child's behavior. Perhaps bullies on the team or an abusive coach is setting off our child. Maybe the level of competition is so fierce that our child is struggling with more adversity than he or she has the maturity to manage. As parents, we need to review these factors before deciding what to do.

Zack's coach soon takes the opportunity to talk to Zack's parents about their son's problem. They reveal that Zack has a long history of reckless behavior in athletics, and though he experiences no cognitive problems in school, other family members have struggled with poor impulse control. With this information in mind, Zack's coach concludes that Zack is not a vicious kid who acts badly on purpose, and he recognizes that it may take the boy a while to fully correct his behavior. Zack may have learned poor self-control from family members and or inherited impulse-control difficulties. By consulting with parents as well as the athletic director, this wise coach was able to create a constructive plan for working with this talented young athlete.

Appealing to Zack's competitive nature, the coach challenges him to a big test. He tells Zack that opposing players will continue to try to distract him as long as they can get a reaction out of him. The goal of his opponents is to bait him and take him off his game. Zack and his coach agree that the way to win is to ignore them, act as if they don't exist, and even laugh at their pathetic attempts to distract him. The coach encourages Zack to be a role model for the rest of his teammates; he has the opportunity to show them that players can learn from their mistakes. In the process, Zack may also prove to himself that he can take control of his passion and use it to play to his best ability.

Some parents might read this and say, "I gave the same speech to my kid and nothing worked." We are sympathetic to these parents. All of us have been in the position of feeling helpless. Sometimes, when we feel like giving up, we have to ask ourselves whether we have given our efforts a chance to work. Yet hanging in there for the long haul to teach our children to control themselves is that little extra effort that can make the difference.

Such was the case with Zack. In time, he made impressive strides in controlling his impulses, although ups and downs occurred along the way. After some games he'd proudly discuss how opponents would try to distract him and how he maintained control. At other times, Zack returned to his old antics. In one instance, he pushed an attacking offensive player who ran into him when trying to score a goal. Zack's coach pulled him from the game immediately, and Zack sat out the following game. He learned to understand the consequences of his actions. In the following days, Zack and his coach talked about what went wrong and what he could do to prevent recurrence of this behavior. Even though this conversation repeated earlier talks on the same theme, it helped remind Zack of his goals and values.

Zack's coach was both firm and caring. He didn't give up on Zack, yet he was willing to enforce consequences, even if they weren't popular with fans or other players. Setting limits and sticking to them can help children learn self-control and build character. By the time Zack was a senior, he had become a role model for younger players as captain of the team. This maturity carried over to other sports he played, proving that the efforts of parents, coach, and Zack himself had paid off.

Firmly establishing rules about emotional control before the beginning of the season can help prevent problems. For example, Zack's coach learned prior to the season that the referees were becoming stricter about bad language. If players shouted obscenities at the refs during the game, an automatic penalty would be called. As a result, Zack's coach shared this information with the team and stated that any time an obscenity was uttered during practice, the whole team, including the coaches, would do ten pushups. While this seemed ludicrous to the players at the time, it became somewhat of a team joke that turned into a bonding experience. A player would say, "Shit!" after a bad play, and the coach would blow the whistle requiring the whole team to drop to the ground and count out loud in unison, "1, 2, 3, 4 . . ." Not once during the season was Zack's team penalized for foul language. Their coach took the time to explain the rules of conduct clearly and enforced the rules when errors were made. When adults teach self-control in a preventive manner, results can be extremely positive.

> An athlete's drive to win can lead to poor tolerance of frustration, particularly when failure is associated with feelings of being unworthy.

CARRIE: THE TEMPER TANTRUMS OF A YOUNG ATHLETE

Carrie, a 9-year-old diver, loses her temper after failing her second dive of an important tournament. She tries to scream loudly under water to get her frustrations out before pulling herself out of the pool; but when she hears the referee announce that she made a failed dive, she yells, "What? No way! I can't believe this!" She throws down her towel, starts to cry, and storms to the locker room. Though she returns to finish the meet, her performance is well below her ability. The judges, perhaps angered by her outburst, score her remaining dives with considerable scrutiny.

In Carrie's next meet, she improves her performance but loses control again when one of the same judges gives her a score of 4 out of 10 on her dive, though the others award a 6. When walking past the referee on her way to sit down, she says accusingly, "You really want me to lose." The referee blows his whistle and warns Carrie's coach that one more comment from her will lead to suspension from competition. After this event, Carrie's mother decides that the girl needs therapy.

Carrie's meet behavior is embarrassing to the team, her coach, and her parents. When she has been openly disrespectful to referees, her coach has tried to bench her, talk to her, and give her time off, but nothing seems to work. Apparently, Carrie is so serious about performing well and pleasing her coach and her parents that anything short of a perfect dive makes her feel like a failure. An athlete's drive to win can lead to poor tolerance of frustration, particularly when failure is associated with feelings of unworthiness. For Carrie, the stakes have become high because winning gives her the feeling that she is making her parents happy. When she loses, she fears that they will no longer care about her.

Such feelings can be particularly intense for a 9-year-old, regardless of talent. In therapy, Carrie eventually shares her feelings about her parents' divorce: she still hopes that they will get back together. Her mother is always working and rarely attends her meets; her father is little involved in her life, and when he does surface, he is concerned about her performance — everyone at the pool can hear him screaming from the stands. Though his comments are typically positive, his presence puts pressure on Carrie: "I have to win. I practice hard. I don't like it when I lose. I shouldn't lose."

Though Carrie will have to learn to manage her emotions, she also needs to hear that she is a valuable, wonderful person regardless of her performance. Carrie believes that her father will love her only if she performs well — perhaps he will come back home if she is good enough. Moreover, she feels obligated to do well for her mother, the person who takes care of her. Carrie interprets anything short of pleasing both her parents as a huge failure, evidence that she is unworthy.

To help Carrie deal with her troubling feelings and their effect on sports experience as a diver, her therapist, coach, and mother find ways to praise her that do not involve athletic performance. For example, Carrie is wonderful to beginning divers on the team; she encourages them and teaches them tricks that come to her naturally. Carrie's mom and coach take every opportunity to praise her for this generosity. Carrie's father is less receptive to trying this approach, however. He agrees to help Carrie relax, but he doesn't much value the therapist's suggestions. Unfortunately, parents do not always agree on how to change a child's behavior — or even concur that a behavior needs to be altered.

Next, Carrie concentrates on devising a plan for handling performance and emotions during meets. Because she is much more talented than her teammates, she often participates alone. In one meet, she discovers that she prefers not to watch the other divers when it isn't her turn. Seeing another diver successfully complete a strong dive makes her nervous, so she decides that after each dive, she will lie down, listen to her Walkman, and visualize her next dive. Then when her next dive is announced, she has no idea how the other divers are doing. This constructive plan of action works. Though she still gets frustrated with poor dives, she has learned to keep a poker face in front of the judges and head to the locker room briefly to collect herself before preparing for her next dive. In essence, Carrie knows how to delay frustration with multiple means of distracting herself from negative feelings and brief failures. The combination of feeling worthy and loved despite how she performs in diving and this improved ability to tolerate failures enhance her confidence, and she goes on to place in the top ten in a huge tournament.

Carrie's relationship with her father, however, remains somewhat strained. Diving is partly important to her because she shares this passion with her dad. Yet she learns not to take his public remarks at meets seriously. Carrie comes to tolerate her father's intensity so that it no longer distracts her. Though she yearns for a closer relationship with him, she is able to separate diving performance from her sadness at her parents' divorce and her own sense of self-worth.

The stories of athletic children reveal that rage and explosive behavior result from the inability to cope with problems. Young athletes need the help of parents and coaches to learn emotional control. Helping athletes and their parents recognize that emotional control leads to better performance is an ideal hook to make their effort to improve a worthy task. A combination of sternness and caring is ideal for the adults trying to help explosive athletes. Staying invested in their improvement, even in the most difficult of circumstances, can help young athletes make needed changes in their behavior. The sports context is an ideal setting in which to teach children of all ages how to control their emotions.

What is apparent in the stories of Carrie, Zack, and many other young athletes is that there is often something else lurking underneath the surface of explosive behavior in sports. Often, they have biological susceptibilities to behaving impulsively. Children with ADD and ADHD lack the capacity to reflect on their feelings and behaviors in the moment and can act impulsively. Problems with mood, anxiety, and family conflicts may also be factors. As a result, we as parents must be open to recognize that impulsive and explosive behavior on the athletic field is an indication that we have work to do. We cannot treat it lightly, nor can we assume that we have nothing to do with the problem. If we cannot resolve the issue on our own, then we must seek the support of others to help guide our children to better self-control and conduct. If we fail to address these problems early, it is likely they will continue to worsen, which will undermine our children's performance and personal development.

> A combination of sternness and caring is ideal for the adults trying to help explosive athletes.

10

QUITTING, BURNING OUT, AND MOVING ON

Helping Children Know When Enough Is Enough

SOONER OR LATER, we all as parents will hear our child make this unsettling statement: "I quit." Usually this is the last thing we want to hear. We wonder if the child is giving up too easily — if he or she always quits when faced with a challenge, how will this kid handle the ups and downs of life? Why start the pattern of being a quitter at a young age? We think to ourselves, "If only our child would try a little harder for a little longer."

Kids might be clueless about the consequences of quitting a sport: losing valuable time with friends, becoming bored or depressed, passively watching too much TV, or gaining weight due to inactivity. Also, the period of time between the close of the school day and dinnertime is risky for drug use, delinquency, and early pregnancy. Without the structure of sports, our kids may take one of these paths, with all its long-term consequences. Quitting a sport at a young age can potentially mean passing up a chance to play at the varsity level in high school or even college and losing out on valuable learning experiences, friendships, and joyful activity.

> Structured activities have become the sole means of social interaction and physical play after school for most children.

When our children want to quit, we as their parents have work to do. What is motivating this decision? Is it reasonable? Some of our kids quit because they hate the coach or their teammates or no longer enjoy playing. They may also come to the realization that they can't compete with their peers. They may say, "Dad, the coach never plays me. I just sit on the bench the whole game. It sucks. He never gives me a chance. I totally try hard, but the other kids are just faster than me. I'm one of the best shooters on the team, but I can't jump very high, so my shots get blocked a lot unless I'm totally open."

In other cases, kids have discovered a passion for a new sport or want to try something different. In more worrisome situations, our kids quit because they're exhausted or burned out. The demands of the sport are too much for them physically and psychologically. "Mom, I have no time to do my homework or even see my friends on the weekends anymore. I spend two hours a day practicing, and tournaments are every weekend. It sucks! I can hardly stay awake in school." Playing on a particular team is simply draining the life out of them, and they can't keep up.

Of course, determining the best solution depends on the nature of our child's specific problem, age, and ability to manage adversity. As parents, we must sort through many factors to arrive at a conclusion and then find a tactful way to address any concerns with our child.

SASHI: SHOULD KIDS QUIT WHEN TEASED?

After the second soccer practice of the season, Sashi, a 7-year-old girl, complains to her parents that playing soccer is no longer fun. With her big brown eyes, she looks up to her mother and says, "Mommy, I don't know if I want to play anymore. I like soccer, but the girls keep on teasing me. I don't know why they do it. I'm nice to everyone."

Having just relocated because of a job change for Sashi's father, the whole family is going through a transition. They know no one in town. Sashi's parents have hoped that soccer would present a nice opportunity for their daughter to meet other girls, particularly because she is an only child. But she is having a hard time. Almost in tears, Sashi says, "No one on the team passes me the ball, ever. The only time I get the ball is by accident. If I make a bad pass, they laugh at me and call me stupid."

Sashi's mother knows that their move has been tough on Sashi, but seeing her daughter suffer from teasing seems unbearable. Sashi's parents consider pulling her from the team and the program, but they are concerned because few alternative sports programs are available. Sashi hates the idea of taking dance or ballet and has no interest in joining her mother for afternoon walks. Her parents hesitate to let Sashi ride her bike without their supervision because they live on a busy street. Yet staying home and doing nothing will not benefit Sashi.

Many of us parents today realize that neighborhood play, a form of physical activity that many children in previous generations enjoyed, is no longer a convenient, safe option for children. We worry that our children might be abducted or hurt if left to play unattended, and we as parents are busy with demanding schedules ourselves. Therefore structured activities have become the sole means of social interaction and physical play after school for most children.

Given these realities, what are Sashi's parents to do? Sashi lacks the maturity and ability to handle these problems on her own. Unfortunately, this places more of the burden of responsibility on her parents to find opportunities that suit her. This task is particularly tough because her parents are already exhausted from their efforts in adjusting to their new life in this unfamiliar town. Sashi's mother is trying to meet other parents in the community, which is a challenge because they know no one. Their house needs significant reconstructive work, and Sashi's father has to work through several weekends. Helping Sashi find the right sport is not top on their priority list, yet Sashi's struggles are becoming too problematic to ignore.

While Sashi's parents don't want to make Sashi more miserable by forcing her to play soccer, they feel that she needs exposure to some social and athletic activities. This is particularly true because Sashi doesn't have brothers and sisters. Only children often need social activities outside home because the lack of siblings makes it more difficult for them to learn to relate well with their peers. Having an only child like Sashi stay at home and do nothing would be an ill-advised path for her parents. Yet allowing her to frequently be teased is also problematic.

It is certainly not surprising that Sashi's parents are more concerned about the teasing. As parents, we are greatly pained when our children are teased in sports, or in any context, for that matter. Why do children tease each other in sports? When children play together in groups, they can feel insecure and fearful about being rejected by their peers. They worry that they won't be as skilled as their peers or that no one will like them. When overwhelmed by such feelings, they can behave in cruel ways to protect themselves from being seen as the outsider. When a group of kids tease an outsider, they may feel more confident about being an accepted member of the group. The term *scapegoat* comes to mind here. The scapegoat takes the negative energy of the group so that everyone else can stick together and feel secure.

Sashi is a scapegoat, the new girl in town. She isn't a great athlete, and she doesn't know how to relate well with girls her own age. Entering a team of girls who know each other well, Sashi is an easy target for teasing, and her desire to quit is an understandable reaction. Her parents, however, are not yet convinced that quitting is in her best interest. Instead, they hope Sashi will learn to behave in a manner that prevents the teasing.

To take action, Sashi's parents first gather more information. They contact the soccer coach, a friendly, enthusiastic young woman. She seems to enjoy working with Sashi but has several concerns: "Sashi really tries hard out there, and I think she likes soccer, but these girls have been playing together for over a year and have more experience than Sashi does. You know kids. When someone is different, they can get teased. Even though I am strict about addressing negative comments, sometimes they say things that I don't notice. I can tell when something is wrong, though, by the look on Sashi's face."

Relieved that nothing appears to be wrong about his daughter's behavior, but still concerned for her, Sashi's father responds, "Well, do you think there is anything Sashi can do to break into the group? Maybe she should quit. She really needs to make friends and to have some kind of activity that excites her, but we don't want to make her suffer."

"I wouldn't give up just yet," the coach replies. "It's still early in the season, and things may improve. One thing I have noticed is that Sashi appears very tuned in to everything the other girls say. When they talk about a TV show, she asks what they're talking about, almost interrupting the conversation. Perhaps you might encourage her to relax and allow herself to learn more gradually about the other girls and what they do. In time I think they'll welcome her in, if she gives them a little space. Also, when she's playing, she often yells to get the ball. It seems the more she does this, the less the other girls want to pass it to her. And let's face it, 7-year-old soccer players don't have the ability to pass to each other. Mostly, they just chase after the ball. I think Sashi may become less frustrated if she expects fewer passes and just goes out and plays."

After discussing together this conversation with the coach, Sashi's parents decide to talk with their daughter. They recognize that her problem involves a combination of factors. Had she been an outstanding player, she probably would have had fewer difficulties with other players. However, her overeager approach to them has caused a negative reaction, and her poor soccer skills serve as a target for their agitation with her. Yet the parents don't want to shame Sashi for trying to make new friends. At the same time, they want to give her helpful hints that might improve the situation. One day after school, they have a family talk before dinner. Her mother says, "Sashi, we know that you have been unhappy playing soccer, but we think a big part of the problem is that you are the new girl on the team. I remember when I was your age, and I was the new girl on the team. It took me time to get to know the other girls and have fun. The more I wanted them to like me, the less they seemed to talk to me. When I just relaxed and played my best, things started to get better. Your father and I know that it is hard being the new girl on a team. It takes time to get comfortable. The other girls may well become friendlier once they get to know you. Just do your best to enjoy yourself when you play. As best you can, listen to what the other girls talk about and watch how they play. In time, things may change. If they don't get better in a few weeks, we'll help you find a different activity."

Some parents might rightfully choose a different path for a daughter in this situation. Pulling her from the team may be justified because ongoing humiliation is unhealthy for a child. Removal from such a situation may preserve self-esteem. Perhaps Sashi would find more success in a different type of activity; yet it's also possible that the same problem could surface in the new setting, making her feel even worse about herself.

Because Sashi's parents took the time to learn about her experience, they can judge what will serve her best interest. They encourage her to continue playing soccer, yet they also provide a time limit — if things don't go well, Sashi can leave the team. In the following weeks, Sashi's parents rarely hear about teasing, and Sashi begins to talk about one girl on the team whom she likes. When her mom and dad ask Sashi if she wants to play soccer again next season, she replies that she is not sure. Sashi's parents express their pride in her for sticking it out through the season; she won't have to play next year unless she wants to.

By encouraging her to "hang in there" and try to improve the situation, Sashi's parents have sent their daughter an important message. Though concerned about the situation, they believe that Sashi has the ability to work through the problem. Furthermore, overcoming the obstacle of teasing is a success that helps the whole family feel positive about their move to a new town.

Understandably, parents in these situations are unsure how to proceed, and there is rarely a clear answer. If Sashi had become increasingly miserable, her parents would have felt that they made the wrong decision. In essence, they

> Young athletes who are exposed to high levels of competition are at risk of burnout.

would have kept her in the sport for two additional miserable weeks adding further pain to Sashi's already humiliating experience. Particularly with younger children, however, parents need to do more investigation to uncover the nature of the problem. Because dynamics in groups can change so quickly with younger children, they were willing to take a chance.

MARVIN: TOUGH COACHES AND BURNOUT

Marvin's parents are shocked to hear their 11-year-old son say, "Mom and Dad, I'm going to quit golf." Marvin has recently become a highly ranked golfer in his state; his parents have no idea that he is unhappy about playing. To the contrary, they've thought that he enjoys his success. Watching Marvin play golf, people note his beautiful swing and excellent touch when putting. Marvin's parents love to see their son play. They attend as many matches as possible, but because they both work, at times they miss a match or two.

Marvin's coach, on the other hand, is very intense about Marvin's training and performance because he feels that Marvin has the potential to be a great golfer. Often he brags to his coaching buddies, "Wait until you see this kid swing the club. We're talking Tiger Woods form here. He can hit the ball a mile." Marvin's coach spends hours working with him on his game, sometimes long after practice is over. They practice proper swing, short-game shots, putting, and chipping seemingly for hours. If Marvin doesn't pay attention or work hard enough, his coach yells at him: "Marvin, what are you doing? You can do better than this. You'll never make the top five if you play like this in tournaments."

At first, Marvin hadn't minded the yelling because he loved playing so much and was having such success. His coach thoroughly understands the game of golf, and Marvin trusted him because he had learned so much from him. The few times his coach's outbursts bothered him, the feeling of stress didn't last long.

Golf started to become a burden for Marvin after he lost a tournament in the quarterfinals to a player with inferior ability and experience. Marvin's coach yelled at him after the first nine holes: "Stop fooling around out there! Make your shots!" After Marvin went eight over par for his first eighteen, his coach came over and said, "You are embarrassing yourself out there. You're playing like an 8-year-old." This statement played again and again in Marvin's head until it became a huge distraction. He couldn't concentrate for the rest of the match and ultimately failed to make the cut in the second round. Each bogie he hit, Marvin became more enraged. At times, he screamed at himself, and once he threw his club. In disgust, his coach just watched him unravel.

Marvin's coach unknowingly planted doubt in Marvin's mind. He made Marvin worry about the future, and this distraction undermined Marvin's focus in the present. It's well known that negative thoughts contribute to tense muscles and poor performance. Good coaches help players reduce the power of negative thoughts, but this coach only depleted Marvin's mental toughness, a skill particularly necessary for golf. Subtle disturbances in a golfer's swing can make the difference between a good and a terrible shot. Disturbed by negative thoughts, Marvin couldn't swing his clubs in a relaxed and confident manner, and it showed.

The walk back to the clubhouse with his coach after the last round was miserable. They did not speak. All Marvin heard was the sound of his golf clubs bouncing rhythmically off his back as he walked. Each bounce was like the tick of a bomb about to explode. The tension became so great that Marvin wished he were somewhere else. Just as he put his clubs in the team van, his coach said, "Be ready to practice tomorrow at 7:30 A.M."

A series of intense practice sessions followed. Though Marvin made the final round of the next tournament, he began to dread the game he had previously loved. Every mistake he made triggered intense criticism. Marvin felt alienated from his friends because he was always practicing—every day after school. He played in tournaments every weekend as well. Marvin started to wish that he could stay home and avoid practice.

After several weeks of this tension, he informs his parents that he no longer wants to play golf. As Marvin's parents discover, young athletes who are exposed to high levels of competition are at risk for burnout (see the table below). Despite the fact that Marvin has the physical ability to compete at high levels and become a strong player, the tension with his coach has killed the fun. Though Marvin has gained confidence through his success, he is so busy playing and practicing that he has few opportunities to spend time with friends. A lack of time to relax magnifies the effect of his coach's criticisms; Marvin has become overly reliant on pleasing his coach. When his performance declines, the criticism increases. Marvin begins to feel bad about himself, and his confidence drops precipitously.

Signs of Burnout in Athletes

1. Increased fatigue or prolonged weariness
2. Increased irritability and/or apathy
3. Increased physical complaints or injuries with no apparent medical cause
4. Consistent feelings of intense ambivalence toward practice or competition including expressed desire to quit
5. Frequent missed practices or skipped games
6. Inexplicable pattern of poor athletic performance
7. Decreased confidence
8. Behaviors that undermine further athletic participation such as poor attitude and effort
9. Participation in fewer age-appropriate activities (such as time with friends) for the sake of sport commitment (especially true for teens)
10. Parents engage in a pattern of risky sacrifice to aid child's athletic career (serious life choices or family decisions based on the parents' view of child's athletic potential)

Source: J. Coakley, "Burnout Among Adolescent Athletes: A Personal Failure or Social Problem?" *Sociology of Sport Journal* 9 (1992): 271–85.

In his surprise to hear of these developments, Marvin's father says, "Why didn't you tell us that your coach was being so tough? We would have talked to him about it."

"It wouldn't have mattered," Marvin responds. "He's just a tough coach. Either you play by his rules, or you quit. I just can't take it anymore. I hate playing for him. In fact, I just hate golf. I get so nervous every time I play. I can't remember the last time I had fun."

Problems occur when a child performs to please others, particularly coaches and parents; the pressure erases the fun. For younger children particularly, when enjoyment disappears, the activity loses its value. Older athletes may be able to treat a conflict with a coach as a short-term problem, but younger kids lack this perspective. They feel wounded and lack the toughness to work through their difficulties with a demanding, even abusive coach. This is exactly what has happened to Marvin.

Marvin's parents decide to talk to the coach despite Marvin's hesitation about it. The conversation goes poorly. When they say that Marvin is quitting because he feels overly criticized, the coach gets angry and replies that Marvin doesn't have the right attitude and enough maturity to play for the team and that his parents don't know what they are talking about — they know nothing about golf or the level of training needed to excel.

Struck by the negativity of Marvin's coach, they walk away feeling bewildered. How could their son have played for such a coach? Why didn't they notice the problem earlier? But most of all, they feel relieved that Marvin recognized the problem. They support his decision to quit.

When our children play for intensely competitive coaches, their first instinct may be not to complain to their parents. Adolescent boys like Marvin are greatly invested in improving their skills, and furthermore, they want to prove to themselves and others that they are tough enough to handle the pressure. A coach can be an important figure in boys' lives. Some believe that constant pushing from their coach means that the coach cares about them and is invested in their improvement. Coaches who act like Marvin's coach are rarely motivated by malice. Rather, they are overzealous and lose perspective. The heat of competition overtakes them, and they forget that playing is about the kids, not the adults.

Pressure can erase the fun and cause the quality of performance to decline.

In retrospect, Marvin's parents see that they might have intervened sooner to prevent burnout, but they did not recognize the warning signs, which include lack of fun in playing the game, nervousness before and during matches, and too much time in practice, at the expense of social life. If they had spent more time talking with their son about his sports experience, they might have discovered the problem with the coach earlier.

As parents, we might also look for more subtle signs of burnout. Do our kids complain before going to practice? Are they not sleeping or eating as well? Do they make excuses for missing games or practices on account of injury, headaches, or stomachaches? Do they come home from practice with a smile or a discouraged and exhausted look? Is a decline in school performance taking place? Some of these symptoms are typical of depression; in fact, we might think of burnout as a form of depression experienced by athletes. It's as if no matter how much children do, they feel helpless to improve the situation. If parents catch these signs early, they might prevent burnout.

Another potential forerunner of burnout is lack of a balanced life. Marvin became exhausted in part because he wasn't spending enough time with friends or experiencing relaxed time just to do nothing. Burning out often reflects the presence of chronic pressures. If the level of competition is high and the nature of the coach is to be abusive, this combination can exceed a kid's physical and emotional strength. Quitting might become the only option. Children are not ready to be pushed like adults. Today the distorted view is growing that children can handle the same level of training and intensity that professional athletes manage. This is simply not the case. They need friends, balance, and relaxation time. Protecting these important elements in their lives can preserve their love of sports and ultimately lead to longer, more successful participation.

MARIA: MOVING ON TO A NEW SPORT

Maria admits that basketball isn't her favorite game. She started to play when she was 8 years old; her teacher suggested basketball because she was so tall. Maria played most of every game because of her size. It was fun to get rebounds and score the most points on the team, even though she was not the most talented. She was always picked first for the team during recess, and this made her feel good about herself. She also developed close friendships through basketball.

When children play for intensely competitive coaches, their first instinct may be not to complain to their parents.

But by the time Maria reached the sixth grade, several of her peers had experienced growth spurts, bringing them within inches of Maria's height. Though she still was the tallest girl, it got harder for her to get rebounds. Though flat-footed and not a very good jumper, Maria has long arms and learned how to position her body to get rebounds without having to jump that high. But over time, the more talented taller players began to score more points than she did. Though this disappointed her, she still enjoyed the girls on the team and the playing time she received.

As the ninth grade approaches, Maria, who has just turned 14, is no longer a starting player. In fact, the coach puts her in only for a few minutes at the end of each half. Maria understands that the team has become more competitive, but she doesn't like sitting on the bench. Most of her good friends had quit basketball the year before and joined the swimming team. Maria's parents encourage her to stay with basketball because she is so tall; they think that basketball might help her get into college, but this is becoming less of a possibility.

We might want to think of burnout as a form of depression experienced by athletes.

In one startling moment, Maria realizes that something has changed for her. Sitting on the bench in the middle of a preseason scrimmage, she finds that she feels no interest or investment in the team. Toward the end of the first half, the coach calls her to go into the game, and she feels no sense of excitement; she couldn't care less. Instead, she experiences this insight: basketball is no longer fun. Maria wants to be with her friends, and perhaps swimming will be more fun. The girls' team needs swimmers, and she has enjoyed swimming since she was a small child.

There is a growing distortion that children can handle the same level of training and intensity that professional athletes manage.

So Maria announces to her parents that she wants to try out for swimming instead of basketball. Maria's mother is particularly disappointed by this news. Formerly a high school basketball player, she did not have the opportunity to play at the college level because of a knee injury. Hearing that Maria is planning to quit makes her relive painful memories. She has long hoped that Maria could have the experience that she never had.

Maria's father swam for a bit as a child, but he lost interest as he entered high school; he is not particularly athletic. He grew up in Puerto Rico and enjoyed playing and listening to music, which became his passion. Sports were not emphasized in his family. His fondest memories involve dancing and singing at weekend festivals with his family and friends. As he grew older, he preferred to watch sports rather than play them. Still, he wants to make sure that Maria is making the right choice, and he doesn't want his wife's disappointment to negatively affect Maria.

Maria's parents then try to work through their feelings. As the three-step approach asks us to evaluate our own feelings and behaviors with regard to our children's activities in sports, Maria's mother struggles to get beyond her love of basketball and support her daughter's decision. In a private conversation, Maria's father says to his wife, "Honey, Maria isn't as talented a player as you were. She has some of my genes. I would love to see her play college basketball, but I don't think it's going to happen. If she really loved playing and was willing to spend the extra time to work on her skills, then I think she would stay with the team on her own accord."

Her mother, frustrated by this comment, can still acknowledge its validity. "I really do think she could have gotten more playing time in high school and become a decent player. She just needed to decide that she was going to devote herself to improving her game as I did. It's frustrating not to see that drive in her eyes. She cares more about being with her friends than winning a spot on this team. I don't know. Maybe she is right. Maybe she would have spent most of the season on the bench."

Conversations like this one rarely go this smoothly. Frequently, arguments and disagreements take place until parents reach an understanding. But here, Maria's father helps her mother separate her identity from that of her daughter, reminding her that Maria is her own person. Thus, both parents give Maria space to feel comfortable with her decision and take a step in defining her own identity.

As addressed earlier, adolescents are in the process of forming their identity. They are making choices about friendships, extracurricular and academic interests, dating, and drug and alcohol experimentation. While in the past they relied on the guidance of their parents to make decisions, more control is available to them to make their own choices. As teams become more competitive, playing time is no longer equal among teammates. At the varsity level particularly, the best players will play most of the game. Players like Maria, who have good size or can fill a particular role, may receive limited playing time. Sensing her athletic limitations and desire to spend more time with friends, Maria chooses swimming, a decision that has positive results.

She makes the swimming team and becomes a successful long-distance swimmer. Her size and long limbs give her an advantage in the pool. She loves the training and the time spent with friends. And though Maria's mother was initially disappointed about her daughter's decision to quit basketball, she eventually grows interested in Maria's swimming, becoming one of her most enthusiastic supporters.

SEAN: MOVING ON AT THE COLLEGE LEVEL

Preseason football is in its second week, and Sean is surprised by his lack of passion for the game. In high school, he was a star receiver and captain of his team, but in college he lacks enthusiasm. Football in his hometown was important to him and his family; his parents attended every game. They cheered from the sidelines while enjoying the company of their friends. The whole community seemed to meet for those home games. Many fathers had played for the same team twenty years before.

But in college, practices are longer and more intense. Weight lifting is scheduled three times per week, and players watch training films every other day. Division I football seems more like a job. Socially, Sean feels alienated. He doesn't know the other players. Athletes are not really respected as students at college. Sean feels labeled as a dumb jock; professors don't take him that seriously.

Sean has described these conditions to his parents, but they fail to understand his dissatisfaction. His father says, "Hey kiddo, just hang in there. I know it's hard, but this is preseason. You've worked really hard to get here. I'm sure things will improve once the season begins."

But playing college football does not improve in the weeks that follow. Sean makes the team, but he feels he can't connect with his teammates. When he spends some time thinking about it, he realizes that he is playing for his father, who is proud to have a son playing Division I football. Also, both his parents love to brag about Sean's ability to the community of parents who had supported his high school football team. His quitting football would amount to a loss for his parents socially. Yet Sean finds himself wondering what it would be like to have autumn free to devote to academics and social life. He worries that he'd miss football if he quit, but the thought of staying makes him miserable.

After another week of deliberating, Sean decides to quit. Though his parents are surprised and a bit disappointed, they communicate their support for his decision. At Sean's age, this decision is in fact entirely his to make; he doesn't have to consult his parents.

The work for Sean's parents begins after they hear of his decision. Sean's mother says to her husband, "Do you think he's depressed? Maybe he's not at the right school. He sounds somewhat distant when I talk to him on the phone."

Sean's father replies, "I don't think he's depressed. I think he's just trying to figure things out."

Not sure what to do, Sean's parents take a trip to visit their son at school; they want to talk to him face to face and assess how he is feeling. During their visit, they sense that Sean feels a little lost at college. He doesn't yet have a set of interesting friends, and he doesn't seem to be his natural, happy, confident self.

> Quitting a sport at the college level may signify something different from quitting high school or youth sports.

His mother asks him directly about this: "Sean, honey, how are you liking college so far? You seem to be a little down."

At first Sean seems annoyed, but then he answers, "Mom, I'm doing fine. The kids here are definitely different than at home. They seem smarter, and some of them are pretty snobby. I'm just trying to figure out who I like."

Sean's father asks, "What about football?"

"Dad, football just wasn't fun. All we did was practice, practice, practice. The players on the team are polite, but there isn't that closeness that I felt in high school. We used to have more fun."

"Of course it's not as much fun as high school. This is Division I athletics. The fun comes later, when you've worked your tail off and are in the best shape of your life. You play in a few games, and you notice how much better you've become. It's a real sense of accomplishment."

"Yeah, I'm sure that's true, but I don't want to go through the work to get there. I just can't keep up with it."

Sean's parents remain a bit concerned about Sean, but think that he is going through a necessary transition. Quitting a sport at the college level may signify something different from quitting high school or youth sports. Sean has been selected for a college sports team, a feat accomplished by few athletes. A successful athlete throughout his career, he has the talent to play at the college level, but something is missing for him. Perhaps he wants to experiment with new activities and interests.

Sean's parents have done the right thing by showing support rather than challenging their son's decision to quit football. Even as young adults make their own decisions, they still need to know that their parents are available if needed, but they don't want parents to interfere aggressively. By allowing Sean to make this choice, his parents give him the opportunity to examine what is truly important to him.

That spring, Sean decides to run track; he throws the javelin and runs on a relay team. He finds track less intense and more enjoyable than college football. He also makes a few nice friends through track and feels satisfied with this sports experience. At the same time, he continues to consider rejoining the football team. Sean is becoming a strong, independent, thoughtful young man. He is not a quitter; rather he is taking time to get to know himself and consider each step on his path so that his ultimate choices in life can be satisfying and rewarding.

As parents, we need to be aware that a variety of factors may influence our children's desire to quit a sport, take a break, or find a new sport. We can see how staying involved in a sport for too long has its risks. As expectations increase for our children to win and perform at unrealistically high levels, they are at a greater risk to burn out from playing sports. We need to recognize when adult expectations are exceeding the abilities of our children. Interrupting this intense form of pressure can preserve the joy of playing and prevent burnout.

Children and teens will experiment with a variety of sports; therefore, it's inevitable that they will make the choice to quit a sport. As they get older, particularly, they will make decisions about which sports they like best and which sports they want to drop. A three-sport high school athlete may decide to play one or two sports in college. In these scenarios and others, quitting a sport is a viable and necessary option.

At the same time, there are circumstances when quitting is not the best option for our children and we have to intervene. Sometimes, our kids need a little encouragement from us to stick it out and try it for a few more weeks before making any rash decisions. Other times, kids want to quit so they can have more free time to do whatever they want in the afternoons. Often this scenario is recognizable when our children say they want to quit but don't have an alternative plan. We encourage those parents to be firm in these circumstances. Choosing to have no activity is not an option. While we prefer to recommend some type of physical activity because of the physical and emotional benefits, other activities such as the arts, community service programs, or a part-time job can be excellent options.

The guiding force for us in helping our children have positive experiences in sports is to pay attention to the sense of balance they have in their lives. When sports overtake important life priorities such as friendship, relaxation, and family time, trouble can emerge for the young athlete. Therefore, we need to listen, attend games whenever possible, and ask questions about children's sports experiences. Sometimes problems will not surface without a bit of probing and investigation.

The key in almost all of these stories was that each athlete, with the exception of Marvin who burned out from playing golf and sports in general, continued to stay involved in sports. They found the activity they enjoyed. Some excelled to high levels in their newly found sports, while others continued to enjoy participating in the sport they selected but at a less intense level. Sports burnout is the outcome that parents want to avoid for their children as it decreases their likelihood of having positive experiences in sports as they grow older. It is absolutely crucial that we preserve the love of sports for all children, regardless of their age or level of experience.

11

DOES THE COACH KNOW BEST?

Knowing When Coaches Are Doing
Right or Wrong by Our Children

IT GOES WITHOUT SAYING that coaches have a significant impact on the sports experiences of our children. Some coaches spend more than two hours per day and up to six days per week working with our kids. In the best circumstances, coaches help them improve their skills, perform to their best ability, and develop strong character. In other situations, coaches can be overly demanding, even abusive. We've all heard horror stories of coaches being physically or psychologically cruel to players. Abusive coaches can turn kids off from sports, force kids into dangerous situations that cause injury, or psychologically damage kids through manipulation.

As parents, we want our children to have the best experiences in sports, yet we also worry that their coaches might treat them unfairly. As the sporting demands on our children increase, it can be difficult for us parents to judge when coaches are behaving in our kids' best interests.

TEDDY AND HIS DEMANDING COACH

It's 5:30 P.M. on a Tuesday afternoon, and Teddy Campbell, a 10-year-old soccer player, is heading to practice for the third day in a row. Teddy's coach, Coach D, has told all parents that in order for their children to be competitive in the town league, they must practice at least four days per week. The Campbells know that Teddy absolutely loves to play soccer. He's a very good player, and all his best friends are on the team. Though sometimes Teddy wishes that he could take a day off just to relax and hang out in the neighborhood, he worries that if he misses practice, he won't get a chance to play. He hears that Coach D has a good relationship with the coach of the local elite team, and missing practices will hurt his chances of playing for that high-level team in the future. Teddy's parents fear that if he doesn't make the elite soccer team, high school coaches won't even allow Teddy to try out when he is a freshman.

But Teddy's mother believes that time off is exactly what Teddy needs. He is having a hard time getting out of bed in the morning and is complaining about having so many practices. Mrs. Campbell worries that Teddy is going to get hurt or start doing poorly in school because of his commitment to soccer. By contrast, Mr. Campbell is less concerned about Teddy's practice schedule. He thinks the structure and physical activity are healthy. Often leaving work early, Mr. Campbell attends many of Teddy's practices. He particularly enjoys it when Teddy plays in tournaments because he often is asked to be an assistant coach. Typically, after games, the whole team goes out for dinner, and Teddy's father shoots the breeze with the other coaches and dads.

Conflict about Teddy's soccer schedule comes to a head when Coach D tells Teddy that he cannot promise him playing time in the future if he misses the upcoming tournament, though Mrs. Campbell wants Teddy to rest this week-

> One season blends into the next, and before we know it, family life revolves entirely around sports.

end because she can tell that he is tired. Mr. Campbell wants Teddy to play in the tournament, but he doesn't like the message that Coach D is giving his son; he thinks it's ludicrous that a 10-year-old should be penalized for missing a few games. Teddy admits that he is tired but says that he still wants to play. The Campbells argue about what they should do and what they think of Coach D's style. Should they follow the coach's recommendations? Where do they draw the line?

The dilemma faced by the Campbell family is becoming increasingly common for parents across the country. Coaches tell kids that they need to practice more frequently these days. Tournaments take place every weekend, often consuming family time on Saturdays and Sundays. One season blends into the next, and before we know it, family life revolves entirely around sports. Family time, downtime, and socializing with friends all suffer. At the same time, we as parents want what is best for our kids, though spouses and partners don't always agree on what is best. We don't want them to miss out on any opportunities. It feels as if we have to choose between our children being overscheduled and feeling bored and alienated from their buddies.

The Campbells might like to challenge the coach: "Our son can't play in the tournament this weekend. He's only 10 years old. We like to have some family time during the weekends. Daily soccer practices are disruptive enough as it is." But these parents fear that their son will suffer for this decision. Coach D may bench Teddy, play him less, or simply cut him from the team at some point. Down the road, when the elite coach asks Coach D about Teddy, he'll say that Teddy isn't a committed player. Teddy's parents would feel horrible about robbing their son of this opportunity, yet there are risks associated with overscheduling children, as well. Fatigue, burnout, and quitting sports altogether are just a few. Even if Teddy is able to get through the rigors of the season and eventually makes the elite team, there are potential costs. He may lose opportunities to explore other sports, school activities, and quality time with a diverse group of friends. Playing soccer may become a chore. How can parents in the Campbells' situation evaluate the advice their son is getting from Coach D and make the best choices?

Unfortunately, there is no straight and easy answer. In these cases, we as parents must continue to ask ourselves several key questions. Are our children having fun? Are they building healthy relationships with peers? Are they sleeping and eating well? Are they maintaining decent academic standing? Are they having a variety of experiences in their lives? These questions will help guide us to consider the fundamental tenets of healthy growth for children. We want them to be healthy, engaged in quality friendships, and competent in a variety of activities. Without these building blocks, our kids are at a disadvantage no matter how talented they are or how hard they train.

Parents cannot rely solely on the perspective of coaches to answer this question. Even when coaches love their kids and want what's best for them, they will not always see the bigger picture; the quest to win often distracts them. Though many fine coaches diligently learn as much as they can about their athletes, it is up to parents to observe their kids and conclude what is best for them. This may entail saying no to a coach — or to a child.

When we speak to parents about these dilemmas, we often discuss how hard it is to say no to a weekend tournament or more frequent practices.

Such efforts need to be fueled by our values, our family mission statement. Being able to make some of the following statements that respect family values such as rest, balance, and time with friends can be difficult.

"No, Coach D. Teddy needs to take this weekend off."
"We can't continue to bring Teddy to practice every day."
"Teddy, you can continue to play soccer, but we have to find a
    different team."

The current of our culture runs completely against these statements. We are told that more frequent and longer practices and high-level competition are the only formula for success. Yet we may not see eye to eye with this philosophy. On a gut level, it may feel wrong to us. We see that our children are able to tolerate the increased and intensified schedule, but we can sense how they are exhausted. In some cases our kids may say they are having fun, even when they are struggling because they want to keep up with their friends, with what everyone else is saying and doing. Or, in Teddy's case, he wants to please his father because he knows how much he enjoys coming to games.

> For some coaches, emphasis on winning is often a distracting factor.

In our work with many families, we have found that the most balanced and centered children have the best chances to become great performers. We know that the message out there is that hard work and early specialization is the key to success for our children. As pointed out earlier, the research does not support this notion. Furthermore, on an intuitive level, we simply don't agree with this philosophy. Devoting hours of exclusive training to one sport at young ages robs many young athletes of the benefits of playing many sports for different coaches. In these diverse experiences, fun, balance, friendship, and competence building are the true keys to a much broader vision of success.

So what if our children fail to make the elite team? It is possible that this will put them at a great disadvantage down the road, as in Teddy's case. But we're not convinced that this is true. We've seen too many cases where the kids we thought were going to be the great players turn out to be very average and the unnoticed players become the dominant ones. Coaches are going to take the kids who can play. Size, talent, and ability cannot be controlled by us or our children's coaches. Training them seven days per week isn't going to change this. Maybe it's going to take some time for our culture and our children's coaches to recognize this. And in some circles, this is already happening.

We believe playing one sport per season at a pace that is reasonable for the family is more than adequate for our children. If our children want to play unorganized sports in the neighborhood with their friends, that's fine. They can play basketball, Wiffle ball, touch football ... you name it. But that is very different from playing for organized teams that involve frequent practice and travel. If kids like Teddy love to play every day and are showing a balance in other realms of life, that's great. But it's our job as parents to keep in mind that we cannot be guided by a "win at any cost" culture, as it rarely leads to winning.

However, there are certain realities that we must consider. We have learned from our conversations with parents that seasons overlap. Soccer tournaments continue into basketball or hockey season at all levels from youth to collegiate. Athletes who want to play for multiple teams in one season will have to negotiate with the coaches involved. This can be particularly difficult because no coach wants to share their players with another team or coach. It is also logistically challenging to keep up with the time commitments of each team and coach. Yet many balanced athletes and their families are trying to find ways to make this work without creating more conflict along the way. As long as we are aware of the importance of maintaining a balance in our children's lives, these transitions and overlaps between seasons, although somewhat stressful, can be manageable if we watch them carefully.

DIANA: COMPLAINTS ABOUT PLAYING TIME

Diana Lee, a 13-year-old girl with dark brown eyes and thick black hair, comes home angry after sitting on the bench during her field hockey game. Although she knows that playing time for all players is not a guarantee, she tells her father that her coach, Coach A, is being unfair. This woman always starts the same players and never gives Diana a chance.

Mr. Lee is not sure whether to discuss this issue with Coach A. He thinks his daughter is an immensely talented athlete with a good attitude, and he can't understand why she's not playing. He knows Coach A has a good reputation in the town, and he doesn't want to make things worse for his daughter. Is he himself overestimating his daughter's talent? All his friends say that Diana should be playing more. Mr. Lee raises his concerns with his wife, and they try to decide on a plan of action.

Complaints to coaches about playing time are common. Parents blame coaches for incompetence, favoritism, or vindictiveness.

"My child is not playing enough!"

"The coach doesn't know what he's doing. His best players are sitting on the bench."

"The coach is playing favorites."

As parents, we know that coaches are imperfect. They can indeed make errors in judgment, but so can parents. Though it is normal and healthy for parents to think highly of their kids' abilities, they may resist acknowledging that other children are more talented or work harder. Maintaining objectivity in situations like Diana's is challenging. We naturally think our child should play and that the coach has the wrong idea in keeping the child on the bench.

Yet coaches must recognize that the evaluation of kids' talent is a dynamic process; they sometimes forget this point. Girls at the age of 13 may improve their skills from one week to the next. If they don't get a chance to shine, the coach may never notice their improvement. This is why we authors value the choice to allot equal playing time to all young adolescents on a team. Coach A may be missing something about the way Diana can play. Perhaps the coach has rigid ideas about who the best players are, and a change in approach is simply not part of her plan.

Because of situations like this, placing younger children on very competitive teams has its risks. Kids who sit on the bench become discouraged and miss out on developing their skills. Children want to participate and be involved. If Diana is regularly prevented from playing field hockey, then she may be in the wrong program. Perhaps she is not as skilled as the other players at this point, and she would be better suited to a less competitive team that promises equal playing time.

Yet there are other factors to consider. Maybe the coach is not playing Diana because of her attitude. Has she listened to Coach A, followed her suggestions, and related well with her teammates? Is Diana giving her best effort? Has she tried to speak with Coach A directly to address the issue of playing time? Does she have an accurate sense of what would be a reasonable amount of playing time?

It's a risky move for parents to confront a coach about their child's playing time. It can annoy coaches because it appears that parents are second-guessing their expertise. And from a logistical standpoint, they simply don't have the time and energy to entertain every complaint and piece of advice from every player's parents. In our consultations with coaches, we hear countless stories about parents giving them advice about game strategies such as in a basketball game for 10-year-olds. Parents with little athletic experience often tell coaches with years of playing and coaching experience how to do their job. Sounds pretty off-base, doesn't it? It is quite possible that parents' input can make matters worse for their children.

Still, consulting with coaches can be a good idea, if done with respect. Such conversations can help parents better understand their kids. Asking a coach about why our child struggles athletically or socially or seeking guidance on how to help our kids focus attention or calm down can be of great assistance. Yet it may be wise to pursue other options first. For example, Mr. Lee might ask Diana about practices and games: "Diana, what does Coach A think is the most important thing about playing field hockey? Do you listen to her in practice? Are you giving your best effort? Do you ever notice that she is disappointed in what you're doing?"

If Diana cannot answer these questions clearly, Mr. Lee might encourage her to ask Coach A directly about her play: "Coach, is there anything I can do to improve? I would love to get more playing time. Is there something I can work on to get better?"

This course of action isn't appropriate for very young athletes because they lack the capacity to evaluate their own ability and to speak objectively with an adult about how to improve. However, a 13-year-old girl like Diana is beginning to get an accurate picture of her abilities. Talking to Coach A about her playing style and attitude could be an important step in becoming more responsible for her own behavior. As former and active coaches ourselves,

> Playing one sport per season at a pace that is reasonable for the family is more than adequate for our children.

we are always impressed when our players approach us in this manner. We feel a certain respect for their direct approach, and we are typically willing to spend extra time to help them and give them an opportunity to play more often.

Of course, there are times when we parents should intervene, especially if a child's safety is at risk. If we are worried that the coach is abusive, we need to get involved immediately, which may include consulting with other parents and athletic administrators before taking action. In less severe cases, if parents feel that they must speak with a coach, it is best to have a conversation away from the field well after the game or match is over. Unnecessary conflicts and arguments may arise when parents complain to coaches in the midst of the game, at halftime, or immediately following a disappointing loss. As parents, we have to wait for the right moment.

If Diana has tried unsuccessfully to speak with Coach A about her playing time and Mr. Lee feels that he must get involved, he might try to speak with Coach A a day or so after a recent practice or game: "Coach A, you've got a great team. Diana really loves field hockey, but I noticed that she is getting discouraged because she's not seeing much time. Is there anything that she can do, or is this just a matter of not being as talented as the other players?"

> Consulting with coaches can be a good idea, if done with respect.

Though this approach puts Coach A on the spot a bit, it is respectful. If Mr. Lee doesn't agree with Coach A's response, it's probably not worth getting into an argument. Instead, Mr. Lee can use this information to help his daughter recognize that she'll have to make the best of the season until she encounters a different opportunity in the future. He can emphasize that it is important to learn to deal with a difficult teacher, boss, or coach; perhaps this season will benefit Diana as she discovers how to handle conflict. Though quitting the team in the middle of the season is an option, it is rarely the right choice if the child is not completely miserable.

> The most effective coaches make each player feel valued for his or her unique contribution to practice and games.

Our children can benefit from these difficult situations if handled appropriately, thus marking how sports teach us valuable lessons about how to live our lives.

For parents in Mr. Lee's position, there are important factors to con-

sider about coaching in general. While Coach A's error might be in not giving Diana enough playing time, a more problematic issue is that Diana is
not feeling appreciated and valued
on the team, leading her to feel bad
about herself and her ability. Good
coaches find ways to create useful
roles for all of their players. Even if
our children receive limited playing time on a competitive team,
they can make some contribution

**Most children don't even
understand the concept
of competition until they
are 6–7 years old.**

to practice and games; good coaches find ways to reward players for attitude
and effort. Even if Coach A plays Diana for only fifteen minutes per half,
during this time she can use her speed to exhaust her opponents; the coach
could encourage her teammates to make long passes down the left wing,
where she can run onto the ball and raise havoc with the opposing team's
defense. Though Diana still might be frustrated about her limited minutes,
she can feel pride as an important part of the team because Coach A gives
her an opportunity to shine, improve, and make an impact. Our children
need to be nurtured and involved. As long as coaches provide this, playing
time is much less of an issue. And if our kids aren't having a positive experience, the great coaches will recognize this early and help us direct our kids
to more appropriate teams or levels.

CAN COACHES BE TOO TOUGH?

Most parents can recall that coach, teacher, or mentor who challenged them
to perform at a higher level. The experience of being pushed can be painful
and exhausting; however, we end up grateful that someone recognizes our
talent and inspires us to maximize it. This can be particularly true in sports.
A good coach can help our children reach higher levels of confidence and
physical ability.

Unfortunately, disturbing stories regularly surface about athletes being pushed too hard by their coaches. Over the past three years, several
professional football players died on account of dehydration during summer workouts. The players were not given enough opportunity to drink
water during practice. Other coaches such as Bobby Knight, the former basketball coach from Indiana University, have gotten so intensely caught up in

games that they have lost control, screamed at players, and thrown chairs onto the court. Coaches can also use psychological manipulation to get the most out of players. Some induce fear; others make the level of competition extremely high. These tactics are understandably worrisome to us as parents because such pressuring can be physically and psychologically dangerous to kids. Our children can get injured or become discouraged or demoralized.

How can parents distinguish between a coach who is appropriately tough and one who pushes too much? Here's an example that shows how hard it is to make this determination. In the movie *Miracle*, the story of the U.S. Olympic Hockey Team's dramatic victory over the Russians in the 1980 Winter Olympics, the coach has the whole team do countless sprints on the ice after they give a poor effort in a scrimmage before the Olympics formally start. The scene is painful to watch: the coach shouts to them after each sprint, "Again!" Some players are close to fainting. Others vomit. Many parents would be horrified to see their children go through anything like this. Was this coaching justified by the fact that the team won the gold medal? The coach was trying to instill a work ethic and a unified commitment to represent the United States with excellence. This hardship helped bring the team together. It is doubtful that many coaches are allowed to conduct workouts like this one anymore, but somehow a coach's job, particularly at the higher, more competitive levels, is to challenge players to perform better and play as a team.

> Coaches who are able to find a way to challenge our children while they also build their confidence and encourage them are typically the best fit.

The fine line between pushing appropriately and pushing too much depends on the age of the children, the nature of the competition, and the personality of the players. It is clear that pushing small children to work harder is pointless and possibly harmful. Children begin to get a sense of competition when they compare their actions and behaviors with those of their peers. In the realm of sports, it is thought that most children don't even understand the concept of competition until they are 6–7 years old, in the early elementary school years. To make them run sprints or challenge them because they are not working hard enough is crazy; they simply will not understand such practices. As already noted, small children play for fun and joy. Sure, they are interested in keeping score, but that is not a big deal. They lack the capacity to take sports seriously and would misinterpret coaching toughness as a sign that they had done something terribly wrong to warrant such treatment.[1]

At what age can good coaches consider pushing their players? A recent article in the *New York Times Magazine* chronicled the story of a well-known high school coach from the South, named Fitz.[2] Having coached varsity baseball for decades, Coach Fitz was a legend; numerous players attested to the powerful way he changed their lives. He was known to be bright, tough, and caring. He'd raise his voice at players who had bad attitudes; he'd challenge them with questions about their character and integrity, often unnerving them and in many cases moving them to think deeply about themselves. But in recent years, his toughness brought criticism from several of his players' parents, who believed he was not giving their children enough playing time or proper respect. A crisis occurred as former players entered the fray to defend Coach Fitz, claiming that his greatness lay in his ability to bring out the best in players; his tactics, while tough, were not unfair or cruel. But the new generation of parents believed his coaching style was antiquated and abusive. Fitz was told to tone down his tough approach. While he tried to do this, the complaints continued, and the problem remains unresolved.

As parents become increasingly involved in the intricacies of their children's daily sports routines, coaches have less room to maneuver. On the one hand, this has the positive effect of protecting children from abusive situations. On the other hand, coaches are becoming self-conscious and overly cautious in response to close parental scrutiny, preventing them at times from motivating and connecting with their players effectively.

This problem is further complicated by the fact that some children respond well to a coach who pushes them, while others do not. Coaches who lack sensitivity to these differences among kids will inevitably run into problems. Good coaches recognize when it's appropriate to push and when it's best to lay off. They know that some children need a simple pat on the shoulder, while others may need more inspiration and encouragement. Research shows that younger players respond much better to positive encouragement than to critical challenges. Good coaches of younger children know this implicitly and conduct themselves accordingly. Older players can handle more of a challenge, but even high-level athletes will not respond well to excessive pushing without positive encouragement.

It is difficult for parents to know whether a coach is striking the right balance. Unless we as parents watch every practice and every game — which we believe is distracting to both coach and children — we must rely on what we hear and observe with our kids. If hearsay labels the coach as really tough but our child is coming home excited about playing and happy about improvement, then perhaps the coach is finding that balance between being nurturing and tough. On the other hand, if our child comes home with physical complaints and concerns about being heavily criticized or discouraged, we may need to learn more. Still, it's important that we do our homework before addressing the coach. It's useless to complain without understanding what is going on.

Sometimes kids harshly criticize the coach because they are unable to recognize their own limitations. Such players may complain to their parents, who may become equally critical. This occurs particularly among high school, collegiate, and professional athletes, when higher levels of competition make it more difficult for players to attain the success they had previously become accustomed to. Rather than recognize the athletic limitations of their kids, these parents blame the coach. This is an unfortunate but common scenario.

Some coaches are outstanding, while others are average. Many coaches, particularly at the youth level, volunteer their time and are not trained in coaching. Some are just unable to motivate children. There is not much we as parents can say to a coach who is limited in this way, but the situation does offer certain teaching opportunities. We can remind our children that it is up to them to make the most of the season, and we can help them set their own goals for enjoying themselves and improving their skills. Ultimately, it is a player's responsibility to find joy in the game and play to his or her best ability. Placing too much responsibility on the coach sets an unhealthy precedent for kids' future achievement-related endeavors.

Therefore, it's important that we take the time to learn about sports programs and teams before we enroll our children. In essence, this is the third step of the three-step approach, Know Your Child's Sports Environment. The coach is the central figure in our children's sports environment. Spending some time to talk to other parents about the coaches and their team philosophies and practices can often help us choose the best environments for our kids and prevent many of these conflicts from occurring.

If we believe that the coach is making an error with our children in one form or another, we need to rule out a couple of important possibilities. Does the coach have a point? Are we getting the full picture from our child? Have we encouraged our child to address his or her concerns with the coach directly? Have we consulted with other parents or athletic administrators before confronting a coach directly? Are we being respectful of the coaches, even when we don't agree with them? If we do decide to confront a coach, we should find an appropriate time, be respectful, and be open to the possibility that the coach may see certain qualities in our children more objectively than we do.

> Coaches are becoming self-conscious and overly cautious in response to close parental scrutiny.

As we know from personal experience, a coach, teacher, or mentor can make a huge difference in the lives of young people. As parents, we must keep our eye out for wonderful coaches yet at the same time be mindful of how well they balance the desire to win with concern for developing the whole child. As Bob Bigelow, the author of *Just Let the Kids Play,* says, the best way to measure a good season and a good coach, particularly at the youth level, is whether children want to play again the next season.[3]

12

WHEN IS A GOOD TEAM BAD AND A BAD TEAM GOOD?

Recognizing Best Team Experiences for Kids

"THE BLAZERS ARE UP 2–0," one parent said to another in disbelief.

"You're kidding, right?" the other said, half laughing.

"No, I mean it. They scored the first two goals, and it's still the first half."

Not only did the Blazers score the first two goals; they scored their first two goals in two years of playing. Bad News Blazers, the Bottom of the Barrel Blazers — they were called all kinds of names, but on this day the Blazers were up 2–0.

> We cannot overestimate the importance of lasting friendships — a huge service to kids' psychological development.

In their first year of youth soccer, the Blazers played an entire season without winning a game or scoring a goal. Frequently, they lost badly. In some games they didn't even get past half field, but they played their hearts out. They prided themselves in the fact that they were playing against older boys. Many of the Blazers were 9 years old, whereas their competitors were often 11. The Blazers even had a girl on the team. She lacked skills, but she was blazingly fast and tried hard.

When the Blazers started to score goals and win a few games in their second season, their morale increased. Though they lost most matches, the players rarely became discouraged. Every member of the team loved to play.

214

One boy boasted that the team was going to be the best in the league in a few years. Though this prediction seemed far-fetched, many players felt that they were improving fast. They counted the fun they had and their small improvements in skill as success. For example, a few players learned how to kick with the opposite foot; another player learned how to head a ball off a corner kick. Such moments were thrilling, a sign that the Blazers were becoming real soccer players. They ended their second season with a record of 2–10, a triumph because it marked an improvement.

Off the field, several players became great friends. On the weekends they would go to one another's houses and play touch football, basketball, and Ping-Pong. The two forwards on the team, Dillon and Mark, played Ping-Pong matches lasting hours at a time. One afternoon, they played forty games and tied, each winning twenty. Being a member of the Blazers enhanced the love of sports and competition. This team established lasting friendships and the foundation for a deep love of the game.

Would anyone consider the Blazers a good team? By most standards, a 2–10 season is a disaster. What makes a team good? What should we as parents look for in teams for our kids?

What made the Blazers' 2–10 season so good was the joy the players experienced and the friendships they developed. We cannot overestimate the importance of lasting friendships — a huge service to kids' psychological development in a consumer, technology-driven culture. By making positive friendships at an early age, they develop a foundation for healthy connections with others. Our children who are growing up in this generation are bombarded with modern technology and infinite distractions that they face in their daily lives. Establishing profound and stabilizing relationships is a tremendous gift to them as they grow older and an ally against potential alienation.

Good teams are formed when the coach has realistic expectations of the players' abilities, both physically and mentally.

Other factors made the Blazers a good team. Head coach Franklin had a passion for soccer and was knowledgeable about the game. But most important, he understood how to keep coaching simple and let the players play. His drills were competitive and skill focused, but they were also enjoyable. He didn't overwhelm the players with sophisticated strategies; kids would learn about advanced plays, strategies, and game plans when they got older. This coach provided a few guiding principles about soccer, and once the game started, he was mostly a cheerleader.

As discussed in Chapter 2, children under the age of 12 have great difficulty keeping complicated sequences in their minds. Their memories and attention spans are limited. When coaches try to teach too much, they overwhelm their players with details and assignments that they can't understand. What these coaches forget is that skill development and fun are the most important aspects of playing. Good teams are formed when the coach has realistic expectations of the players' abilities, both physical and mental. When these expectations exceed the players' abilities, players perform worse and have less fun. This is true for athletes competing at the youth, high school, college, and professional levels.

Also, Coach Franklin had realistic expectations about winning and losing. Although the team began to win more games, they continued to experience tough losses. On one occasion, after a particularly frustrating loss, he told the team about an experience he had as a player when losing badly in a championship game. When the ball bounced in his direction in his penalty box, he kicked it as hard as he could. He said the ball sailed all the way down the field toward the other team's goal; their goalie was playing too far out, and the ball bounced over his head and into the goal. It was the only goal his team scored in their disappointing loss.

> When coaches try to teach too much, they overwhelm their players with details and assignments that they can't understand.

Coach Franklin's story stayed with the team for the rest of the season. How to strive in the face of adversity and find joy and success in dark moments is what Coach Franklin taught them. In the way he told this story the young players could sense his passion and frustration. He had that same desire to win that they did. Yet his smile implied that no matter how intense or frustrated he felt, it was still just a fun game, a message that helped the team keep their win-loss record in perspective.

As we already noted, good coaches find ways to give each player an important role. Coach Franklin identified players to serve as goal scorers, good passers, good headers, hustlers, tough defenders, speedsters, smart players, and leaders. Everyone mattered. The smallest and least skilled player was often instructed to defend a good player from the opposing team. Though this player often struggled in this role, it gave him a sense of purpose, and his small successes made him feel great. Like this little boy, the rest of the team felt important and valued.

Had Coach Franklin become frustrated with the team's losing, his negative attitude would have undermined their ability to perform. Comments like "Damn, you guys need to try harder to win" or "What do I have to do to help you guys win? I can't go out there and play for you" would have taken the wind out of the sails of the entire team. Instead, Coach Franklin created an environment for his players to engage in the game without worrying about the past or the future, and in time, the team started to win more games, even though they had already become winners where it counts.

Up in the stands, twenty yards away from the field, parents of the Blazers huddled together at almost every game. They laughed, cheered, and generally enjoyed themselves. One father complained about the refs, but that occurred rarely. The parents recognized that something special was happening for their children. The team spirit and passion were evident, even from the sidelines. A group of kids came together one or two times a week and played with passion, regardless of score. They were determined, and they never gave up.

The parents noted that their children were invested in and improving their skills. They felt positive about the relationships on the team, and as a result, they continued to cheer the team on, even when circumstances seemed dire. Their support and enthusiasm fueled the team. The players handled the frequent losses because they knew they were loved and supported.

Like Coach Franklin, the Blazer parents were not distracted by the fact their children were losing regularly because they recognized that their children were winning in other ways. When we as parents are proud of qualities such as effort and dedication, it can do wonders for kids' athletic and personal development. The Blazers only had to play hard and have fun to gain approval. This was an achievable task. Had the parents begun to complain about the losses, which unfortunately is typical in our present youth sports culture, players would have begun to have problems as well. Some would have quit, while others would have developed bad attitudes. Skill development and joy of the game would have been threatened.

Another way to evaluate the success of a team is to track the athletic careers and experiences of team members over time. It is worth exploring what happens to kids who play for certain teams. Do they continue to play sports or do they quit? Years after the Blazers graduated from the league and went their separate ways, a group of the boys formed the core of a successful high school team. The team went 13–3 that year; they were ranked in the top ten and missed the state championship by one game. Several players from the original Blazers went on to play college soccer, while others played different college sports. The drive required to reach higher levels of excellence was founded and nurtured in their experience as Blazers. Their love of the game inspired them to work harder and reach higher.

The story of the Blazers shows that good teams are fostered by strong coaches and supportive parents. Values such as trust, hard work, commitment, and integrity help teams perform to their potential. When coaches and parents set this foundation for the team, players value individual improvement as well as team unity. Good teams also consist of talented players, but the qualities that make a good team are the same. For example, a girls' high school gymnastic team had a very successful record. They were one of the top teams in their state tournament, and they attributed their success to the strong relationships and commitment to team success that had been fostered over the years. The athletes treated one another with respect, regardless of talent. Although the less talented players shared limited time in the limelight, they took pride in pushing the more talented players. Hard work and consistent practice formed a standard the whole team embraced. While practice was often hard work, they enjoyed each other.

When a Good Team Is Bad

Several years ago, a Division III women's hockey team in the Northeast was expected to have an outstanding season. Hopes were high since the team was returning seven seniors and one junior All-American. The previous season, the team just missed the tournament by one game. The whole school expected that they would make the tournament this season and even go far into it. They recruited a new coach, Ms. Dunn, a former Division I hockey player. Though she was in her early thirties, she could still strap on the skates and run circles around the players. Immediately, she gained the respect of the team, and she set out to get them into the best shape of their lives.

Practice sessions were longer and more intense than in previous years. The team watched videos from the previous season and lifted weights three days per week, and the coach established strict rules about off-the-field conduct. Players were warned that if they were caught with alcohol or even seen at a bar, they could possibly get kicked off the team. Initially, players were a little resistant to these changes; however, the seniors were so intent on making the tournament that they were willing to make the sacrifice.

> Good teams are fostered by strong coaches and supportive parents.

Creating high standards is often essential for creating a successful and healthy team. As adolescents make the transition into adulthood, they thirst to be respected and challenged. Coach Dunn communicated that she believed that they could be successful, and she was willing to show them how to maximize their ability through hard work. But, when the team finally got on the ice, Coach Dunn made practices very intense. With a strong belief in toughness and a winning attitude, she set up competitive drills, with the implicit message that no player was guaranteed a starting position. Even the All-American player was told that she would have to prove herself in practice in order to play. As a result, practices grew vicious. Occasionally, arguments broke out as tempers flared. Coach Dunn did not bat an eyelash.

Coach Dunn's competitive coaching style triggered skill improvement and a competitive edge in all players. However, something was lost. The notion of teamwork and selfless play began to fade; individual performance became the focus. Practices became an obligation rather than an opportunity to enjoy the game. Many teams can still excel in these circumstances because of exceptional talent, but eventually, the selfishness can catch up with the initial improvement and success.

By the time the season started, the team was in fantastic physical condition. The women were stronger, faster, and more confident than ever. In their first match, they completely outplayed their opponent and won, 6–0. Coach Dunn announced the starting team the day before the game. She did not want the players knowing that far in advance whether they had earned a spot, so that practices would remain competitive. As the season progressed, players were taken out of the game when they made mistakes. Sometimes they would sit on the bench for a while, and then Coach Dunn would send them back in. At other times, they would lose their spot and not see the ice for weeks. Some players complained that this was unfair, as their errors were minor. As a result, many players became anxious about making mistakes, and their performances suffered.

By midseason, the team was 8–2, a significant improvement from their start the previous year. Home game attendance had increased substantially. In the past, students would show up minutes before the game and find a great seat. Before the tenth game of this season, however, a long ticket line had formed. The team was the talk of the campus.

Halfway through the second semester, the team lost a few close games to lesser opponents. Then parents watching from the sidelines began to bash the coach: "Does she know what she's doing out there? How hard is it? They should be winning games against crappy teams like these." The grumblings of parents trickled down to the players, so eventually, in the locker rooms, players began to complain as well. A few parents considered approaching the athletic director, but because the team's record was decent, they decided to wait and see.

Intense competition, divisive cliques, and poor communication can sink a very talented team.

At this time, students were taking midterm exams, requiring players to burn the candle at both ends: their study load increased, but their practice did not diminish. As a result, some players got sick. Others had to miss practice on occasion, and Coach Dunn was not happy about that. Having heard through a few players that dissension was growing among some parents and players, she was beginning to feel pinched to perform well. Although Coach Dunn knew that the school valued academics more than sports, she felt pressured to achieve some wins. As a result, she let her players know that the team would suffer if their commitment dwindled.

One player, Kim, who had been benched in the previous game for making a bad pass in the defensive end that led to an opponent goal, missed two practices because of a lab and a study session. Coach Dunn literally ignored her for the first two practices upon her return. In their next game, Kim did not play even one minute. As a senior and starter, she was furious. Kim's parents were livid too, particularly since Kim had been a faithful team member and a four-year starter for the team. They decided to talk with the athletic director about the coach. This conversation seemed to go well; the athletic director acknowledged that other complaints about the coach had surfaced and that she had spoken with her. Kim's parents were pleased to hear this but became frustrated when Coach Dunn's behavior remained unchanged.

As we watch our teens develop into young adults, we will witness their struggles to manage conflicts between competing priorities in their lives. Part of what a college education teaches our young adult sons and daughters is how to manage their various life commitments and make them work. While there are situations where coaches have to enforce rules when players fail to follow the team rules, good coaches know how to make exceptions for extraordinary situations. In Kim's case, she had a legitimate conflict. Coach Dunn was not sensitive to Kim's dilemma, and by punishing Kim, she was punishing the team.

At the same time, dissension among parents and athletes was creating a difficult environment for Coach Dunn. She was losing the support of parents and the respect of her players. After talking with the athletic director, she began to feel less certain about the stability of her job. She knew the players were pressed, but she didn't feel comfortable backing off when the team was performing so poorly.

What progressed in the weeks to follow was painful for all of the girls. Kim had to miss playing against one of the better teams, and her team lost in overtime. Coach Dunn was furious. She questioned the team's commitment. At the same time, players began to point fingers at one another; the offense blamed the defense for letting in so many goals, and the defense criticized the offense for playing soft. During the practices that followed, a sense of paranoia settled over the team. Players stopped passing to one another. Before and after practice, they talked together less. There were fewer smiles and laughs; in fact, it seemed as if the girls practiced in silence.

> Values such as trust, hard work, commitment, and integrity help teams perform to their potential.

Because practices intensified during exams, stress started to take its toll. More players were getting sick and injured. One broke her wrist, and another separated her shoulder and was out for four weeks. Eventually, the team's winning momentum slowed. For the last ten games, the team won four, lost four, and tied two. But since they had achieved such a strong start, they still made the tournament; 12–6–2 was a respectable record.

Ironically, the girls were scheduled to play the team they beat 6–0 in the first game of the season. As expected, they jumped to an early lead in the first period; however, midway through the second period they allowed three straight goals, which tied the game at 3–3. The third period was tense. Both teams had chances to score. One shot hit the post; another went off the goalie's skate. The crowd was going crazy. The girls grew tenser as their coach screamed at them to play harder. They tried to block out the yelling and forget about the divisiveness that had infected their team. But they had gotten so used to ignoring one another, it was hard to regain positive team play. With about thirty seconds left, the other team scored the winning goal.

The team was distraught afterward. The fans for the opposing team screamed and cheered, while their own fans slowly walked out of the arena with their heads down. It was obvious that they had lost a game they should have won. In the locker room, the coach had little to say. She challenged the girls' desire to win and said she hoped that they were as disappointed as she was. She asked them to remember what this moment felt like, so that next time they would summon up the drive to win.

A bad aftertaste lingered in the off-season. A few bench players quit; others tried to organize a group to fire the coach. The seniors, who had given so much to the team and school, graduated with feelings of sadness and frustration.

Though coaches often take the heat for team problems, Coach Dunn was not the only one responsible for this disappointing season. Complaints from parents

Talent does not make a good team, nor does it guarantee a winning record.

helped fuel the unrest that led to difficulties. When coaches, players, and parents are sniping at one another, everyone suffers. Instead of coming together to resolve their differences, those involved with the team pulled the players apart. As a result, many young women began to play for themselves alone, a recipe for disaster, particularly at higher levels of sports.

The stories of the Blazers and the women's college hockey team make it clear that talent does not make a good team, nor does it guarantee a winning record. Positive player chemistry, strong coach leadership, and supportive parents are the combination that works. Challenging but realistic expectations encourage players to work hard, but within their ability. Overly competitive environments may foster initial improvements in skill and the win-loss record, but ultimately, they undermine team spirit. And no matter the level, teams that have fun are much more willing to work hard.

Athletes may struggle at the college level because they never learned how to deal with adversity as younger athletes.

As parents, we cannot control whether our children's team will be great or not. However, we can thoughtfully select good programs and coaches that have a reputation for encouraging players to improve skills, creating team unity, and having fun even when the competition increases. Particularly as it applies to youth sports and junior high school teams, the crucial goal is to have fun and develop skills. These younger players are simply not ready to compete as adults. Being on a dominant winning team may not be the best environment for them because they aren't challenged. Placing our younger children in good teams that experience both winning and losing will prepare them to manage the adversities inevitable at higher levels of play. We have seen many collegiate athletes struggle at the college level because they never learned how to deal with adversity as younger athletes. Consequently, we should not confuse early winning records with developing a well-prepared young adult athlete.

Although winning becomes more important as our children enter their teens and young adult years, the same principles that make good teams apply. Our kids need to be relaxed enough to play in the moment. Teammates need to support one another. The coach needs to create valuable roles for each player to keep team morale at its peak. Players need to believe in their coach, and parents need to remain supportive at a greater distance. There are many distractions along the way that make these seemingly simple qualities difficult to maintain. As is often the case, the good coaches know how to preserve these qualities, and we as parents can help by directing our children to play for these good leaders.

13

OVERWEIGHT CHILDREN

Surviving the Teasing and Prejudice and Finding Healthy Exercise and Eating Patterns

"DON'T PICK HER. She's too fat to play."

"Hey, what's wrong with that kid? Looks like he can barely make it up those stairs."

"Mom, I'll never be good enough to play. I'm too fat."

Statements like these are only too common. Too many kids have poor eating habits and not enough physical activity. Given the rise in obesity in our country and around the world, more parents are confronted with the challenge of finding the right physical activity for children in a society that is unforgiving about weight problems. For overweight children, playing for a team is a daunting task. They are at a disadvantage because others think they look funny in gym shorts, they can't run after the ball, or they easily get winded. They are also at risk of being teased, humiliated, and excluded by other kids. The benefits sports can offer in developing physical and social skills are lost to these children because of their fear of embarrassment.

It starts early. Children who can compete in sports relatively well have an avenue to friends and popularity; athleticism does not guarantee these outcomes, but it certainly helps. When we as parents witness our heavier children struggle on the athletic field, both physically and socially, we naturally become concerned. Such children are vulnerable to harsh, cruel teasing, and kids can be relentless at this. Chronic verbal and even physical pounding are likely to con-

> Overweight children are at risk of being singled out, teased, humiliated, and excluded by other kids.

tribute to a poor sense of themselves and their bodies. Heartbroken by this suffering, we as parents desperately want to help.

Understanding is the first step, and all we have to do is review our own experience to develop some empathy. How many of us know we should go to the gym to get into better shape but find some excuse not to? Sure, it's often difficult to find time to work out, but a more typical deterrent for overweight adults is being considered fat by others at the gym. We look at ourselves in the mirror and say, "There's no way I can go to the gym looking like this. I look like a beach ball compared to those young, hard bodies." The prospect of being humiliated, embarrassed, and ashamed makes some of us stay away.

> **Approximately 50 percent of overweight children become overweight adults.**

Still, adults don't have to put up with the treatment that overweight kids get. Imagine if we went to the gym and someone called out, "Hey, fatso, you need to spend another year on that treadmill before you lose that enormous gut." Some children fear this kind of experience when they play for sports teams. In the locker room, will they be teased and insulted? Will someone whip them with a towel when they're not looking, just to get a laugh from the other kids? Such worries can be paralyzing for overweight kids, and the consequences of such negative interactions can be serious. Young children suffer tremendously when they are unable to make friends and feel competent; they may experience negative consequences, such as a poor self-image, problems in decision making, and lack of social interactions with others, well into adulthood.[1] Wounds from teasing and feeling alienated can last a lifetime and may include discomfort with one's body, insecurity, and even self-loathing. For some overweight children, eating becomes the only way to feel good, and weight gain multiplies. Chances of finding a suitable physical activity decrease as health risks rise. This cycle, if not interrupted, can get worse year by year.

Though we don't want to be alarmists, we think parents should be concerned about sedentary, overweight kids. Obesity has become one of the top health problems in our nation's child and adult populations, and obese children are likely to be obese as adults. Approximately 50 percent of overweight children become overweight adults.[2] Type 2 diabetes, hypertension, and cardiovascular illness threaten overweight children and adults. The health costs for weight-related illnesses in our country amount to billions of dollars, and the problems keep getting worse. The American Obesity Association reports that over 15 percent of children ages 6–19 are obese, and over 30 percent are overweight. Over the past twenty-five years, the prevalence of obesity for children ages 6–11 has quadrupled, and the prevalence for adolescents ages 12–19 has more than doubled.[3] We are facing a health crisis, and our kids stand to be the ones most affected by it.

CHALLENGING TRENDS

Many factors in our culture make it difficult for our children to create healthy eating and exercise habits. First, it has become harder for kids to make the team these days. Starting at young ages, there are tryouts and cuts even for kids as young as 6 years old. The culprits causing this selectivity are the travel and elite teams. Out of a drive to win, these programs cut players early, and as a result, an emphasis on outcome trickles down to the town and recreational leagues. Many parents protest this trend, believing that all kids should be guaranteed equal participation in youth sports until the age of 12 or 13, but lots of kids are being cut from sports earlier. The chances that overweight children will make these selective teams, receive playing time, and feel valued as they participate rapidly drop.

Even overweight children with decent coordination are at risk of being cut simply because they can't keep up. The book *Travel Team,* by Mike Lupica, illustrates that even talented young athletes are getting excluded from sports.[4] Imagine how much harder making the team becomes when you add fifteen, twenty-five, or fifty pounds to the frame of a kid. There's just no chance. Unfortunately, adults who are driven to win at any cost are influencing the landscape of youth sports. Teams are picked and designed to win immediately. There is less room for a variety of talent and ability. Kids of all ages are getting squeezed out, and overweight kids are often the first to go.

> Over 15 percent of children ages 6–19 are obese, and over 30 percent are overweight.

But the problem is more complicated. As illustrated in great detail in Eric Schlosser's book *Fast-Food Nation,* our country is dominated by the quick, cheap, unhealthy, yet seductive meal.[5] Fast-food franchises are prominent on streets and in the media, and our children are their target audience. Pressed for time, families rarely eat dinner together. Often, both parents work to make ends meet, and children spend time alone after school. Some children use this time to play with friends; others participate in sports or other extracurricular activities. Yet a growing group of children must fend for themselves; they are more prone to getting into trouble and making unhealthy choices with regard to food.

Many parents are unsure about what to do. Because casual, unsupervised recreational activity for kids is largely unavailable, how can we get overweight kids to play organized sports that may bring them embarrassment and humiliation? Even positive sedentary activities can exacerbate weight problems, so they are not a solution. Finding ways to get these kids active and involved with others is no easy journey.

SALLY: OVERWEIGHT BUT TRYING TO PLAY

It's 3:15 P.M. and Sally, a 7-year-old second-grader, meets her mother at the bus stop after school. Sally looks clearly upset, so her mother asks, "What's wrong, honey?"

"They were mean to me at school," Sally blurts out.

"Who was mean to you? What did they do?"

"At recess, we started to play kickball, and they were picking teams, and one of the third-graders said, 'Don't pick her. She's too fat to play. She can't even kick the ball right.'"

"Oh, honey, I'm so sorry. Who was that girl? I'm going to have to call the school."

"No!" Sally shouts. "Don't do that. I just want to go home."

Sally's parents never thought their daughter was fat—perhaps a little chubby. Her weight had never been a concern before. The pediatrician told them that Sally was ten pounds overweight for her age but would likely thin out as she grew taller. They were given the name of a nutritionist, but they never called her. It seemed that Sally enjoyed playing sports, so they are surprised to hear of any lack of coordination. Now they wonder what to do. Should they start Sally on a diet? They also wonder if this incident is a rare occurrence or part of a pattern of teasing.

After asking Sally more questions and doing the work of the three-step approach, her parents discover that this is the second time someone has teased her about her weight. Another child called her Miss Piggy while they were having milk and cookies at snack break. Sally admits that it made her angry, but she didn't say anything about it at the time.

Teasing is one of the most unfortunate realities for many overweight children. When kids like Sally are teased, they begin to doubt themselves and lose their confidence. Sally now feels self-conscious and ashamed of her body: "I'm fat. People make fun of me. Nobody likes me. I'm bad."

As parents with overweight, nonathletic children, we want our kids to have a positive body image and become healthy and active. And of course, we want the teasing to stop. Herein lies the problem: the confidence kids need to combat teasing is gained through positive playing experiences with other kids — exactly what it is hard for overweight kids to attain. It seems that parents have to send them back into the jaws of the lion to give them the experience they need. But instructing Sally to keep a stiff upper lip while continuing to play with these teasing children could make matters much worse, leading to further humiliation and failure.

Though Sally's parents cannot control how coordinated their daughter is, they can help her develop confidence and physical skills. This may mean spending time on the weekends in the backyard, playing catch, kicking a ball, and perhaps including friends or neighbors who can ignore Sally's weight. This task requires time and perseverance; many neighborhood kids may be involved in organized teams and activities and lack time for informal play. Yet finding some noncompetitive kids and parents

Casual, unsupervised recreational activity for kids is largely unavailable.

may build a supportive group that allows Sally to play and gain skills without being ridiculed or embarrassed.

Physical activities outside of traditional organized sports may be just the thing for kids in Sally's position. These include biking, yoga, walking, karate, and dance, all of which yield significant health benefits and take place in an environment that is more accepting and less competitive than popular team sports. Finding the right activity may involve a fair amount of trial and error, but in the end the effort is worth it. When our overweight children find an activity that they enjoy, their whole world lights up and they feel relieved, and so do parents. Active kids tend to be more sociable with their peers and more upbeat at home.

Our overweight kids may have a genetic predisposition to digest food slowly, leading to weight gain. They may also eat to deal with emotional needs or boredom. Increasing physical activity, then, addresses only a part of the problem. Our children need to be educated about proper nutrition and how to choose foods that benefit health; they need awareness about eating when hungry and stopping when full. If they are eating for reasons related to emotion or boredom, parents need to teach them better ways to cope with feelings; too often, ads on TV make it look as if food makes people happy and solves problems. Children need other ways to manage stress, disappointment, anger, boredom, and loneliness. A combination of healthy eating and increased activity will likely succeed for children like Sally. The better the balance, the greater the chance that she can have positive, lasting experiences in sports.

ANDREW: WEIGHT DIFFERENCES AMONG SIBLINGS

On a brisk fall day, the perfect setting for the annual Thanksgiving classic between two rival high school teams, Andrew, a 12-year-old boy, is thrilled to watch his 18-year-old big brother, Mark, play quarterback for the home team, the Greyhounds. Andrew's family sits together in the stands, participating in Greyhound cheers and adding a few of their own for Mark.

It's an exciting game. Mark throws a touchdown and runs for another, and his team leads 14–10 at halftime. Andrew is beaming, thrilled with the success of his older brother. Cold and hungry from sitting in the stands for the past hour, Andrew asks his mother for a few dollars to get a snack and a hot chocolate.

"Okay, Andrew," she says. "Why don't you get a hot chocolate and a pretzel. Let's stay away from the candy."

"All right, Mom," Andrew says, annoyed. Food selection has been an area of concern for Andrew and his family. Whereas Mark is six feet tall with zero body fat, it seems everything Andrew eats goes right to his stomach. Mark can eat a huge dessert, and nothing seems to happen; the family often jokes that he has a hollow leg. In contrast, Andrew's metabolism is slower, much like that of his mother, who has to watch her weight. From the age of 6, Andrew has been overweight. Despite his parents' efforts to encourage exercise and healthy eating, Andrew's weight has grown more problematic; he has tried several diet programs and his parents have consulted with a nutritionist recommended by Andrew's pediatrician.

At the football game, it's no surprise to Andrew's parents that in addition to the hot chocolate, he also bought a pack of M&Ms, his favorite candy. Concerned for their son's health and somewhat annoyed that he did not obey them, Andrew's parents watch their son labor slowly up the steps. They can almost see how weight is making it difficult for him to breathe.

Before they can say anything to Andrew, a parent sitting two rows in front of them turns to friends and says, "Hey, look at that kid. He can barely make it up the stairs." Both Andrew and his parents hear the comment. With hurt feelings, Andrew tries to put the M&Ms in his pocket and nearly drops the hot chocolate, causing a few kids in the stands to laugh at him. Andrew's parents are furious at the insensitive parent and sad to think how Andrew must be feeling.

Ads on TV make it look as if food makes people happy and solves problems.

Although Mark leads the Greyhounds to an exciting victory, the mood at the family Thanksgiving gathering is dampened by Andrew's bad experience at the game. While Mark piles large portions of turkey, gravy, and stuffing on his plate, Andrew quietly picks at a few pieces of white meat and asks to be excused before dessert is served.

It's painful enough to watch a child be ridiculed by others, but to reexperience the pain daily at the dinner table adds to the agony. In his big brother, Andrew sees everything that he is not: He's not tall. He's not thin. He's not particularly athletic. And he can't eat whatever he wants. In fact, if he eats three quarters of what his brother eats, he gains weight.

Parents in such situations often wonder whether it's fair to other family members to make them adjust their eating habits to accommodate one or two weight-watching members. At the same time, they worry that it's borderline abusive to serve ice cream and high-calorie foods when weight is such a problem for some. Maintaining fairness among siblings is hard; kids are very sensitive about equality of treatment. For children like Andrew, it feels unfair to not be able to eat what his brother eats. It's unfair that he is not particularly athletic when his brother is a star. At the same time, Mark may also feel that it's unfair that he can't eat ice cream at home because his brother is overweight.

No matter what decisions we make, we feel that someone is going to suffer. We worry that we will damage one child's health and self-esteem for the sake of the other, and this kind of discrepancy creates unrest for us. Andrew does not have the metabolism and athletic talent of his older brother. Sports and healthy weight simply come easier to Mark. While it's possible that Andrew could still experience a growth spurt, thin out, and become more physically able to compete, it is unlikely that he will attain his brother's level of success. And though Andrew clearly admires his big brother, he of course harbors some feelings of jealousy and resentment.

Parents can't protect children entirely from sibling rivalry but can help them establish and appreciate their individual strengths. Andrew has a great sense of humor. He excels in science, and he has a keen knowledge of sports trivia. Finding ways to celebrate his knowledge, his personality, and his strengths will make him feel that he too has something to offer, and this builds confidence. Often when our children perceive themselves as operating at a deficit, they become needy for approval and reassurance. When they don't get this from friends and family, they resort to unhealthy practices such as eating or restricting food, abusing drugs and alcohol, or engaging in impulsive sex.

Like Sally, Andrew needs to seek the physical activity that fits him best. He may never be a quarterback or even a football player like his brother, but he still can find joy in another activity or sport. Once he does find something he enjoys, it will be impor-

Parents who force overweight children to play in a sport they hate are setting the kids up to hate exercise in general.

tant for his parents to give adequate attention to his efforts. While it's easy to assume that the whole family should support their very own superstar quarterback, the other kids need to feel that their activities are valued. To parents, Mark's love of football should not be any more important than Andrew's love of his sport or physical activity.

As part of their efforts to address the great differences in the family with regard to diet and athleticism, Andrew's parents return to their core family values. They review how they value effort, honesty, patience, and good health. They feel their decision to serve healthier foods at dinner and encourage adequate portions fall into their value of good health. As a result, inconsistencies and complaints about lack of fairness are greatly reduced.

Cookies aren't served frequently at the table because they aren't as healthy as other options.

When Andrew observes that the entire family is adjusting their eating patterns, he is less likely to feel shamed and left out. And while his brother may continue to excel in sports, this may also inspire Andrew to pursue some type of sports activity as well. If Andrew's newfound sport or physical activity is complemented with recognition of his other talents, he is in a much better position to grow and evolve without the self-consciousness of feeling damaged and overweight. He is more likely to develop the confidence and perseverance to continue to stay active and engaged. In time, if he remains active and sustains reasonable eating patterns, his weight will likely level off as he grows into his adult body. And if he remains a bigger boy and young man, he will still have developed a stronger sense of himself and a healthier style of eating and being active.

MARY: WHEN WEIGHT PROBLEMS LEAD TO QUITTING

In the beginning of her second season playing varsity field hockey, Mary, a 17-year-old junior in high school, struggles to keep up with the rest of the girls during tryouts. At five feet, six inches and 170 pounds, she usually trails behind everyone else in a sprint. After one particularly difficult practice, she tells her parents that she no longer wants to play: "I hate it. I'm miserable every day in practice. I don't like the way the coach teaches us about the game. I'm just not having fun. I can't keep up with everyone in the sprints."

> The pressure on young women to be thin gets worse and worse.

Worried that her daughter is just being impulsive, her mother says, "Oh, Mary, you always hate field hockey in the beginning of season, but once you get into shape, you start to enjoy it again."

In private Mary's father says to his wife, "We don't want to teach Mary to be a quitter. Sometimes I think she just needs a push. If she doesn't play field hockey, she's going to end up in front of the television after school. Plus, she's such a good player. The coach likes her. I just don't understand. Field hockey may also help her get into college. What is she thinking?"

In a heart-to-heart conversation with her mother, Mary says, "It's not just that I hate the running in practice. I don't think the coach understands the game well, so it's not as much fun. Plus, I don't really like the girls on the team. They are so superficial. There's such a field hockey clique, and I'm not into that. Believe me, I don't want to be overweight. You have no idea how much it bothers me."

"Well, what would you do if you quit?"

"I definitely want to play something, maybe water polo, or I may even consider trying out for soccer goalie. I have pretty good hands, and I can kick the ball. And I want to lose weight. I'm ready to try anything."

It is noteworthy that in Mary's decision-making process she recognizes the importance of being engaged in a physical activity and exercising. She doesn't want to quit playing sports; she just wants to quit field hockey. If we as parents force our overweight children to play in a sport they hate, we are setting them up to hate exercise in general. If instead we listen to them and respect what they say, we give kids a better chance to enjoy being active well into adulthood.

Of course, sometimes we as parents wonder whether we truly under-stand kids' reasons for quitting. What if Mary is just giving up because of her weight? Maybe she thinks she won't have to work as hard in water polo or soccer. Do parents cave in too easily? Perhaps our children will say years later, "Mom and Dad, I wish you had pushed me to stick with field hockey. I was pretty good and could have played in college." The best we parents can do is understand as well as possible why our child wants to quit. We can en-courage him or her to consider the importance of watching weight and being active as well as working through challenging times and not quitting in the face of adversity. If, after exploring all of these issues, Mary continues to say that she is miserable playing field hockey, then her parents are in a better position to support her. The fact that Mary wants to play another sport and is serious about losing weight suggests that she is not running away from her weight problem.

As part of incorporating the three-step approach, it will be important for Mary's parents to assess the impact of team and coach influence. Are the other girls on the team making comments to Mary? Does the coach make subtle or not-so-subtle comments about overweight players? Coaches can have a significant impact on the self-perceptions of players. At times, they are not even aware of the potential damage they are inflicting. Taking the time to learn more about the daily dialogue between coach and players can give a better idea of what's going on. In Mary's case, her parents learn that the coach is mostly supportive, and therefore they focus on understanding and helping Mary deal with her weight difficulties.

Talking to a teenage girl about her weight, even if sports is the main focus, is a precarious endeavor. The pressure on young women to be thin gets worse and worse. While many of us assume that girls and women in certain sports such as gymnastics, figure skating, and running are the ones most scrutinized for their weight, a growing number of girls and women in competitive team sports at the high school and collegiate levels, such as soccer, basketball, lacrosse, and field hockey, are becoming increasingly self-conscious about their weight. These girls and young women are made to feel defective if even slightly overweight. Some of these messages may come from their coaches. Other times, they may hear it from teammates or opponents. As a result, any criticisms or suggestions we might make about their weight are taken to heart. Drawing attention to a young woman's body in a negative manner is typically an invitation for self-loathing. This puts parents in a bind. A mother might say, "If I don't say anything, she's going to become increasingly overweight and unhealthy. She'll feel self-conscious and miserable. If I do say something about her weight, she'll become self-conscious in a different way. She'll obsess about her weight and maybe even become bulimic."

Late adolescent and young adult female athletes like Mary are at the greatest risk for the development of eating disorders. In our work with overweight female athletes, they often feel that their parents are completely insensitive to their weight issues. They complain that their fathers make thoughtless comments about their weight. They may call them chubby or a little plump in what seems to be a benign manner and fail to recognize how devastating their comments are. Mothers, on the other hand, are often criticized for being too involved, too tuned in to everything they eat. These are good kids with very supportive parents, yet they still feel pressured and misunderstood.

Many of us parents feel paralyzed and helpless. We begin to watch every word to avoid sending our kids into a downward spiral of negativity. We wonder how we will ever be able to help. The key is to find the right moment to raise concerns in a nonjudgmental manner. Mary's decision to quit field hockey can be an opportunity for the parents to learn more about her body image and possibly help in her efforts to address weight concerns.

Luckily, Mary is raising the issue herself. She wants to drive the change in her behavior, allowing her parents to take a supportive position.

In their discussion about field hockey, Mary's mother suggests that Mary consult with a nutritionist and the family doctor. This succeeds because Mary appreciates her mom's support of her decision to quit field hockey, and Mary is motivated to lose weight. Without this motivation, weight loss rarely occurs.

When we have the opportunity to meet with overweight girls and young women, one of our first questions is "Why are you here today? Whose idea was it for you to come for this evaluation?"

More often than not, we hear "My parents want me to be here. I really didn't want to come."

This response often indicates that this is not the right time to focus on weight loss. When our overweight daughters feel this way, they are likely to undermine and even sabotage efforts to lose weight. In these situations, we might spend time talking to parents about ways to back off a bit on the topic of weight loss until their daughter states that she wants to lose weight.

Putting children on diets and signing them up for gyms and exercise programs will often fail if they are not interested in participating.

It's quite challenging for an athlete like Mary to cut back on eating while simultaneously training hard to keep up with her teammates in a new sport. At first, she may be hungry, uncomfortable, and irritable. She may not see the benefits of her efforts for at least a few weeks. Her parents can help by being mindful of the food they bring home and discouraging eating while watching TV. So in Mary's case, it's fine that she quits field hockey, but sitting home in front of the TV every day after school is not an option. She will have to choose a physical activity that she plays every day after school and that is supervised by a coach or adult. This way, we are not letting a resistant adolescent fall through the cracks or plunge deeper into weight gain.

The temptation for many of us as parents with overweight children in sports is to seek the quick solution: put them on a diet, sign them up for more physical activity, and watch them like a hawk. This approach may pro-

duce short-term benefits of minor weight loss and potential long-term consequences of weight obsession and resistance to healthy eating and exercise.
To help children sustain healthy eating and exercise patterns, we as parents
must take the long view, assisting kids in finding the physical activity that
works best for them and expecting this to take a while. Stocking the refrig-
erator with nutritious foods, regulating mealtimes, offering healthy snacks,
and modeling balanced eating and exercise habits can be very effective. And
when uncertain or overwhelmed, we as parents can seek the counsel of professionals. Like other issues related to children in sports, healthy eating and
exercise are more likely to fall into place for kids if they are tied to a core values system. Rather than focus on the outcome — weight loss — wise parents emphasize taking care of the body in order to enjoy life and engage in
meaningful activities. In the end, our goal is not that our kids will be superstars, but that they have found a relationship with eating and exercise that
sets the foundation for healthy adulthood.

14

EATING DISORDERS, BODY IMAGE, STEROIDS, AND SUPPLEMENTS

SPORTS CAN HELP our children maintain a healthy weight and positive self-image, but some kids become so intensely focused on being physically fit and looking good that they follow unhealthy diets, exercise excessively, and experiment with dangerous drugs. Some of our daughters and even our sons will drastically restrict their food intake; they may also experiment with hazardous medications to reduce the appetite in order to stay thin. Some athletes may take steroids and legal but possibly harmful supplements to build muscle in order to gain a competitive edge in their sport.

Messages to our children to lose weight and build muscle are embedded in our culture. Girls inevitably read something like this in a magazine: "Too fat? Is your weight slowing you down? Do you feel unattractive? Take this pill. You'll lose weight while toning your body to perfection." Boys are the target of a different message: "Too skinny and scrawny? Are you still that weakling boy who lacks confidence and gets bullied on and off the field?" or "Are you looking for that extra edge to make it to the next level? Take this pill, and you will double your strength and finally know what it's like to feel confident and dominate your opponents." The pressure to perform makes kids vulnerable to often dangerous quick fixes such as steroid and supplement abuse as well as disordered eating. Girls and boys push themselves too hard and lose perspective, taking measures that may place their health and performance in sports at risk.

Eating disorders have received a fair amount of attention, but many of us parents know little about steroids and so-called dietary supplements. Sure, we have heard about alleged steroid use in professional baseball in the cases of Jose Canseco, Jason Giambi, and Barry Bonds and in international track in the cases of Kelli White and Marion Jones. But we can't imagine that our own kids are experimenting with these drugs. Most of us are surprised by how our kids become so focused on their appearance and performance, and we are at a loss as to how they get their hands on drugs and steroids. In fact, we may be ill-equipped to recognize warning signs.

AMANDA: SIGNS OF AN EATING DISORDER

Amanda, a 16-year-old junior on the track team, is having a great season. In the past two meets, she has finished first in the 800- and 1,500-meter races. Though her parents are thrilled with her success, they are becoming concerned about her weight loss. Her clothes are beginning to hang off her body, and at dinner she eats only salad. When her mother encourages Amanda to eat some meat or pasta, she'll put a little bit on her plate, pick at it, but not eat it. When her parents ask her why she is eating so little, she shrugs and says, "I'm just not that hungry. I had a big lunch at school." Not knowing exactly what their daughter ate earlier in the day, Amanda's parents cannot challenge her reply. They want to believe her but have their doubts.

Over the next few weeks, Amanda's parents notice that she is spending long periods of time in the bathroom. They know she is not taking a shower because the water isn't running. When they knock on the door and ask if she is okay, Amanda snaps, "I'm fine. Can't I have a little privacy?"

Then, Amanda's parents receive a call from the school athletic trainer. Amanda's recurrent problem with shin splints has worsened, and he suggests that she see an orthopedic doctor. During Amanda's visit with the doctor, her parents learn that she has a mild stress fracture in her shin and ankle. As they leave the clinic, the doctor pulls Amanda's parents aside and says that Amanda likely has an eating disorder. Her bones are thinning and her weight is dangerously low. At five feet, four inches, Amanda weighs only 101 pounds. This news is understandably alarming to Amanda's parents. They want to get help for her immediately, but first they want to better understand Amanda's condition and how she got this way.

> Bingeing and purging form a secret code, and no one wants to break it because of potential shame and embarrassment.

The presence of eating disorders can surface in unusual ways. Who would think that an orthopedic doctor would be the one to diagnose such a disorder? Yet when orthopedic doctors treat recurrent stress fractures in adolescents and young adult athletes, particularly girls, they may suspect an underlying problem with eating. The condition of Amanda's bones suggests one component of the female athlete triad,[1] a sports medicine term that refers to three physical and behavioral problems that are risk factors for female athletes: disordered eating, amenorrhea (no menstruation), and osteoporosis (thinning and weakening of bones).

In Amanda's case, the combination of weight loss and stress fracture draws her doctor's attention. When he learns that Amanda has missed two menstrual periods, he is certain that she needs professional help. If an eating disorder progresses quickly, her life may be in danger. As many eating-disordered females in high-intensity sports have discovered, overtraining (the relentless pounding of feet on the track) and starving the body will eventually lead to a breakdown. Amanda's doctor recommends a range of professional help because a host of other behaviors probably contribute to Amanda's problems with eating.

Amanda's doctor is right: weight loss and a stress fracture form only the tip of the iceberg. Amanda's overtraining is exhausting and damaging to her body, yet her drive to be thin blinds her to the dangers of overtraining and restrictive eating. Therefore she may be at risk for two well-known eating disorders: anorexia nervosa and bulimia nervosa.

The Diagnostic Statistical Manual–IV (DSM-IV), which describes psychiatric disorders, defines anorexia nervosa as a condition present when a young woman or man weighs less than 85 percent of her or his normal weight; so if a girl's normal weight is 100 pounds, she must weigh less than 85 pounds to be diagnosed as having this condition.[2]

Even when athletic girls exercise intensely in sports such as track, cross-country running, swimming, and gymnastics, they should remain at a normal weight. Amanda's normal weight should be approximately 120 pounds. Any weight below 102 pounds places her below that 85 percent cutoff number used to diagnose anorexia. At 101 pounds, Amanda is in that danger zone.

Anorexic girls fear becoming fat and are highly self-critical about their appearance; this problem can be particularly striking for female athletes. Even though they are in great physical condition, they still feel dissatisfied with their body. For example, when Amanda looks in the mirror, she sees a fat person, whereas her parents and coaches view her as dangerously thin. Amanda also reveals that she has missed two consecutive menstrual periods; if she misses a third, she will meet all the criteria for anorexia nervosa.

The other major eating disorder that Amanda may have is bulimia nervosa. In order to meet its criteria in the *DSM-IV*, the individual must binge-eat at least twice per week over a three-month period. During a binge-eating episode an individual eats an unusually large amount of food in a short time while feeling a loss of control. Then, to compensate for overeating, the person will vomit, fast, exercise excessively, or use laxatives, diuretics, enemas, or other medications and practices to prevent weight gain.[3]

To the untrained eye, bulimic athletes may be difficult to detect. They may eat regularly in public yet binge and purge in private. Some may look healthy when in fact they are abusing their bodies and suffering emotionally. Interestingly, teammates may know what girls with bulimia are doing. In fact, it's not uncommon for several girls on a team to struggle with bulimia without openly confronting one another. Bingeing and purging form a secret code, and no one wants to break it because of potential shame and embarrassment. Unfortunately, the affected girls suffer silently. This may be particularly difficult for parents as we may not suspect our daughters of an eating disorder when their weight seems to be normal, and we fail to notice any of the other signs.

Bulimic athletes are similar to the high-functioning alcoholic who hides the liquor and drinks in secrecy. Unless the alcoholic is caught red-handed, the problem may remain hidden — until the person begins to perform poorly at work or fail miserably in relationships. However, if we pay attention to facial coloring and the smell of an alcoholic's breath, we may infer a problem with drinking.

Though some of our athletic girls may not meet the full criteria for anorexia nervosa or bulimia nervosa, they may very well have a serious condition related to eating. Many who struggle with eating and body-image problems have just a few symptoms of anorexia or bulimia, which don't amount to a clear diagnosis. Such a case may be categorized as an eating disorder that is not otherwise specified (NOS).[4] Though this diagnosis differs from full-blown anorexia or bulimia in magnitude, treatment is essential to preventing more serious problems.

As part of the secrecy of eating disorders, athletic girls frequently lie about what they eat. Like Amanda, when offered food they will say that they have already eaten. Increased time in the bathroom is a warning sign that a girl may be vomiting (purging) to keep her weight down. Because it may be hard to ascertain that Amanda is purging, her parents have to look for specific symptoms of this behavior. For example, Amanda's skin may become a pale yellowish color. Broken blood vessels may appear under her eyes as a result of vomiting, and scratches on the back of her fingers and knuckles, made by her teeth, may indicate that she sticks her fingers down her throat to make herself vomit. A breakdown in the enamel of her teeth may result from exposure to stomach acid during vomiting. Amanda may also have chronic sore throats and chest pain and become tired and depressed. Like many eating-disordered athletes participating in endurance sports, she may feel fatigued and may withdraw from having fun socially with her teammates. And her performance may decline for no obvious reason.

When Amanda's parents ask her about eating problems, she denies that she binge-eats but admits that she has tried to make herself vomit on occasion. She insists that no real eating problem exists. The parents tentatively conclude that their daughter's efforts to stay thin and focus almost entirely on eating less and exercising more are characteristic of anorexia nervosa.

Most girls with eating disorders will deny the problem and react defensively.

Amanda's parents are ashamed that they did not notice the problem sooner. The orthopedic doctor recommended that the entire family consult with an eating-disorder specialist, and Amanda's parents decide to speak directly about this with their daughter.

Before dinner, Amanda's mother says, "Amanda, the doctor says that you will need to rest for a bit so your leg can heal. But he also said that your weight is way too low. He thinks you may have an eating disorder. Honey, we need to get you some help."

"What are you talking about? There's nothing wrong with my weight. Why are you always so focused on my weight? You're obsessed. I don't want to talk about this."

The direct approach backfires. Amanda refuses to meet with an eating-disorder specialist and claims that her eating is fine. Her parents ask the pediatrician for advice, and she explains that confronting girls about eating disorders can be tricky. Most will deny the problem and react defensively. For athletes especially, a good deal of their sense of competency and confidence is generated by having control over their bodies. When parents, coaches, or peers raise the topic of eating disorders, they feel attacked on three fronts: how they eat, how they look, and how their body functions. They feel protective of their bodies and enormously ashamed of their behavior. Therefore, parents must seek guidance from trained counselors and physicians and use tact when confronting their daughters.

> Numerous physical and psychological risks accompany the use of ephedra. This stimulant is extremely dangerous and should never be consumed.

In some cases, girls need to be hospitalized for treatment of eating disorders. Our colleague from Massachusetts General Hospital and Harvard Medical School, Dr. Paul Hamburg, is an expert in eating disorders, among his other specialties. He notes that hospitalization often comes as a relief to an adolescent caught between failing bodily health and the inability to stop restricting intake of food. But when Amanda's parents meet with an eating-disorder therapist on their own to discuss whether they should consider hospitalizing their daughter, they learn that Amanda's weight loss has not progressed to the point at which emergency hospitalization is required. Instead, the therapist urges them to invite Amanda to help create an outpatient treatment plan. During this meeting, the therapist coaches Amanda's parents to focus on Amanda's happiness. They are encouraged to share their concern about their daughter's fatigue and depression, her lack of enjoyment of sports and school, and her obvious unhappiness. This approach has more success. Amanda agrees to see her school counselor, someone she knows from health education classes. Together, the family begins to address why Amanda is feeling unhappy — how she feels a tremendous amount of pressure to do well in sports and school and is terrified about not being good enough in either to get into a good college. As their relationship strengthens, the counselor persuades Amanda to see a nutritionist to help her develop a healthier diet. In turn, the nutritionist has Amanda weigh in once a week at the school nurse's office and initiates an eating plan that will produce a slow but steady increase in weight. In the following months, Amanda gains weight gradually and begins to feel better about herself. She slowly returns to running after explaining the situation to her coach. They discuss how to avoid overtraining.

To address their concerns with their daughter, Amanda's parents incorporate the three-step approach. Despite the urgency of the problem, they take a step back and try to learn more about their daughter and the characteristics and causes of her eating disorder. They learn that changes in the body of an adolescent girl may feel like a loss of control to her. Some girls accept and embrace these changes, but others may attempt to return their bodies to a preadolescent shape through weight loss and excessive training, possibly laying the foundation for an eating disorder. Amanda may be particularly vulnerable because of her desire to excel in school and sports so that she can get into a fine college. Her school environment is extremely competitive. All the popular girls are skinny, smart, and athletic. At the same time, Amanda is playing a sport that encourages hard training.

Amanda's parents also ask themselves about their role in her difficulties. Though parents are rarely the sole cause of an eating disorder, the family environment as a whole is worth exploring. Subtle pressure to excel beyond reasonable bounds may be present, though not overt or intentional. Eating-disordered athletes may overvalue success and physical appearance because our culture lionizes them and girls also observe that their parents work hard and push themselves — they may feel a need to keep up in order to please their parents. Eating-disordered athletes may fear disappointing their parents or restrict eating in an attempt to gain control over some aspect of life. Some may be affected by family problems such as marital conflict or substance abuse; in these stressful circumstances, controlled eating becomes a child's way to assert power over an otherwise unstable life.

Though Amanda's parents show support for her sports activities, they sense that Amanda may worry that she will disappoint them if she doesn't perform at peak levels. Achievement-oriented in their professional lives, Amanda's parents are passionate about their jobs, and Amanda may confuse this passion with an expectation that she must excel in school and sports with the same level of enthusiasm and success. Also, as an only child,

Amanda does not have the opportunity to see a brother or sister experience the ups and downs of growing up. In a way, she is living in an adult world and expects herself to meet adult standards of accomplishment. Amanda uses restrictive eating and increased exercise to manage the feeling that she is not keeping up with others; she has become so concerned with winning and doing well in school that she loses perspective. Her parents conclude that they are not causing the pressure that Amanda feels but could help her reduce tension and regain balance in her life.

As parents of athletic daughters, we have to watch for clues that indicate feelings of being alienated and overly pressured. It is wise to keep our eyes on their basic needs. Do they feel accepted by their peers? Do they feel loved for who they are rather than what they do? Do they have balance in their lives? Are they engaged in a variety of activities? Do they connect well with other adults such as coaches and teachers? Often, problems develop when these needs are not being met. Eating disorders, anxiety, and depression can occur when our children are deprived of these basic life necessities.

Because our athletic daughters are strong and appear healthy, we as parents rarely suspect problems with eating. Girls will not discuss them directly, so we have to use indirect methods of gathering information if we suspect a problem. For instance, we can ask about the players on their teams, the intensity of training, and their own self-care habits. Are they getting enough rest and drinking enough water?

Andro can stunt growth and may cause other negative side effects such as liver cancer.

Listen carefully for any stories of problems between players or coaches. Often, we can learn quite a bit by how they talk about their friends and the struggles they may have. At the same time, we can talk to other parents who have children on the team. What do they think of the team and the coach? Hints of a problem may emerge during these conversations. If an eating disorder seems likely, it is wise to discuss the matter with a medical or mental health professional. Involving the coach or other players may shame the girl and increase her defensiveness and resistance to help. A pediatrician, nutritionist, or eating-disorder counselor can provide guidance on how to approach this sensitive issue and interpret possible symptoms of a disorder, such as exhaustion, anemia, abnormalities in electrolyte levels, changes in pulse rate or blood pressure, and mood disturbance. This serious, even dangerous condition can easily pass below parents' radar screen. Symptoms can surface, disappear, and then reemerge. Therefore, it is absolutely essential to take this problem seriously.

STIMULANTS AND DIETARY SUPPLEMENTS

There are other means by which our children can abuse their bodies that extend beyond eating problems. They can experiment with drugs and dietary supplements that are largely untested and often risky to health. Some of our kids are drawn to stimulants in order to lose weight; others use stimulants and dietary supplements to beef up sports performance and build muscle. As parents, we must try to remember what it was like to be a vulnerable, self-doubting, and at times confused adolescent. If kids are uncertain about their looks and their identity, they may be susceptible to quick-fix remedies to what they perceive as their problems or inadequacies.

The false promises are everywhere:

"In just a week, lose ten pounds and fit into that new bikini."
"Take this supplement, and develop muscles and strength you
    thought you would never have."

The lure of the quick fix can lead to experiments with stimulants and dietary supplements. For some kids, these choices can lead to dangerous consequences. For example, kids hoping to lose weight quickly may experiment with stimulants such as ephedra. Ephedra is a stimulant used to lose weight, improve sports performance, and enhance energy. Though the FDA reports that ephedra may produce short-term weight loss and short-term performance enhancement, numerous physical and psychological risks accompany its use. This stimulant is extremely dangerous and should never be consumed. Side effects include nausea, vomiting, irritability, heart palpitations, anxiety, and mood changes. The effects of ephedra on adolescents have not been adequately researched, and it's possible, in fact likely, that the risks may even be greater for our children.

Energy drinks are becoming increasingly popular dietary supplements for adolescents. Some teens want to lose weight or simply lose their appetite; others, and this group consists mostly of boys, want to improve their performance. Ann S. Litt, sports nutritionist for the Washington Redskins and author of the book *Fuel for Young Athletes*,[5] reports that adolescent girls and boys are experimenting with a variety of energy drinks, such as 180, Arizona's Energy X, Energy, Sobee Adrenaline, and Red Bull. These beverages provide a burst of energy and at the same time deceive the body into acting as if it doesn't need more fuel. Kids feel their metabolism speeding up. Yet the risks far outweigh the potential short-term benefits. According to Litt, many energy drinks contain large amounts of sugar, which often causes nausea, vomiting, and dehydration; they also produce a burst-and-crash effect. Our children experience a short-term increase in energy, lasting for thirty to forty-five minutes, and this burst may improve athletic performance. But then a sugar crash follows, making reflexes slow down. Kids may experience dizziness, a decrease in muscle power, and, in fact, a decline in athletic performance.

Many energy drinks also contain caffeine, which creates a boost for some and a problem for others. Some athletes derive a kick of energy from caffeine, which helps their performance; others instead become distracted, hyperactive, and irritable. All children can become addicted to caffeine, meaning they have to drink more to get the desired effect; this pattern increases the likelihood of dehydration. As we have seen over the past decade at the high school, collegiate, and professional levels, dehydration in hot weather can have terrible consequences in sports. In the most extreme examples, athletes have died from heat exhaustion and stroke.

But many of our kids try using substances even more hazardous than energy drinks. In one statewide study in Iowa involving male high school football players and female volleyball players, up to 8 percent of the male athletes and 2 percent of the female athletes were using some type of food supplement or steroid.[6] These percentages are alarmingly high. Since our own kids may be experimenting with drugs and supplements without our knowledge, it is important to become aware of this trend and its potential risks.

Creatine, one of the most popular dietary supplements, has garnered mixed reviews in terms of effectiveness and safety. Creatine is an amino acid that helps build protein. Athletes take creatine to improve performance and build strength. According to some researchers, when athletes use creatine, they experience less fatigue during intense physical activity such as sprinting and weight lifting, and they improve their recovery time after exerting themselves. This substance gives them a burst of energy and also, over time, may increase lean body mass, which leads to greater muscle tone.[7]

Given these positive reports, it's no surprise that many of our kids are drawn to creatine. In fact, up to 17 percent of high school athletes, including 30 percent of high school football players, use it. At the college level, creatine use is even higher: 28 to 41 percent of NCAA Division I athletes take it.[8]

However, the negative reports on creatine use are not as well ad-

> A tremendous sense of self-doubt and a distorted view of their bodies often underlie the drive in these adolescent boys and young men to be fit.

vertised. In fact, some research indicates that the effectiveness of creatine is questionable, particularly as it relates to athletic performance. In other words, our kids are not getting the hoped-for boost. And on top of this, the supplement has dangerous side effects — creatine use may do long-term damage to kidney function. Also, almost all studies of creatine have involved adult populations, so the effectiveness or risk of creatine use for children and teens is largely unknown.[9]

Since the news broke that professional baseball home-run legend Mark McGwire reportedly used androstenedione (andro), a hormone thought to be a precursor to the development of testosterone, its popularity has skyrocketed. Athletes of all ages and experience began using andro to build strength and improve performance. In response to this trend, which increased in momentum when McGwire broke the home-run record in 1998, the Endocrine Society,[10] a well-known organization that conducts research on hormones, issued a statement strongly condemning andro use. First, the society identified andro as a steroid rather than a dietary supplement. Though taking andro leads to the development of testosterone, which may increase strength, it can also promote the development of the female hormone estrogen. Too much estrogen development can lead to the shutdown of testosterone production, which can shrink the testicles. To drive this message home to boys, some clear imagery may be helpful: their testicles could conceivably shrink from the size of grapes to that of raisins. Although andro use was condemned, it is still available in stores and through the Internet.

Andro can also stunt growth and cause other serious side effects such as liver cancer. Like many unregulated over-the-counter supplements, andro dosage may not be consistent, so users can't really tell how much they are taking. Furthermore, no evidence proves that andro actually builds muscle size and strength or improves athletic performance. So our kids could be taking andro without receiving any benefit yet incurring much risk.

In addition to creatine and andro, a whole range of protein supplements is offered over the counter in drugstores and markets and on the Internet, making them easily available to our kids. Countless brands of protein shakes and powders advertise the benefit of building strength. Tara Mardigan, a sports nutritionist who works with kids and professional athletes, warns that overuse of protein supplements can be dangerous. Large amounts of protein can lead to overload. Those trying to lose weight on high-protein diets such as the Atkins diet should know that the increased protein can turn into fat and subsequent weight gain. In more serious cases, kidneys fail to process this surfeit of protein, causing kidney stones and gout.

Perhaps the greatest concern is the notion that if supplement use has positive results, using more will be even better. This misguided assumption may lead to harmful consequences, many of which we cannot anticipate yet but will likely surface in the coming years. Athletic trainer BJ Baker of Train Boston reports that despite his recommendations about what he believes is proper use of supplements for a small population of athletes, many will ignore his warnings about overuse.

It's fairly easy for our children to buy supplements despite the risks involved. Andro has been condemned by the medical community, but it remains available; ephedra sales have been banned by the FDA, yet it can be obtained through prescription or illegal means. Other products can be purchased at health and nutrition stores. For example, our kids can buy a five-pound jug of creatine for fifty dollars or less. A wide range of protein powders and amino acid products is also readily available. Though labels on some brands strongly recommend consultation with a dietitian or a physician, our kids

> The kid who is told that he has no chance of making the team unless he gets stronger is particularly vulnerable to steroid use.

still have easy access to the products. If they can find the money, they can buy them.

Should we as parents forbid use of these supplements? How should we handle the discovery that our child is using them? Mardigan suggests that parents should ask the child about the supplements and their use; then through consultations with a primary-care physician and through research, parents can team up with their kid to assess how supplements work and whether they are safe, legal, and tested, identifying potential health risks. Finally, parents and their child can discuss whether the potential risks are worth the questionable gains. Detailed guidelines about how to talk to our children about eating problems and supplements are also available in Nancy Clark's well-known book *Sports Nutrition Guidebook*.[11]

Because these supplements and steroidlike agents are not well tested and may have health risks, nutritionists like Litt emphasize healthy eating for adolescents in place of supplement use. Though adolescents are notorious for awful eating habits, if they can focus on creating healthy, balanced meals, they will get all the nutrition they need to build their bodies. For this reason, many nutritionists are devoting time to teaching kids how to improve their habits.

ADAM: THE RISKS OF ANABOLIC STEROIDS

Of average height and somewhat skinny, Adam, a 14-year-old boy, is not the typical candidate for high school football. Before the summer of his freshman year, the freshman coach tells Adam that his chances of making the team are slim to none because of his size.

This feedback is particularly painful for Adam, for he has always been a bit self-conscious about his size. In fact, he is self-conscious in general and is struggling with low-grade depression, which many people have misread as shyness. He has few friends and has never had a best friend or a girlfriend. Inspired to make the team and boost his self-confidence, Adam commits himself to build muscle and strength and secretly begins to experiment with steroids. Over the summer, he spends much of his time in the weight room, becoming increasingly antisocial, moody, and obsessed with his diet. His parents at first are puzzled by their son's behavior. Then, when looking at a photograph from their spring vacation, they notice how much bigger and stronger Adam has become in a short time. When they ask him how he accomplished this, he avoids answering. His mood is disagreeable, and everything his parents say seems to irritate him, which is unusual.

A surprising number of young men, ranging in age from the teens to the late twenties, are totally consumed with improving their physique. They stare at themselves in the mirror, work out compulsively, and are obsessed with gaining muscle. It's normal for young men to be somewhat concerned about body image—they want to be attractive to others and feel a sense of masculinity—and generally, parents don't need to be concerned about this. Problems occur when fitness and body image overtake all other priorities in their lives.

This fixation is described in the book *The Adonis Complex*,[12] which deals with male body image and the dysfunction that comes with body obsession, including the insecurity and imbalance that drive young men to focus on the body so much that they sacrifice relationships and professional or academic endeavors. Some use the terms *reverse anorexia* or *muscle dysmorphia* to describe this condition. Whereas the anorexic girl has a distorted sense that she is fat, the reverse-anorexic boy has the distorted sense that he is weak and thin. The defining feature is the distorted view of one's appearance. This is the case for Adam. Even as he grows stronger, he still sees a skinny, weak boy when he looks in the mirror.

For boys in this category, life revolves around gyms and workout routines. They can become depressed, anxious, and isolated. They may avoid spending time with friends and family because it conflicts with their workouts. Their lives become ritualized and routine oriented. Their workouts and their obsession with the body take over until nothing else matters. If their obsession with fitness and appearance reaches these peaks, they need a consultation with a counselor specializing in athletics, body image, and eating disorders. The goal of this consultation would be to address causes and practices related to this imbalanced lifestyle and distorted self-perception.

Some teens and young men experiment with anabolic steroids. According to our colleague Dr. Hamburg, anabolic steroids are powerful hormones, both naturally occurring and synthetic, that are related to the male sex hormone testosterone. Anabolic steroids stimulate appetite and cause a dramatic increase in muscle mass and weight gain. They are also toxic to the brain and the liver, cause severe acne, arrest growth, increase the risk of heart disease, promote male baldness and the development of breasts, and suppress normal sexual function. The more frightening risks related to steroid use include "roid rage"; approximately 10 percent of steroid users become violent. There is no way to tell which steroid users will be susceptible to this dangerous side effect. What's more, the long-term impact of steroid use on younger adolescents may well be even more damaging than its effect on fully grown athletes. Secrecy is a common trait of steroid users, making it hard to determine whether a child such as Adam is partaking of this substance. Also, as trainer BJ Baker notes, parents are often surprised to discover that a child is using steroids or may even deny it: "My son would never take steroids. That's too dangerous. He's too smart to do something like that."

But research statistics confirm that many kids are steroid users. The National Institute on Drug Abuse conducted a national study on steroid use called "Monitoring the Future Survey."[13] Among boys and girls, rates of steroid use peaked in 2002 at 2.5 percent for twelfth-graders and 2.2 percent for tenth-graders. Eighth-grade steroid use peaked at 1.7 percent in 1999 and 2000. Statistics indicate that among adolescent boys in 2003, 1.8 percent of eighth-graders, 2.3 percent of tenth-graders, and 3.2 percent of twelfth-graders had used steroids during the past year. This means that out of a class of one hundred students, at least a few boys may be experimenting with steroids.

Male steroid users are more likely to have low self-esteem, high incidence of depression and suicide attempts, and high rates of eating disorders and substance abuse.

Statewide studies raise even greater concern. A decade ago, one such study in Georgia, targeting high school freshman boys and girls, revealed that up to 6.5 percent of boys and 1.9 percent of girls had been using steroids. More recently, in a statewide study in Minnesota of over four thousand male and female middle and high school students, researchers found that 5.4 percent of males and 2.9 percent of females were using steroids.[14] Surprisingly, steroid use was more pervasive among middle school students; younger adolescents are at a greater risk than many had realized.

Adam is a model candidate for this high-risk group. As trainer BJ Baker informs us, the kid who is told that he has no chance of making the team unless he gets stronger and spends more time in the gym is particularly vulnerable to steroid use. Too young to know the risks and insecure enough to try anything, he impulsively selects the quickest way to get stronger. If a young boy like Adam instead consults a multidisciplinary team of doctors, he will get sound advice, which may involve nutrition and weight-training education but never steroid use. But at the local gym, he may not receive appropriate guidance, and unfortunately, at some gyms steroids are readily accessible.

Initially, parents may be glad to see a son heading for the gym to exercise. Once at the gym, the boy asks some older, bigger young men how to build his body. In addition to getting advice about weight-lifting regimens and techniques, he may learn that many of the

> Supervised gyms, staffed with trained, trusted professionals, are best for young athletes.

weight lifters use performance-enhancing drugs. Sadly, the culture of the gym often doesn't challenge this behavior. Instructors there are typically big and strong and help others achieve the same results. Thus many of those in charge will look the other way when steroid use comes up. Parents should be aware of the culture of a particular gym. Supervised gyms, staffed with trained, trusted professionals, are best for young athletes. Based on the three-step approach, this is part of knowing a child's sports environment.

How our kids take steroids is also worrisome. Oral steroids are often taken at high dosages because of a "more is better" rationale, though this heavy use can lead to liver damage. Alternatively, steroids can be taken through shots into the muscle, which pose additional risks, including infections transmitted through dirty needles, since injections are not monitored by health professionals. HIV or hepatitis can be spread by such needle use.

Male steroid users like Adam are typically vulnerable to a host of problems, such as low self-esteem, high incidence of depression and suicide attempts, and high rates of eating disorders and substance abuse. They are also more likely to participate in sports that value weight and have parents who are concerned about weight.[15] Though Adam has never attempted suicide, he has a history of untreated depression fueled by a poor self-image. Since he has joined the local gym, he has not abused substances other than steroids, but he is noticing how readily available other drugs are. By using steroids, he may be more likely to develop a dependency on other danger-ous drugs.[16]

Steroid use is more prevalent than most people realize. Some studies suggest that more than one million people use steroids in the United States. Once athletes start using them, it may be hard to stop.[17]

For high school boys, a powerful deterrent is finding out that steroid use stunts growth in terms of height and healthy development of organs. Parents of a 14-year-old son like Adam, who is interested in building his body, can remind him to think twice about using steroids because they may have the exact opposite effect of what he hopes to gain from them. Unfor-tunately, most adolescents are unaware of this fact.

Rather, they see that the short-term effects of steroid use are enticing. Steroid users grow stronger and become more aggressive. They experience improved sports performance and confidence. They also feel more positive about their body image. Despite the long-term risks to health, the short-term boosts are powerfully attractive.

Going to the gym can be a risk factor for initiating steroid use. Some gyms are a central location for body building and steroid use. Steroid users need to lift weights to build muscle; they can't see significant effects without training. Therefore, gyms attract individuals who share an interest in build-ing muscle, and some use steroids to accomplish this. While this does not mean that parents shouldn't allow their teen to lift weights, it does mean that they should be mindful of their son's behavior. For example, Adam's parents may feel less worried about their son if he is working out at the school gym under the supervision of familiar coaches rather than at gyms where no one is watching out for his best interest.

In reacting to the growing use of steroids in professional and amateur sports peaking in the spring of 2005, Dr. Nora Volkow, director of the Na-tional Institute on Drug Abuse (NIDA), expressed her strong beliefs about the dangers of steroid use:

> Let me be clear: while anabolic steroids can enhance certain types of performance or appearance, they are dangerous drugs, and when used inappropriately, they can cause a host of severe, long-lasting, and often irreversible negative health consequences. These drugs can stunt the height of growing adolescents, masculinize women, and alter sex char-acteristics of men. Anabolic steroids can lead to premature heart at-

tacks, strokes, liver tumors, kidney failure and serious psychiatric problems. In addition, because steroids are often injected, users risk contracting or transmitting HIV or hepatitis.[18]

Adam's parents decide to consult with their family doctor after noticing their son's increased muscle mass and irritability. They learn that they were right to be concerned about such a significant change in his appearance and his mood. The doctor confirmed that these are typical signs of steroid use, so Adam's parents decide to discuss the matter with him.

In a heated discussion, Adam at last admits that he has used one cycle of steroids in the beginning of the summer. Adam's parents forbid him to go on taking steroids and discuss steps to get him help. Together they decide to consult with a sports nutritionist to help Adam review healthier ways to build his body and also set up an appointment to meet with a counselor to explore questions like these: Why doesn't Adam have a stronger belief in himself? Do issues in his family life, school relationships, or social interactions contribute to a negative view of himself? Though he wants to compete in sports and his limited size is an obstacle, why did he choose steroids to bulk up, placing himself at risk of serious physical and mental health consequences?

In sessions with the therapist and after a few family meetings, Adam's parents learn that he has always felt inadequate both in school and in sports. His average grades have not drawn positive or negative attention from his parents; he seems to fall between the cracks in contrast to his older sister, who is praised for her academic achievements. Adam has always been envious of her talent and stellar grades. His desperation to find an activity to attract positive attention from peers, coaches, and family in part fueled his decision to use steroids. He wants to be noticed and valued.

Approximately 10 percent of steroid users become violent.

Moved by their son's struggles, Adam's parents make an effort to become more involved in his life. They support his attendance at counseling sessions and occasionally check in with the sports nutritionist to ensure that Adam is eating and exercising in healthy ways. Although Adam does not make the football team his freshman year, he hears about openings on the water polo team and decides to try out. Although he continues to go to the gym frequently, his parents are less concerned that he is using steroids because his mood has improved and he has begun to develop new friendships.

These types of positive outcomes are not always the case. It's no surprise that many incidents of adolescent steroid use go unnoticed and undetected. Some of our kids will experiment briefly for a season or two and then never use this substance again. For this reason, it is important that we and our children are educated about steroid use and its dangerous risks. Unfortunately, some of our kids don't realize these risks until it's too late. They may be laying the foundation for long-term health problems. As we have mentioned, they may get involved in serious drug abuse, and in some cases, become dangerously violent or suicidal.

As our athletic children train their minds and bodies to compete in sports at the junior high school through college levels, we have to be aware of their vulnerabilities. We need to be aware of their eating and training patterns. We need to explore with them what their friends are doing to lose weight or build muscle. We need to watch out for warning signs like depression, irritability, quick changes in weight, acne, and skin color changes among many other symptoms. While it's difficult to keep up with the most recent weight loss medications, trendy supplements, and newly developed steroids that are readily available to our kids, we can stay on top of how our kids are functioning in this increasingly competitive sports world. We need to remind our kids that no matter how they perform, they are valued for who they are as opposed to what mountain they climb.

15

Tips for Top Performance
The Art of Being SHARPP

We have developed a series of tips that will help all children in sports improve, whether they are all-star athletes or temporarily sitting on the bench. For our children to acquire a consistent sense of personal achievement and enjoyment, they must develop good character habits along with fitness, strength, and sports skills. Over the years we have developed a way to help kids, parents, and coaches join together in their desire to win yet build character. We have found that to teach children good character habits there must be clear, concrete behaviors that represent the higher-level conceptual ideals such as justice, moderation, and compassion. The acronym *SHARPP* denotes this program, initially developed for the Savin Hill Little League in Boston. The SHARPP method can be used by any parent or coach to guide young athletes in sports.

The SHARPP Approach

The behavioral expectations of the Savin Hill Little League are encapsulated in the components of SHARPP:

Be SHARPP	
Play with	**S**PIRIT
Always	**H**USTLE
Pay	**A**TTENTION
Be	**R**ESPECTFUL
Be	**P**OSITIVE
	PRACTICE, PRACTICE, PRACTICE!

256

Playing with spirit reminds parents, coaches, and players that sports are to be fun. Bringing spirit to the game ensures that kids experience passion and joy. Competition can bring out the best performance and teach many things, but the first rule should be "I play the game because I love to play." Though this concept may seem basic, it is devastating how many young athletes are not playing because they love it. They play for the hope of scholarships; to please their parents, friends, or coaches; to be popular; to get into college; or simply because their identity is so wrapped up in the sport that they cannot imagine themselves doing anything else. It is possible to either hold tightly to the love of playing or to reclaim it. Most kids began a sport because they thought that playing or competing was fun. It is important to encourage our kids when they simply play with enthusiasm. And unquestionably, playing with spirit — passion and love for the sport — is one of the ways to give the athlete the best chance of optimizing performance.

Always hustle means players must try their best in any situation and demonstrate the love of participation whether they feel like it or not. Developing the habit of hustle shows respect for the sport, the players, and everyone else involved — coaches, parents, referees, and spectators. As parents we can encourage our children to think, or aspire to thinking, "I give my best at all times!" This can be a point of pride regardless of what the scoreboard says.

Pay attention means players must listen to the coach by remaining quiet, with eyes focused on him or her. In a game, it means that players watch the ball and focus on their task. The first rule of becoming competent in any endeavor is to pay attention. Athletes can be encouraged to think, "I keep my eyes on the prize and the task at hand" and "I give full attention to the game (rather than be distracted by my thoughts or others around me)." Paying attention at all times is challenging even for successful veteran players. Children can learn to do this incrementally but will need encouragement. Attentiveness represents the good character habits of self-control and integrity.

Be respectful means players take care of the athletic field, the equipment, and their own bodies. Umpires and opponents are to be treated with respect. Players shake hands in victory or defeat, which represents the spirit of good sportsmanship. Training properly, eating nutritious food, staying away from harmful substances, and treating injuries with care show respect for the body. Coaches deserve respect as teachers and mentors in sports; referees and umpires deserve respect as protectors of fairness and safety; opponents deserve respect as coparticipants in the game. The game itself as well as school, community, and fans merit respect. Without these peoples' contributions to the game, no one could play. Therefore, they deserve appreciation and respect. With this approach, everyone feels supported and can give the game their best. Players might say to themselves, "I give respect to get respect. I am grateful for the opportunity to play."

Be positive means that players learn that sports involve both success and failure. They must overcome failure, learn from losses and adversity, and improve without dwelling on shortcomings, their own mistakes, or the mistakes of others. They must learn that staying angry will not help anyone play better; it's more effective to shift into a constructive approach. Searching for the lesson to be taken from setbacks and striving resiliently to improve are the key to playing with grace and joy. Players might say to themselves, "I'll give it my best shot, no matter what" and "I can play this game."

Practice, practice, practice! There is no substitute for working at getting better. Our children need to learn to practice well and practice hard to improve in any endeavor. Athletes tend to perform in the way that they practice; therefore it is critical to practice with full focus on the task at hand. The old adage "practice makes perfect" holds true in sports; long-term improvement comes only from hard work. Joy in sports is the product of fitness, improved technique, and working as an individual or as a unit, and these are attained through practice. Kids might remind themselves, "I work hard at my game."

The concept of SHARPP, when implemented, allows kids to merge with the games or practice — free of dread, worry about outcome, and excessive pressure from others. They can fully engage in the activity that they love. This type of training helps simultaneously develop top-level performance and good character habits.

DEALING WITH DISTRACTIONS

Distractions may consist of feeling physically tired or sore, worrying about what an opponent or coach said (or didn't say), obsessing about who is playing in which position at a particular moment in a game or match, or trying to meet the expectations of a parent or coach. Athletes must learn to deal with or put aside a variety of distractions.

These preoccupations may be physical, emotional, social, or mental in nature. Physically, a player might be bothered by not having enough to eat prior to competition, being too thin or overweight, or a nagging minor injury.

Social distractions are a big challenge for our children, particularly adolescents, to overcome. They are hypersensitive to the opinions of friends, teammates, and coaches. And whether they overtly demonstrate it or not, they are also very aware of parental expectations and hopes. All types of parental behavior — from quietly watching games to screaming from the sidelines — can distract a child from optimizing sports performance. The hard part is that our children are not necessarily responding to what we actually want or think; they are responding to how they evaluate what we want: it is their perception of us that counts. For example, you may try staying away to give them personal space and not put pressure on them, and they may interpret the lack of presence as meaning you don't truly love them. To deal with this, parents can directly talk with their child about how the parent's level of involvement makes the child feel.

> Currently, the most damaging and prevalent emotional distraction in sports is fear of failure.

Emotional distractions include a wide array of negative, disempowering feelings that arise from physical, social, or even self-created mental problems in sports. Triggers may include a fight with a boyfriend, an argument with a parent, significant disappointment in a recent performance, or dread regarding an upcoming competition. Fear, anxiety, and lack of inspiration can have adverse effects on the ability to focus on the game, getting in the way of doing one's best and enjoying the process.

Currently, the most damaging and prevalent emotional distraction in sports is fear of failure. Many of our children worry about what will happen if they are not successful. This causes their bodies to tighten up, a physical effect referred to as "bracing." This gets in the way of doing their best.

Mental distraction, interdependent with the other types already mentioned, can be described as any thought that takes attention away from thinking about how to practice or perform well. A common source of mental distraction, particularly for postadolescent athletes, is negative assessment of ability, potential, self, or performance. Concern about how the competition might play out is another typical preoccupation.

Rebecca: Determining the Causes of Distraction

Rebecca, a star basketball player, is coping with all types of distractions. A first-year high school student who is a starter for her varsity high school basketball team, Rebecca has been doing great for the first few games but then begins to pass out on the court. After a number of physicians tell her that no physical explanation exists for her fainting spells, she turns to sport psychology to figure out if psychological issues are causing her to collapse physically. It soon becomes clear that a prominent physical distraction is affecting her. When she feels pressure, she does not eat on the day of competition because she simply is not hungry, and eating makes her feel worse. Of course, during the game she feels a lack of physical energy. One intervention that she undertakes immediately is to determine what type of food she actually can eat when feeling nervous and to keep this food on hand.

Rebecca is also experiencing serious family troubles. Her divorced parents still spend quite a bit of time together and consequently argue a lot. Rebecca finds these almost weekly blowouts very stressful. Her fainting episodes typically happen a day or two after a big fight between her parents. In addition, as a freshman starting player on a varsity team, Rebecca feels the jealousy of certain upperclassmen — especially those who sit on the bench as Rebecca plays. And finally, because her family is less well off financially than those of her classmates at the private school that she attends, Rebecca also consistently feels like an outsider. These social and emotional distractions make it hard to focus on the game.

Rebecca also experiences mental distractions. She often finds herself thinking about whether she will pass out and dwelling on other people's expectations of her. Together, her preoccupations can make her feel anxious and lonely.

Rebecca eventually makes a radical shift in how she deals with this troubling situation and puts a stop to the fainting episodes. She learns how to become aware of distractions and how to prevent them from ruining her ability to participate and shine in her sport. Her parents and coach used the following tips to help Rebecca make progress.

Tips for Handling Distractions

TIP 1: Help children become aware of their DISTRACTION. Awareness and refocusing on the sport itself can help improve performance.

Most kids don't realize that something is distracting them or know how to deal with it. The answer is to think about doing the sport better. For example, the swimmer needs to think about how to swim better in terms of technique and confidence. Words that depict how they want to swim — such as "powerful," "smoother," "easy" — can be repeated mentally to pull concentration away from distraction and back to the task at hand.

TIP 2: Help children use FOCUSED THOUGHTS to become aware of negative thinking and replace it with empowering thinking.

Our kids may need help to become aware of their negative interpretations of a given situation. Once aware of negative thoughts, they can then learn to replace them with encouraging and supportive ideas. For example, a tennis player worried about windy weather might automatically think, "This sucks! It's impossible to control this stupid ball in these crazy wind blasts. I'm going to play like shit today." This type of thinking sets up the athlete to play poorly. A more constructive way of thinking is this: "It's really windy out. It will be fun to see how well I can place the ball with this crazy wind. Whoever can focus better will probably win." Parents and coaches can help children reframe their thinking in similar ways. Even a subtle change in wording can make thinking more positive. For example, a child who has trouble catching the ball might think to herself, "Don't drop the ball this time!" But the wording "I can catch it" is more likely to yield good results because it accentuates capability and confidence. Parents who have knowledge and experience in a particular sport and know that their child enjoys receiving feedback from them (back to Know Yourself and Know Your Child) can be most helpful at framing positive mental statements. For example, a parent could say, "Everyone is dealing with the wind. Just focus on one point at a time, and keep your eye on the ball. Just make a game out of who can handle the wind better."

Here are further examples of how to turn negative thinking into positive thinking:

NEGATIVE THOUGHT	POSITIVE, EMPOWERING THOUGHT
"I want to give up. I hate being behind."	"I've worked hard for this. I'll push through and make myself proud."
"I'll never be as strong or as fast as she is!"	"I'm doing my best and getting stronger every day."
"I can't win so I might as well not try."	"I'm getting better and better."

Furthermore, our kids must believe that reframed thought is true; otherwise the positive self-talk won't work. Through practice they will gain examples of how this strategy can work for them. Parents and coaches can review these examples if kids start to doubt the power of their positive thoughts. It can be helpful to model working through negative thoughts with our kids. If we are able to become aware of our own negative thoughts and practice shifting them — and share this process with our kids — they might be more open to trying the strategy themselves.

TIP 3: Help children use mistakes and failures as opportunities to improve.

Many of our kids in sports assess their competitive performance in a negative way, often in comparison to their teammates. The sports world has trained our kids to judge performance in terms of what is wrong with it so that they can improve — a wonderful thing. With this habit of assessment our kids can learn from their mistakes. However, this habit can backfire if our kids focus on only what is wrong, forgetting to take the next step and use the mistake as a learning tool. Helping the young athlete become aware of this pattern of thinking is the way to start. Then teaching kids to value their mistakes as doors to further skill development can translate into great leaps forward in athletic performance. Instead of getting stuck in the drama of having made an embarrassing play, they can gain insight into how to improve.

TIP 4: Help children use positive images to picture how they would like to perform.

Young athletes up through adolescence generally have amazing ability to create mental imagery that can be used to visualize and rehearse skills and techniques. When asked to recall one of their best experiences in sport, most athletes can almost relive it. Jessyca, a high school swimmer, could immediately recall and imagine her best swim meet. When asked to describe what she was seeing in her imagination, she said, "My strokes are long. I feel really strong in the water. I feel confident that I'll do well. I'm ahead. I feel a good rhythm . . . it was a great race!" Many children can even recapture sounds,

> If our children can get in the habit of learning from their failures or mistakes, their performance and enjoyment will be greatly enhanced.

smells, and emotions as they mentally replay a given event. This technique can be improved with practice.

Our kids who can visualize how they would like to perform or how it would look and feel to acquire a new skill are more likely to achieve their goals. It can be beneficial to imagine how they would like to feel and what they would like to think while competing in sports. If they play these personal "mind videos" only a few moments a day, it can help sports performance in real life. However, young athletes often waste this natural ability or unwittingly use it to their disadvantage. Some kids spend time imagining how their performance will go wrong. Few of our children actually spend time dreaming about achieving their best.

Adult mentors and parents can encourage children to mentally rehearse how they want to perform and to remember and talk about participating in their sport when they performed well and really enjoyed it. Have them describe the experience, using as many of the senses as possible (sight, smell, sound, touch). The more they imagine an optimal experience throughout competition — not just winning at the end — the better chance they have of achieving their best.

TIP 5: Help children to set daily goals to maximize chances of success.

Goal setting can be helpful to all athletes. Short-term goals — those that can be achieved today — are especially productive because goals that are set for a time too far away can seem unreal and lack motivational power. The best way to learn is to set an achievable task to accomplish today.

Most kids have no understanding of or experience in goal setting. The acronym *SMART* can help remind them of important aspects of goal setting. First, goals should be *specific*. Setting the goal of running a mile in eight minutes is more specific than simply planning to run faster. Second, goals should be *measurable* so that children know exactly what they are striving for and whether they attain it. Running a mile in eight minutes is a measurable goal — it is objective and stipulates results that are observable.

Third, goals need to be *adjustable*. Sports present many surprises — from unexpected quick success to disappointing injuries or being cut from teams. Helping our children adjust their goals when they are struggling with pressure or boredom can help them achieve a balance of just enough but not too much challenge. This can inspire them to be fully engaged without fear of failure.

TIP 6: Help children learn to control temper and emotions.

Negative emotions, such as anxiety, dread, fear, and hopelessness, can ruin our children's athletic experience. Taking our children's emotional experience seriously is critical; it can be tempting to dismiss our kids' feelings and tell them how they ought to feel or respond to a sports situation. This treatment can inflame negative emotions and make the child feel resentful and ashamed. By contrast, adults' empathy can help them relax and learn how to cope with an explosive temper, embarrassment, or frustration. This begins with listening to and respecting the child's reported emotions.

For example, if a child feels dread before a Little League game, it is important for adults to acknowledge and try to understand that fear. Then the parent or coach can suggest alternative ways of facing the challenge at hand, such as taking a few deep breaths to slow down and regain focus. Paying attention to kids' emotions before helping them develop different responses is essential. We as parents also need to remind our children that we love and care for them regardless of their sports performance.

TIP 7: Encourage children to focus on playing the game, not on what others think.

A major distraction for our kids at all levels of play is concern for what others think. Many children are obsessed with how their coach might evaluate them or how a parent might assess their performance, and they can't focus on playing the game. It is more constructive, however, to concentrate on things that they can control, such as the effort to build skills, fitness, and strength. Kids won't be able to control what others think or say about them, though parents can help them through difficult times when they deal with criticism or teasing. By being open and available to our kids to talk, we can help them make sense of these hard moments and help them learn how to overcome them.

TIP 8: Teach children how to strive for moderation and integrity in sports.

Striking a balance is hard—typically, our kids are either not trying hard enough or sacrificing themselves body and soul for sports. The sports culture seems to encourage extreme behaviors, which can put the child athlete's body, mind, and heart in danger.

The challenge of being asked to push themselves to extremes must be taken seriously. Some coaches will push groups of athletes extensively in hopes that the top few survivors will produce for them. When considering whether a coach is pushing your child too hard, it is important to again consider your child's interests and abilities. When athletes are asked to push too hard for extensive periods of time, this can lead to burnout and either a significant reduction in enjoyment to ultimately dropping out of sports. This is where the Aristotelian idea of moderation can shed light on

The sports culture seems to encourage extreme behaviors, which can put the child athlete's body, mind, and heart in danger.

the right amount of exercise and training. Moderation refers to the right amount and right degree of action. This rightness can vary, depending on a child's motivation, physical make up, and talent. If a child is getting injured, expressing significantly less interest in playing, or demonstrating a change in personality, a change may be in order. A serious conversation may reveal whether the child needs a different team or coach or a break from sports participation. The child's experience may have been too intense.

Lack of investment is another sign of imbalance. Sometimes children who are gifted or simply not challenged in sports won't give it their all. They may need to be involved in a sport that better captures their interest or may need to compete at a higher level. On the other hand, they may simply need some encouragement to motivate them to try harder and give more. Often if a parent emphasizes doing one's best — giving it the best shot — it is enough. Children are freed up to engage and play their best.

When our kids are learning to do their best, personal integrity is important. For example, the intensity of a workout should be the same whether others are watching or not. The goal for a race should be to do one's best, whether the race will be close or not. Stressing the importance of this idea can help children demonstrate integrity in hard moments when they don't feel like pushing themselves. In the same vein, it takes integrity for a young athlete to step away from practice or competition when injured and take time to heal from injury. Courage is needed to demonstrate respect for one's body consistently, whether others are watching or not.

TIP 9: Encourage children to face and accept fears and to accept failure in order to achieve success.

Many of our children fear what will happen if they don't do well. When kids spend time and energy worrying about what will happen if they don't achieve success, it can be helpful to remind them that they will survive regardless of how they compete. The fear of failure can also be defused by confirming to children that they are worthy, good people, whether or not they meet some mark of success in sports.

If a child has a particular fear, such as not making a team, parents might suggest that he or she spend a little time thinking about how to handle negative consequences such as social embarrassment and personal feelings of disappointment. Eventually the child will realize that though it may be difficult, he or she can handle the heartache and get over it — ready to focus afresh on a new athletic goal. Thus acceptance of failure can free kids to imagine new possibilities and goals.

TIP 10: Support that idea that "your best is good enough" to help children establish compassion for themselves.

Today the belief that only winning counts extends to athletes at a very tender age. When you see 6-year-old kids crying at the end of a soccer game because they lost, you know something is wrong. Though parents cannot single-handedly change the ideals of today's sports culture, they can give their kids the message that their best is good enough. A child who fully embraces this idea experiences the joy of participation in sports. Many problems in athletics today stem from players' unwillingness to put aside the notion that they must be the best or it just isn't worth participating. The idea of winning has overtaken the importance of friendship, fitness, strength, and the celebration of the ability to move physically and learn continually.

We as parents can help our children believe that doing one's best is the best! This attitude confers freedom from emotional and mental distractions. It also promotes compassion for oneself. We as parents can reinforce the link between best effort and compassion with appreciative statements like these: "Son, I'm so proud of you. You've made such great progress in such a short amount of time. You'll make me proud as long as you do the best that you can out there!"

> Many children fear what will happen if they don't do well.

In sports our children learn to respect and appreciate their bodies and learn how to become physically and muscularly fit. Our kids can learn how to control their emotions and how to develop excellent focus. Yet also in sports, terrible habits can become ingrained, from taunting others to purposely hurting them. No matter what their age, our kids need us. They need our guidance and our unconditional love. We need to remind them that they matter, not because of how high they can jump or how fast they can run, but because they are human, our special beloved ones. Our love and attention form the foundation for them as they learn to be good people, allow themselves to be passionate and dedicated, develop the ability to persevere, and form the habit of integrity and maintain it whether others are watching or not. Our kids will forever look to us to help them make sense of what they are going through. They care deeply about everything we say and do. We can use this amazing influence to help them do the very best that they can on the field and in their lives.

16

Questions and Answers

Finding Solutions for Kids' Dilemmas in Sports

OUR BEST TEACHERS are parents. The following is a series of questions raised by parents during our talks and workshops. The answers offer general guidelines for parents to consider as they address the challenges that emerge as children of all ages participate in sports.

STARTING SPORTS AT A YOUNG AGE

Q: *I have a 2-year-old boy. I take him to tennis lessons once a week. He cries and complains about going every time. Once he's there, he does really well for about twenty minutes, but for the second twenty minutes he doesn't like it. Am I crazy to make him do this? What should I do?*

A: Early exposure to sports is much less of a problem than premature pressure. It's always hard to know how much to encourage a child. Perhaps it is best to limit this boy's playing time to twenty minutes and see if his attitude improves. If parents can find a way to encourage a child like this one to persevere just a little bit, then it might be worth trying that for a while. However, if the boy continues to challenge his parents at each lesson, it might be a message to back off a little, give him a break, and perhaps try again a month or two later.

A child's development can be unpredictable. One day he may resist tennis but on the next may want to try again. The key is to make his experience in sports joyous and fun, with an emphasis on safety, a positive connection with parents, and an opportunity to explore physical activity.

EARLY SPECIALIZATION

Q: *I have a 5-year-old daughter who takes gymnastics once a week. She has a really intense coach who loves her. He pulled me aside the other day and said that he thinks my daughter has great talent. He wants her to practice three times a week and once on the weekend. I wasn't an athlete in a competitive way. My husband and I aren't really sure what to do. She seems to like this activity, but we worry that it might be too much for her.*

A: As we have mentioned earlier, the sports culture has embraced the notion that early specialization is necessary to future athletic success, particularly in sports such as gymnastics, ice skating, and hockey. However, no empirical evidence supports this idea. Therefore parents need to make a judgment call. If the girl increases the number of her weekly practices, she may risk losing time to relax, play, and rest each day. She may become tired and eventually burn out. Other possible negative consequences include poorly developed friendships outside sports and academic struggles later on. On the other hand, she may greatly enjoy the friendships she makes on the team and the feelings of competence she gains from practicing and competing. Parents need to protect the long-term development of their child as sports involvement intensifies. Is she having fun? Does she have friends? Is she doing okay in school? Does she have time to relax and be a kid? Does she really want to practice more? Answering these questions may target problems early.

> Sometimes the rush to become great has the opposite effect.

To give the coach's idea a try, the parents might increase the girl's weekly practices by one day and see how she handles it. If she is not having fun, she will likely complain or quit. And if she really wants to practice more, she may announce this to her parents herself. It's always better to err on the side of caution with younger children. Sometimes the rush to practice and become great has the opposite effect.

ARE TEAM SPORTS ESSENTIAL FOR ALL CHILDREN?

Q: *I have a 5-year-old boy. Because his father works long hours, my parents have been telling me that I need to teach the boy how to throw a* *ball. But when we talk about this with him, he gets tense. He doesn't have great hand-eye coordination, but he is having fun in other sports. Should we make a concerted effort to teach him how to throw? We worry that he might get teased or miss out on opportunities in recess in the future if he doesn't learn now.*

A: Given the prevalence of teasing among children, it's no surprise that parents are concerned about it. Some adults recall the horror of being picked last for teams at recess and how this damaged their self-esteem. Though they hope to prevent this from happening to their children, sometimes it is inevitable. Yet it is not clear why this boy feels tense about catching and throwing. Perhaps he feels concern because his family keeps bringing it up or he worries about his inability to catch and throw. Most likely it's a combination of both.

The good news for this boy is that he has competencies in different sports, which gives him ways to feel good about himself physically. Forcing him to catch and throw when he is anxious or not interested is typically not the best route. A better alternative would be to ask indirectly about baseball and throwing. Ask him what kids do in recess and see how he feels about it. Be open to spontaneous play around the house in which things can be caught or thrown without triggering the tension and anxiety the boy might feel at school. The home environment can be a safe haven for him to experiment with sports skills without being judged.

This boy is still quite young and may be ready to learn to throw a bit later. However, if he never learns to throw well, his parents can remind him of what he does do well and encourage him to remember this at school or recess. A little more opportunity to play spontaneously with his father would not hurt either. Fathers might decrease the

> A boy can be a winner on a losing team if he sees improvement in his skills.

pressure to perform by welcoming the chance to simply enjoy themselves: "Hey there, kiddo, you don't have to be a great baseball player. But it might be really fun if you and I could play some catch and throw . . . just the two of us. We'll play for a few minutes and then we'll go visit Mommy and Grandma at the house."

Some boys may respond well to this kind of approach; others may feel pressured by it. Knowing the child's temperament can help a parent select the best path. And while challenging a son or daughter to try hard, the parent can stress values such as effort and experimentation rather than pushing for a particular outcome.

Winning and Losing

Q: *My 7-year-old son really loves the Red Sox, and every time they lose he gets incredibly upset. How do I teach him about winning and losing?*

A: Since the authors of this book are avid Red Sox fans, we can understand having passion for the team. If this boy's mother and father are avid fans as well, he might watch their reaction to inform his own. What has this boy learned from his parents about winning and losing? Which other role models show him how to deal with losing? Answering these questions is the first step. If the parents of this boy express anger and discontent in reaction to loss, their child may learn to respond similarly. If a parent is unhappy, the child senses it as well, which may create some anxiety. Losing may seem unbearable not only because his team loses but also because his parents become agitated.

Second, as mentioned earlier, 7-year-old children are just beginning to embrace the concept of competition. As they navigate the developmental stage of latency from 6 through 12 years of age, they learn new skills and make friends. Like many adults who watch the Red Sox, they may identify with the successes and failures of their team. When the Red Sox win, this boy may feel great. When they lose, he may feel bad, as if he were a player on the team. It is important to acknowledge and even share with him this disappointment: "Yeah, I was really sad they lost too. How do you feel about it? What do you think they could have done better?" After a brief commiseration, the next step might be to help the boy recognize the achievements of the team, such as effort, focus, and fun, even in the face of defeat. This effort can reframe the idea of loss. Surely it is okay to be disappointed, but what did the team accomplish? What can they learn from the loss? Parents can create a learning experience to teach this boy how to manage and overcome adversity.

Sports offer wonderful teaching tools like this one. The stakes are not very high because the competition is just a game; however, children take games seriously and gain valuable lessons from what they learn and observe in play.

PLAYING ON A LOSING TEAM

Q: *My 11-year-old child is playing for a team that always loses. What do I say to him to keep his spirits high?*

A: Parents need to help their children redefine what it means to be a winner. Of course, it is no fun to lose all the time; no one plays to lose the game, and it is important for parents to acknowledge the disappointment involved in losing. When someone wins, it often confirms his or her ability and capacity to be competent; similarly, losing can raise doubt about a person's competence.

However, as we discussed in Chapter 12, a losing team is not necessarily an unsuccessful team. Eleven-year-old boys are most concerned about improving skills and having good relationships with teammates; therefore, this boy can be a winner on a losing team if he sees improvement in his skills. Parents can also help children on losing teams by praising their attitude in the face of disappointment: "Son, I am very proud of you because no matter the score, you give your best effort and treat your teammates and opponents fairly. Just keep doing this, and you'll see the benefits for the rest of your life." As we've mentioned before, difficulties and setbacks in sports provide wonderful teaching opportunities. Praising values in the face of losing can be a great boost to a young boy. And he won't always play on teams that lose. This season will give him some perspective about how to be a respectful competitor because he knows the humility gained from losing.

PROBLEMS WITH COACHES

Q: *My 11-year-old daughter plays for a bad coach who isn't fair about playing time. My husband and I think we should pull her from the team. Is this a good idea?*

A: Certainly bad coaches exist, but more often, good people have bad coaching moments or tendencies. Most coaches, whether they are volunteer or paid, enjoy working with kids and coaching sports. Identifying the good in a coach is an important step toward finding a way to approach him or her in a positive manner, particularly when the main objective is to register a complaint. A parent might say, "Look, I really appreciate your knowledge of this sport and your dedication to the kids, but . . ." As we discussed earlier, a parent who plans to confront a coach needs to recognize that coaches are sensitive too. Their jobs involve constant public exposure, and it's not easy to manage a large group of children whose parents watch closely. Appreciating this vulnerability may help get the conversation started on a more positive note.

However, in some situations it is difficult to find anything positive about a coach. Parents may worry that the experience is damaging to their child. If chronic intense criticism or issues regarding a child's safety exist, pulling the child out of the program may be necessary.

> A parent who plans to confront a coach needs to recognize that coaches are sensitive too.

If the child is a teenage athlete, the first step may be to encourage the athlete to approach the coach and ask what he or she can do to have a better experience on the team. If the coach is not responsive, the player may then ask the athletic administrator for assistance. If this does not work, then it would be appropriate for the parents to get involved. This process is important because it allows the teenage athlete to address problems independently, a skill he or she will need later in life.

For parents of younger children, a good option is to set up a meeting with the coach away from the athletic field and in the privacy of an office. Even if a lot of problems exist, a parent might say, "We really value having our daughter in sports. And we are grateful for the opportunity to have her play in this league. However, we have some concerns, and we need to know from you how to address them. She's just not playing very often, and we're wondering if there is anything we or she can do to improve this situation." If this meeting is not successful, then finding another program may be the best option.

DEALING WITH DIFFICULT PARENTS

Q: *Yesterday at my 12-year-old daughter's hockey game, I sat next to a screaming mother who was driving me nuts. She was so negative and distracting. I didn't know what to do. Should I talk to her?*

A: Parents love their children, but sometimes parents behave badly when they want their kids to do well. Parents can lose perspective especially when they have difficulty separating themselves from the outcome of their child's performance. When their investment becomes too great, bad behavior can follow. Such behavior may range from subtle pressure to yelling or even physical abuse. Other parents who witness such behavior should follow a certain code in dealing with it: physical abuse needs to be reported to the league officials and authorities immediately; violence in sports has to be addressed quickly and taken seriously.

As we discussed earlier, it is challenging, even risky, to confront another parent who is yelling and acting out. People hesitate to interfere in the matters of another family. Yet someone who knows the yelling parent might try to find a quiet moment, perhaps at halftime or well after the game, to talk about the situation. A sport psychologist might say, "I know you want your child to perform at her best. I can see how much you care. But yelling at your daughter seems to have a negative effect. Athletes of all levels and abilities perform best when they feel relaxed and positive. Intense yelling and pressure from coaches or parents often result in poor performance. So if you really want to help your child win, give her positive support and comfort so she can relax and perform her best." Or this message might be phrased more informally: "Wow, your kid is really great. You can tell that when she feels confident, she seems to play her best. She's just like my kid, and it's the strangest thing. The second my daughter starts to get down on herself, she starts to play worse. I try to cheer her on, but it gets hard after a while, if you know what I mean. I really enjoy watching your daughter. I'll keep cheering for her."

Allying with, instead of alienating, the parent can result in a positive interaction. This is, however, more difficult to manage if the parent is not a friend or acquaintance. In these circumstances, it may be hard to do anything. One possibility is to encourage another parent who knows the person to discuss the issue; informing the site administrator of the problem is another option.

Overtraining and Overplaying

Q: *My 13-year-old boy plays soccer three times per week and also plays in two hockey leagues. He seems to enjoy it, but I worry that it's too much. How do we know when we need to cut back?*

A: This question raises an issue that can be especially difficult for parents. On the one hand, they want to expose their kids to as many sports as possible so they have positive experiences and find the sports they love to play. On the other hand, they want them to specialize so they have the opportunity to become great in one sport, which may provide a scholarship or acceptance to a college farther down the road.

As we have discussed earlier, playing different sports has many advantages. Kids can make a lot of friends. They can learn how to deal with different coaches and coaching styles. They can develop athletically by learning a variety of skills in different contexts. Such diversity in skill and experience can be of benefit later if they choose to focus on one sport. This child may become a more effective scorer in hockey because of his years of playing soccer, a sport that requires great field vision and persistence in attacking the goal. Similarly, the aggressiveness, speed, and passing sequences in hockey will help him become a tougher, more intelligent soccer player. Tennis stars such as Boris Becker and John McEnroe were former soccer players. Some argue that the conditioning, leg strength, and athleticism gained from soccer made them better tennis players. On the other hand, playing two sports at once may be too much for a child.

Unfortunately, some parents overload their children with too many sports. Some kids are playing on two, three, or even four different teams. They become exhausted or, worse yet, get hurt. It's worth considering a rule that limits kids to one sport per season. Sometimes a little overlap occurs between seasons, but in general this rule protects the child's time, body, and spirit. Playing one sport per season, or four sports per year, allows for plenty of exposure to different games and skills. This guideline also protects the sanity of parents.

Setting this limit may involve saying no to other parents and coaches, and this can be very difficult. Parents worry that their kids will simply miss out. They won't get the training they need and will

It's worth considering a rule that limits kids to one sport per season.

feel bored by spending more time at home. Parents may also miss out socially by not attending games and other functions related to sports their kids don't participate in. They lack interaction with the other moms and dads who support these events. Thus it is important for parents to have a strong sense of their values before the season begins. If family time, schoolwork, and plain old leisure are important to them, they may have to buck the tide of constant overscheduling, which many families give in to.

Yet some parents may go too far in narrowing a kid's scope by having him or her pick one sport and specialize in it year round. This approach has its own risks. As mentioned earlier, no empirical evidence confirms that early specialization leads to better results for young athletes. Rather, a diversity of sports experiences of less intensity offers benefits not available when one sport is the focus. Eventually, young athletes who continue in sports will make their own choices about specialization. For example, a 14-year-old, eighth-grade boy may choose soccer over football because his size and quickness suit soccer. Such decisions emerge over time.

As parents strive to achieve a balance for their kids, they can learn a lot by careful observation. When children start to complain, develop excuses for not going to practice or games, and begin to seem withdrawn or tired, it may be time to reduce sports activities. A decline in academic performance or a reduction in social activity may also be a warning sign. Kids vary in their ability to juggle multiple activities. If a parent suspects that a child is overloaded, it could well be time to cut back.

Too Much Travel?

Q: *My husband is absolutely obsessed with our 14-year-old son's performance in baseball. He coaches him every day, travels with him on weekend tournaments, and talks about baseball all the time with him. Is this too much for my son, and if so, what should I do?*

A: When a spouse or partner is intensely invested in the success of a child, it is extremely difficult to make adjustments. Though this type of parental behavior is becoming more common, its roots are uniquely specific to each family. A parent may have a variety of reasons for behaving this way. He may be an experienced athlete himself who believes that he knows what it will take for his son to succeed. He could be a frustrated athlete who wants his son to excel beyond what he was able to accomplish. He may be a nonathlete who never had success in sports and is experiencing his son's play as therapeutic. Or this father may

> For every Tiger Woods and Serena Williams, there are at least ten children who have burned out or quit a sport in which they were encouraged or forced to specialize.

simply enjoy the experience of being with his son and sharing the camaraderie that comes with involvement in team sports. Often a combination of these factors is at play, making it difficult for a spouse to address potential problems.

A key to the situation is observing the son's reaction to the father's gung-ho attitude: How is this boy handling his father's behavior? Does he seem to enjoy it? Is it becoming apparent that he is feeling pressured by it? The attentions of an overly invested parent, and the energy and pressure the parent may generate can be exhausting to a child. As much as he might enjoy spending time with his dad, the stakes of the game become so high that it becomes emotionally taxing. If this is the case, it is likely that action is needed.

> The disadvantage for some former athletes who become coaches is that they forget what it is like to be a kid.

This boy's mother might consider beginning a conversation with her husband by asking an open-ended question: "Honey, you've been so great with all the coaching you've done with our son. I can see how much he enjoys having you there with him. I am noticing that he seems to be getting tired more frequently, and he's complaining about some of the long trips on the weekends. What do you think would help him get rested up so he can continue to enjoy baseball?"

Some might find this comment too indirect, but because the father is so devoted to baseball, a more direct and demanding interaction like this one might be ineffective: "Honey, I don't know what's gotten into you, but you're driving our son way too hard. He's only 14. This isn't the pros. Why are you pushing him so much?" In response, the father may become defensive, entrenching both parents more deeply in their positions.

Success can be achieved when both parents collaborate to focus on the health of the child: "How do you think our son's doing? Is he getting enough rest? How will we know if he's pushing himself too hard? What should we do if that happens?" This approach prevents taking sides. Instead, parents are on the same side. Also, if parents agree on their family's sports values, it will be easier to navigate the uncertainties that crop up about sports participation. Consulting with a counselor is another option. Rather than make the consultation about parental pressure, focus on helping the child reach peak performance. We have found in our clinical work that ambitious fathers are much more receptive to our help if they feel we are equally concerned about helping their child improve performance. This can also be true with a resistant adolescent. If the adolescent believes that we are acting to improve sports performance, we have more flexibility to talk about broader issues such as balance and parental pressure that affect both performance and psychological well-being. As we have pointed out throughout this book, good performance and healthy psychological development go hand in hand. If we can present health and performance as mutually inclusive, there is more room for negotiating and working through challenging issues for our children in sports.

PARENTS WHO COACH

Q: *I just signed up to coach my son's town rec soccer team. The players are 11–13 years old. I am a former high school athlete. What are the three most important things I should know before starting this coaching position?*

A: Soon-to-be coaches who were former athletes have many advantages. They know how to compete, train, and work with a team. They understand skill development and the importance of confidence and practice. The disadvantage for some former athletes who become coaches is that they may forget what it is like to be a kid — that fun is the absolute most important ingredient in youth sports. They might also forget that the brain of a child is not sophisticated enough to handle adult-level instruction and that many kids of ages 11–13 aren't as competitive as high school athletes. They want to feel good and have fun.

> Create an environment in which kids feel good and have fun.

So the first suggestion is to create an environment in which these kids feel good and have fun. As we have noted earlier, one of the best measures of success for a youth sports program is whether the kids want to play the next season: this should be any youth coach's standard of excellence. If kids want to continue playing, they will gain the skills, friendships, and wonderful experiences that sports offer. In fact, a nonathletic first-time coach who understands the importance of fun will be more successful than the sports guru first-time coach who misses the point of joy in sports for kids.

A second consideration is the league's rulings on playing time and level of competitiveness. Town rec teams for this age group may be more competitive than, say, the program for kids of ages 6–10. Some parents may expect equal playing time for their children; others may want the most talented players to play most of the game. It is important to clarify these parameters before the beginning of the season; an informal meeting with parents can launch a successful season. Make sure parents understand your mission, so you can avoid problems down the road.

Whatever the level of competition, all kids deserve to enjoy playing for a coach who finds meaningful ways for them to contribute to the team. If coaches play only the top players, the bench players may become restless and dissatisfied. Kids want to play; they all deserve this experience. When coaches lose track of this, the less-skilled players and their parents will likely complain.

Last of all, talking to experienced coaches is also a wise move, both for gaining information and enjoying strong peer support.

Sports Injury

Q: *My 17-year-old daughter broke her ankle during the first game of the soccer season. As a senior, she was hoping to have a great season. Now that she is out for the season, college scouts won't be able to see her play. She's miserable. What do we do?*

A: There are several issues to address in this difficult situation. First, it can be overwhelming and scary to experience a season-ending injury. Because adolescents and young adults see themselves as invulnerable, this experience can be destabilizing and disorienting. First and foremost, such athletes need a sense of safety and reassurance. Though a broken ankle is a serious injury, most athletes can recover from it and return to playing if they follow the proper rehab program. Dr. Arthur Boland, an orthopedic surgeon and sports medicine doctor at Massachusetts General Hospital and Harvard Athletics often reassures injured athletes by telling them that throughout a career, an athlete will usually experience at least one major injury and then announce, "And this is your injury." This puts the injury in context and lets athletes know that getting injured is simply a part of playing sports. Such reassuring comments can alleviate an athlete's fear and uncertainty.

Second, this young woman must process a series of losses. Besides losing out on the utter joy of playing the sport she loves, she will also miss the opportunity to impress college scouts. College acceptance is often foremost on the minds of high school children, so this girl will need a lot of support from coaches and parents in recognizing how to handle recruiting. Perhaps she has tapes of past games or reports from her coaches that may help with college admissions. At the same time, her injury undeniably may hurt her chances of being recruited. She may feel legitimate anger at the unfairness of her situation. Giving her space to experience these feelings while helping her see this setback as an opportunity to work through a challenge will help empower her to take back control over her body and make it stronger.

> Some athletes become so identified with playing their sport and being an athlete that they feel lost when they aren't engaged in their sport.

Finally, some athletes become so identified with playing their sport and being an athlete that they feel lost when they aren't engaged in their sport; it's as if they no longer know who they are. In this situation, some athletes cannot tolerate sports events because they remind them of what they are missing. They lose team camaraderie too. Getting this young woman involved in her sport in some meaningful way that she can tolerate may help her. For example, she may assist the coaches during practices and games; she can support her teammates in furthering their success. And she can devote her energy to a rigorous and purposeful rehab that develops strength in different parts of her body, so that when she returns, she will be even stronger. Though this process will not guarantee that she will compete in college, it gives her something to shoot for.

PROBLEMS WITH ALCOHOL

Q: *My 18-year-old son got caught drinking over the weekend. Not only did he break a team rule, but he also betrayed our confidence. Though we have allowed him to have a beer at home, we've clearly stated that we don't want him drinking when he's out over the weekend, particularly when he is driving.*

He's one of the star basketball players on the team, and we wonder whether we should suspend his play for the next week as a punishment. Unfortunately, it's the last week of the season. If the team loses a game, they won't make the tournament. The coach wants to discuss the situation with us. What do we tell him?

A: These parents are correct in wanting to send a strong message to their son, letting him know that he has violated the law, betrayed their trust, and possibly endangered himself or others. When athletes mix alcohol with going out at night, they are tempting fate. To ignore the seriousness of this behavior in order to serve the short-term success of the team is short-sighted and possibly dangerous. While many teammates, and even teammates' parents, may disagree with imposing a suspension, doing so will remind all the boys that this kind of behavior is dangerous and will result in consequences.

Whether the boy should be suspended for one game, two games, or the rest of the season is not easy to decide, however. If this represents the young man's first problem involving alcohol, he will probably learn what happens when he breaks rules and endangers himself if he is given a single-game suspension. When the opportunity arises for him to again break rules or the law, he will be likely to think twice. If this is the second or third infraction, however, then more serious consequences are advised. A suspension for the remainder of the season may well be in order, and consultation with an alcohol counselor, at least so the boy can be evaluated for a more serious problem, is strongly recommended.

Notes

Introduction

1. T. W. Rowland, "Clinical Approaches to the Sedentary Child," in *Exercise and Children's Health* (Champaign, IL: Human Kinetics, 1990), 259–74.
2. E. Michael Jones, *Degenerate Moderns: Modernity as Rationalized Lust* (San Francisco: Ignatius Press, 1993).
3. Philip Cushman, "Why the Self Is Empty," *American Psychologist* 45, no. 3 (1990): 599–611.
4. Kenneth Kaye, *Family Rules: Raising Responsible Children Without Yelling or Nagging* (New York: St. Martin's Press, 1990), 17–18.
5. Richard Ginsburg, "Violence in Youth Sports," *Massachusetts Psychological Association Quarterly* 46, no. 3 (November 2002): 11.

1. Your Child's Development and the Three-Step Approach

1. Jon Finkel, "Athletic Dreams and Demands: Our Kids Want to Compete, but Are We Pushing Them Too Hard?" www.Parenthood.com (2005).
2. Raphael Brandon, "A Fitness Specialist Says: If You're Training Child Athletes, Remember Not to Treat Them as Adults in Miniature," ed. Bob Troop (London: Peak Performance Publishing, 2004), 14.
3. Daniel Siegel and Mary Hartzell, *Parenting from the Inside Out* (New York: Penguin Books, 2003), 4.

2. The Early Years (Ages 1–5)

1. Erik H. Erikson, *Identity: Youth and Crisis* (New York: Norton, 1968).
2. Richie Poulton and Barry J. Milne, "Fearless Children Likely to Shine at Team Sports," *Behavioral Research and Therapy* 40, no. 10 (2002): 1191–97.

3. A. P. Humphries and P. K. Smith, "Rough and Tumble Friendship and Dominance in School Children," *Child Development* 58 (1987): 201–12.
4. Karen Clarke-Stewart, "And Daddy Makes Three: The Father's Impact on Mother and Child," *Child Development* 49 (1978): 466–78.
5. Ibid.

3. THE ELEMENTARY SCHOOL YEARS (AGES 6–12)

1. Brian Mackenzie, "Coaching Young Athletes," *Successful Coaching* 4 (August 2003): 1–2.
2. T. W. Rowland, "Clinical Approaches to the Sedentary Child," in *Exercise and Children's Health* (Champaign, IL: Human Kinetics, 1990).
3. Russell Pate, Stewart Trose, et al., "Sports Participation and Health-Related Behaviors Among U.S. Youth," *Archives of Pediatric and Adolescent Medicine* 154 (September 2000): 904–11.
4. Frank L. Smoll and Ronald E. Smith, *Children and Youth in Sport*, 2nd ed. (Dubuque, IA: Kendall Hunt Publishing, 2002), 57–58.
5. John L. Haubenstricker and Vern Seefeldt, "The Concept of Readiness Applied to the Acquisition of Motor Skills," ibid., 66–71.
6. Jim Thompson, *Positive Coaching: Building Character and Self-Esteem Through Sports* (Portola Valley, CA: Warde Publishers, 1995).
7. Frank L. Smoll, Ronald E. Smith, and N. P. Bartnett, "Reduction of Children's Sport Anxiety Through Social Support and Stress-Reduction Training for Coaches," *Journal of Applied Developmental Psychology* 16 (1995): 125–42.
8. Albert Bandura, *Self-Efficacy: The Exercise of Control* (New York: Freeman, 1997).
9. American Academy of Pediatrics: Committee on Sports Medicine and Fitness, "Intensive Training and Sports Specialization in Young Athletes," *Pediatrics* 106 (July 2000): 156.
10. Ronald E. Smith and Frank L. Smoll, "Coach Effectiveness Training: A Cognitive-Behavioral Approach to Enhancing Relationship Skills in Youth Sport Coaches," *Journal of Sport Psychology* 1 (1979): 59–75.
11. Shane Murphy, *The Cheers and the Tears: A Healthy Alternative to the Dark Side of Youth Sports* (San Francisco: Jossey-Bass, 1999).
12. Roger Reinhardt, "The Outstanding Jet Pilot," *American Journal of Psychiatry* 126, no. 6 (December 1970): 732–36.

5. HIGHER LEARNING AND HIGHER STAKES

1. David Shields and Barbara Bredemeier, *Character Development and Physical Activity* (Champaign, IL: Human Kinetics, 1995).

6. SHOULD WE PUSH OUR CHILDREN? HOW MUCH?

1. G. L. Stein, T. D. Raedeke, and S. D. Glenn, "A Developmental Overview of Child and Youth Sports in Society," *Child and Adolescent Psychiatric Clinics of North America* 7 (1999): 725–44.
2. R. E. Smith and F. L. Smoll, *Way to Go, Coach! A Scientifically Proven Approach to Coaching Effectiveness* (Portola Valley, CA: Warde, 1996); I. R. Toffler, R. Knapp, K. Penelop, M. J. Dell, "The Achievement by Proxy Spectrum in Sports: Historical Perspective and Clinical Approach to Pressure and High-Achieving Adolescents," *Journal of the American Academy of Child and Adolescent Psychiatry* 38 (1999): 213–16.
3. Mary Pipher, *Reviving Ophelia: Saving the Selves of Adolescent Girls* (Toronto: Ballantine, 1995).
4. M. W. Passer and B. J. Wilson, "Motivational, Emotional, and Cognitive Determinants of Children's Age-Readiness for Competition," in *Children and Youth in Sport: A Biopsychosocial Perspective*, ed. F. L. Smith and R. E. Smoll. (Dubuque, IA: Kendal Hunt Publishing Company, 2002), 83–103.
5. Pat Conroy, *My Losing Season* (New York: Doubleday, 2002).

7. WHEN THE APPLE FALLS FAR FROM THE TREE: WHAT TO DO WHEN KIDS' ATHLETIC ABILITIES AND INTERESTS DIFFER FROM OUR OWN

1. D. W. Winnicott, *Home Is Where We Start From: Essays by a Psychoanalyst* (New York/London: Norton; Harmondsworth: Penguin, 1986).

8. BOYS AND GIRLS: SIMILARITIES AND DIFFERENCES IN SPORTS

1. Harvard School of Public Health, "Report Finds Girls Lag Behind Boys in Sports Participation," 2004. Press release. www.hsph.harvard.edu/press/releases/press02032004.html; National Council of Youth Sports, "Report on Trends and Participation in Organized Youth Sport, Stuart, FL," 2001. www.ncys.org.
2. K. Davison, M. Earnest, and L. Birsch, "Participation in Aesthetic Sports and Girls' Weight Concern at Ages 5 and 7 Years," *International Journal of Eating Disorders* 31, (2002): 312–17; K. Robinson and F. Ferraro, "The Relationship Between Types of Female Athletic Participation and Female Body Type," *Journal of Psychology* 138, no. 2 (2004): 115–28; E. Parsons and N. Betz, "The Relationship of Participation in Sports and Physical Activity to Body Objectification, Instrumentality, and Locus of Control Among Young Women,"

Psychology of Women Quarterly 25 (2001): 209–22; L. Smolak, S. Murnen, and A. Ruble, "Female Athletes and Eating Problems: A Meta-analysis," *International Eating Disorder Journal* 27 (2000): 371–80.

3. D. Gardner, A. Naylor, and L. Zaichkowsky, "Drug Use Patterns Among High School Athletes and Non-athletes," *Adolescence* 36 (2001): 627–39.

4. E. E. Maccoby, "Gender and Relationships: A Developmental Account," *American Psychologist* 45, no. 4 (April 1990): 513–20.

5. Ibid.

9. Rage and Explosions

1. Jack Nicklaus (n.d.) *Sports Illustrated.*

2. John McEnroe, *You Cannot Be Serious* (New York: Penguin Putnam, 2002).

11. Does the Coach Know Best?

1. L. A. Festinger, "Theory of Social Comparison Process," *Human Relations,* 7 (1954): 17–140; M. W. Passer and B. J. Wilson, "Motivational, Emotional, and Cognitive Determinants of Children's Age-Readiness for Competition," in *Children and Youth in Sport: A Biopsychosocial Perspective,* ed. F. L. Smith and R. E. Smoll. (Dubuque, IA: Kendal Hunt Publishing Company, 2002), 83–103.

2. Michael Lewis, "Coach Fitz's Management Theory," *New York Times Magazine,* March 28, 2004.

3. Bob Bigelow, *Just Let the Kids Play.* (Deerfield Beach, FL: Health Communications, 2001).

13. Overweight Children

1. K. J. Thompson and D. Tantleff-Dunn, "Assessment of Body-Image Disturbance in Obesity," *Obesity Research* 6 (1998): 375–77; S. J. Erickson et al., "Are Overweight Children Unhappy? Body Mass Index, Depressive Symptoms, and Overweight Concerns in Elementary School Children, *Archives of Pediatric and Adolescent Medicine* 54 (2000): 931–35.

2. W. H. Dietz, "Health Consequences of Obesity in Youth: Childhood Predictors of Adult Disease," *Pediatrics* 101 (1998): 518–25; S. Kirna, R. P. Nelder, and G. J. Lewendon, "Deprivation and Childhood Obesity: A Cross-Sectional Study of 20,973 Children in Plymouth, United Kingdom," *Journal of Epidemiology and Community Health,* 54 (2000): 456–60.

3. USA Today, Health and Behavior, Report: "Children's obesity now 'modern day epidemic.' " 3/23/04.

4. Mike Lupica, *Travel Team* (New York: Penguin, 2004).

5. Eric Schlosser, *Fast-Food Nation* (New York: Penguin, 2001).

14. EATING DISORDERS, BODY IMAGE, STEROIDS, AND SUPPLEMENTS

1. J. A. Hobart and D. R. Smucker, "The Female Athlete Triad," *The American Family Physician* 61 (2000): 3357–64, 3367.
2. American Psychiatric Association, *Diagnostic Statistical Manual of Mental Disorders–IV* (Washington, DC: APA, 1994).
3. Ibid.
4. Ibid.
5. A. Litt, *Fuel for Young Athletes: Essential Foods and Fluids for Future Champions* (Champaign, IL: Human Kinetics, 2004).
6. M. A. Mason, et al., "Use of Nutritional Supplement by High School Football and Volleyball Players," *Iowa Orthopaedic Journal* 21 (2001): 43–48.
7. R. B. Kreider, "Creatine, the Next Ergogenic Supplement?" in *Sportscience Training and Technology,* Internet Society for Sport Science (1998). www.sportsci.org/traintech/creatine/rbk.html.
8. T. A. McGuine, J. C. Sullivan, and D. A. Bernhardt, "Creatine Supplementation Among Wisconsin High School Athletes," *Clinical Journal of Sports Medicine* 11 (2002): 247–53; M. Labotz and B. W. Smith, "Creatine Supplement Use in an NCAA Division I Program," *Clinical Journal of Sports Medicine* 9 (1999): 167–69; M. Greenwood, et al., "Creatine Supplementation Patterns and Perceived Effects in Select Division I Collegiate Athletes," *Clinical Journal of Sports Medicine* 10 (2000): 191–94.
9. M. A. Pecci and J. A. Lombardo, "Performance-Enhancing Supplements," *Physical Medicine and Rehabilitation Clinics of North America* (2000): 949–60.
10. Endocrine Society, "Alert: ANDRO Use by Athletes," (2000). www.endo-society.org/news/press/2000/20000201.cfm.
11. Nancy Clark, *Sports Nutrition Guidebook,* 3rd ed. (Champaign, IL: Human Kinetics, 2003).
12. H. G. Pope, K. A. Philips, and R. Olivardia, *The Adonis Complex: The Secret Crisis of Male Body Obsession* (New York: Free Press, 2000).
13. National Institute on Drug Abuse, "Monitoring the Future Study," (2003). www.nida.nih.gov/Infofax/HSYouthtrends.html.
14. R. H. Durant, et al., "Use of Multiple Drugs Among Adolescents Who Use Anabolic Steroids," *New England Journal of Medicine* 328 (1993): 922–26; L. M. Irving, D. Neumark-Sztainer, and M. Story, "Steroid Use Among Adolescents: Findings from Project EAT," *Journal of Adolescent Health* 30 (2002): 243–52.
15. Ibid.
16. D. Arvarry and H. G. Pope Jr., "Anabolic-Androgenic Steroids as a Gateway to Opioid Dependence," *New England Journal of Medicine* 342, no. 20 (2000): 1532; J. D. Wines Jr., A. J. Gruber, H. G. Pope Jr., and E. S. Lukas, "Nalbuphine Hydrochloride Dependence in Anabolic Steroid Users," *American Journal of Addiction* 8, no. 2 (1999): 161–64.

17. "National Household Survey on Drug Abuse," (1994). www.icpsr.umich.edu; K. J. Brower, F. C. Blow, J. P. Young, and E. M. Hill, "Symptoms and Correlates of Anabolic Androgenic Steroid Dependence," *British Journal of Addiction* 86, no. 6 (1991): 759–68; K. B. Kashkin and H. D. Kleber, "Hooked on Hormones? An Anabolic Steroid Addiction Hypothesis," *Journal of the American Medical Association* 262, no. 22 (1989): 3166–70.

18. Nora Volkow, www.drugabuse.gov/about/welcome/MessageSteroids305.html.

FOR FURTHER READING

FOR PARENTS

Books
Rotella, R. J., and L. K. Bunker. *Parenting Your Superstar: How to Help Your Child Get the Most Out of Sports.* Champaign, IL: Leisure, 1987.

Journal Articles
Barnicle, M. "Many Little League Parents Should Be Called 'Out'!" *New York Daily News.* www.nydailynews.com/news/col/story/76898p-70958c.html (accessed April 19, 2003).

Web Sites
Center for Sport Parenting: www.sportparenting.org.
Drake University: A Parent's Guide to Youth Sports Participation: www.drake.edu/ icd/pdf/ParentsGuideSports.pdf.
Fatherhood: Sports and Recreation: fatherhood.about.com/cs/sportsrecreation/.
Texas A&M University: Parents Could Learn Lesson from Children About Youth Sports: www.tamu.edu/univrel/aggiedaily/news/stories/00/032700-9.html.
Youth, Sports, and Self-Esteem: A Guide for Parents, by Dr. Darrell Burnett: www .djburnett.com/sports.htm.
Youth Sports Parenting Information: www.momsteam.com.

Web Site Articles
Burnett, D. "Hey, Mom and Dad, Your Attitude Is Showing!": www.youth-sports. com/getpage.cfm?file=/topics/121198-4.html&userid=60463951.
Colacurcio, Joseph. "Parent Defends Involvement in School Sports": www .recordonline.com/archive/2002/11/04/view04.htm.
Edwards, Rebecca. "Parent Involvement in Athletics Bibliography": www.unt.edu/ cpe/library/rbibliog/parentinvbib.htm.

Murphy, Shane, Ph.D. "Successful Development of the Young Athlete: Guidelines for Parents": www.momsteam.com/alpha/features/cheersandtears/.

———. "'The Cheers and the Tears'": Tips for Soccer Moms and Dads: www .calstatela.edu/faculty/dfrankl/soccer/brvw_murphy1.htm.

YOUTH SPORTS AND CHARACTER

Books

American Academy of Orthopedic Surgeons and American Academy of Pediatrics, "Care of the Young Athlete," in *Care of the Young Athlete*, ed. J. A. Sullivan and S.J. Anderson. Elk Grove Village, IL: American Academy of Pediatrics, 2000.

Danish, S. "Teaching Life Skills Through Sport," in *Paradoxes of Youth and Sport*, ed. M. Gatz, M. Messner, and S. Ball-Rokeach, pp. 49–60. Albany: State University of New York Press, 2002.

Elmore, T. *Nurturing the Leader Within Your Child*. Nashville: Thomas Nelson Publishers, 2001.

Gatz, M., M. Messner, and S. Ball-Rokeach, eds. *Paradoxes of Youth and Sport*. Albany: State University of New York Press, 2002.

Mastrich, J. *Really Winning: Using Sports to Develop Character and Integrity in Our Boys*. New York: St. Martin's Press, 2002.

Parcells, B., and J. Coplon. *Finding a Way to Win: The Principals of Leadership, Teamwork, and Motivation*. New York: Doubleday, 1995.

U.S. Department of Health and Human Services, Centers for Disease Control. *Guide to Preventive Services: Physical Education Classes in Schools Are Strongly Recommended to Increase Physical Activity Among Young People*. Washington, D.C.: U.S. Government Printing Office, 2001.

Journal Articles

Centers for Disease Control. "Guidelines for School and Community Programs to Promote Lifelong Physical Activity Among Young People." *Morbidity and Mortality Weekly Report* 46, no. RR-6 (March 7, 1997): 1–36.

Ewing, M., L. Gano-Overway, C. Branta, and V. Seefeldt. "The Role of Sports in Youth Development," in *Paradoxes of Youth and Sport*, ed. M. Gatz, M. Messner, and S. Ball-Rokeach. Albany: State University of New York Press, 2002.

Lee, M., J. Whitehead, and N. Balchin. "The Measurement of Values in Youth Sport: Development of the Youth Sport Values Questionnaire." *Journal of Sport and Exercise Psychology* 22 (2000): 307–26.

Web Sites

Character Counts: Josephson Institute: www.charactercounts.org.

Institute for the Study of Youth Sports: Michigan State University: www.uthsprts@ pilot.msu.edu.

Mendelson Center for Sport, Character, and Culture: University of Notre Dame: www.nd.edu/~cscc.

National Alliance for Youth Sports: www.nays.org.

Wellesley College: National Institute on Out-of-School Time: www.wellesley.edu/WCW/CRW/SAC/.

Youth-Sports.com.

Web Site Articles

Agbayani, Caroline. "It's Not About Winning or Losing, It's How You Play the Game." Sports Rage: www.soc.hawaii.edu/leonj/409as2001/agbayani/sports_rage.htm.

"Choosing the Right Sport and Physical Activity Program for Your Child." Youth Sport Council and The National Association for Sport and Physical Education: www.aahperd.org/naspe/pdf_files/pos_papers/resource-choosing.pdf.

Dewey, Todd. "Youth Sports Group Stresses Fun on Field." View News: www.viewnews.com/2000/VIEW-Nov-25-Sat-2000/NWest/14869709.html.

Shalala, D., and R. Riley. "Promoting Health for Young People Through Physical Activity and Sports." Department of Health and Human Services Web site: www.hhs.gov/news/press/2000pres/20001129.pdf.

EXPERTS ON YOUTH IN SPORTS

Web Sites

Ask Coach Mike. Dr. Michael A. Simon: www.askcoachmike.com.

Positive Pushing. Dr. Jim Taylor: www.positivepushing.com.

Web Site Articles

Stratton, Richard K., Ph.D. "Coaching Youth Sports." An Electronic Newsletter for Coaches, Athletes, and Parents: courseware.vt.edu/users/rstratto/CYS.

———. "Coaching Youth Sports: Motivation in Young Athletes": www.youth-sports.com/topics/031398-2.html.

PROBLEMS IN SPORTS

Books

Engh, F. Why Johnny Hates Sports: Why Organized Youth Sports Are Failing Our Children and What We Can Do About It. New York: Avery Publishing Group, 1999.

Journal Articles

Ginsburg, R. D. "Violence in Youth Sports: How Sports Can Help and Hurt Our

Youth." *Massachusetts Psychological Association Quarterly* 46, no. 3 (2002): 9–11.

McGrath, D. "Athletes: Culture Tells Them Rules Don't Apply." *Chicago Tribune.* June 15, 2003.

Satcher, D. "Call to Action to Prevent and Decrease Overweight and Obesity." *Report of the Office of the Surgeon General of the United States:* Doc. #017-001-00551-7. Washington, D.C.: U.S. Government Printing Office, 2001.

Web Sites

Steroid World: www.steroidsinfo.com.

Web Site Articles

Abdal-Haqq, Ismat. "Violence in Sports." Child Development Institution: www.childdevelopmentinfo.com/health_safety/violence_kids_sports.shtml.

Bach, Greg. "National Community Requirements for Youth Sports Will Be Released This Fall by the National Alliance for Youth Sports." Combating Violence in Youth Sports: www.lib.niu.edu/ipo/ipo10927.html.

Heinzmann, Gregg S., Ed.M. Director, Youth Sports Research Council. "Parental Violence in Youth Sports: Facts, Myths, and Videotape." Rutgers, The State University of New Jersey: youthsports.rutgers.edu/parental_violence.html.

Mann, Denise. "Experts Suggest Ways to Stop Parents' 'Sports Rage': Fatal Beating Calls Attention to Problem at Youth Sporting Events." Positive Coaching Alliance News: www.positivecoach.org/news/20000715_mann.html.

Morrison, Gwen. "Parent Rage in Youth Sports: Giving the Game Back to Our Children." Pre-Teenagers Today: preteenagerstoday.com/resources/articles/parentrage.htm.

Rorem, Brad. "A Cause for Concern about Youth Sports." Island Forum: www.mi-reporter.com/sited/story/html/110419.

Help Centers

Center for Education on Anabolic Steroid Effects (CEASE), Atlanta, Ga. 1-877-STEROID

National Association of Anorexia Nervosa and Associated Disorders, Highland Park, Ill. 1-847-831-3438

Obsessive Compulsive Disorder Foundation, New Haven, Conn. 203-325-2190

The Body Image Program at Butler Hospital/Brown University, Providence, R.I. 401-455-6466

PERFORMANCE

Journal Articles

Miller, P., and G. Kerr. "Conceptualizing Excellence: Past, Present, and Future." *Journal of Applied Sport Psychology* 14 (2002): 140–53.

Web Site Articles

Marriott, Lynn, and Pia Nilsson. "Golf Parent for the Future": www.juniorlinks
.com/features/fullView.cfm?aid=264.

NUTRITION

Books

Litt, A. *Fuel for Young Athletes: Essential Foods and Fluids for Future Champions.*
Champaign, IL: Human Kinetics, 2004.

Journal Articles

Arvary, Drew, and Harrison G. Pope. "Anabolic-Androgenic Steroids as a Gateway
to Opioid Dependence." *New England Journal of Medicine* 343 (2000): 1532.

Clark, Nancy. *Sports Nutrition Guidebook,* 3rd ed. Champaign, IL: Human Kinetics,
2003.

Coleman, Ellen. "NO Supplements? No Way!" *Sports Medicine Digest* 26, no. 6
(2005): 70–71.

Durant, R. H., et al. "Use of Multiple Drugs Among Adolescents Who Use Anabolic
Steroids." *New England Journal of Medicine* 328 (1993): 922–26.

Goldberg, L., et al. "The Adolescents Training and Learning to Avoid Steroids Program: Preventing Drug Use and Promoting Health Behaviors." *Archives of Pediatrics and Adolescent Medicine* 154 (2000): 332–38.

Irving, L. M., D. Neumark-Sztainer, and M. Story. "Steroid Use Among Adolescents:
Findings from Project EAT." *Journal of Adolescent Health* 30 (2002): 243–52.

Kindlundh, A. M., et al. "Adolescent Use of Anabolic-Androgenic Steroids and Relations to Self-Reports of Social, Personality, and Health Aspects." *European
Journal of Public Health* 11, no. 3 (2001): 322–28.

Mason, M. A., et al. "Use of Nutritional Supplement By High School Football and
Volleyball Players." *Iowa Orthopaedic Journal* 21 (2001): 43–48.

Pecci, M. A., and J. A. Lombardo. "Performance-Enhancing Supplements." *Physical
Medicine and Rehabilitation Clinics of North America* (2000): 949–60.

Rawson, Eric S., and Priscilla M. Clarkson. "Scientifically Debatable: Is Creatine
Worth Its Weight?" *Gatorade Sports Science Institute* (Sports Science Exchange 91) vol. 16, no. 4 (2003).

WEIGHT-RELATED ARTICLES

Ara, I., G. Vicente-Rodriguez, C. Dorado, J.A. Serrano-Sanchez, and J.A.L. Calbet.
"Regular Participation in Sports Is Associated with Enhanced Physical Fitness and Lower Fat Mass in Pre-Pubertal Boys." *International Journal of Obesity* 28, no. 12 (2004): 1585–93.

Brooks-Gunn, J., Carolyn Burrow, and Michelle P. Warren. "Attitudes Toward Eating and Body Weight in Different Groups of Female Adolescent Athletes." *International Journal of Eating Disorders* 7, no. 6 (1988): 749–57.

Davis, Caroline, and Shaelyn Strachan. "Elite Female Athletes with Eating Disorders: a Study of Psychopathological Characteristics." *Journal of Sport and Exercise Psychology* 23, no. 3 (2001): 245–53.

Davison, Kirsten Krahnstoever, Mandy B. Earnest, and Leann L. Birch. "Participation in Aesthetic Sports and Girls' Weight Concerns at Ages 5 and 7 Years." *International Journal of Eating Disorders* 31, no. 3 (2002): 312–17.

Robinson, Kirsten, and F. Richard Ferraro. "The Relationship Between Types of Female Athletic Participation and Female Body Type." *Journal of Psychology* 138, no. 2 (2004): 115–28.

Thomas, Non Eleri, Julien S. Baker, and Bruce Davies. "Established and Recently Identified Coronary Heart Disease Risk Factors in Young People: The Influence of Physical Activity and Physical Fitness." *Sports Medicine* 33, no. 9 (2003): 633–50.

GENDER-RELATED ARTICLES

Chappell, Susan. "How Much Athletics Is Too Much?" *Daughters Newsletter* (2004): 13.

Decker, David. "Participation in Youth Sports, Gender, and the Moral Point of View." *Physical Educator* 52, no. 1 (1995): 14–21.

DeFrancesco, Charmaine, and Paulette Johnson. "Athlete and Parent Perceptions in Junior Tennis." *Journal of Sport Behavior* 20, no. 1 (1997): 29–36.

Freedman-Doan, Carol, et al. "What Am I Best At? Grade and Gender Differences in Children's Beliefs about Ability Improvements." *Journal of Applied Developmental Psychology* 21, no. 4 (2000): 379–402.

Howell, Melbourne F., James F. Sallis, Bohdan Kolody, and Thomas L. McKenzie. "Children's Physical Activity Choices: A Developmental Analysis of Gender, Intensity Levels, and Time." *Pediatric Exercise Science* 11 (1999): 158–68.

Humphries, Charlotte A. "Opinions of Participants and Nonparticipants Toward Youth Sport." *Physical Educator* 48, no. 1 (1991): 44–47.

Jacobs, Janis E., et al. "Changes in Children's Self-Competence and Values: Gender and Domain Differences Across Grades One through Twelve." *Child Development* 73, no. 2 (2002): 509–27.

Jambor, Elizabeth. "Parents as Children's Socializing Agents in Youth Soccer." *Journal of Sport Behavior* 22, no. 3 (1999): 350–59.

Kidman, Lynn, Alex McKenzie, and Brigid McKenzie. "The Nature and Target of Parents' Comments During Youth Sport Competitions." *Journal of Sport Behavior* 22, no. 1 (1999): 54–68.

Klomsten, Anne Torhild, Einar M. Skaalvik, and Geir Arild Espnes. "Physical Self-Concept and Sports: Do Gender Differences Still Exist?" *Sex Roles* 50, nos. 1–2 (2004): 119–27.

Kutner, Lawrence. "Helping Young Athletes Keep Their Feet on the Ground as They Pursue Their Interest in Sports." *New York Times*, Feb. 3, 1994.

Leff, Stephen S., and Rich H. Hoyle. "Young Athletes' Perceptions of Parental Support and Pressure." *Journal of Youth and Adolescence* 24, no. 2 (1995): 187–203.

Lesyk, Jack J., and Alan S. Kornspan. "Coaches' Expectations and Beliefs Regarding Benefits of Youth Sport Participation." *Perceptual and Motor Skills* 90 (2000): 399–402.

Marino, Jennifer. "Sportsmanship 101 for Parents." *Parenting* 18, no. 5 (2004): 242.

About the Authors

Sports have been a central part of **Richard Ginsburg**'s life starting in childhood. His parents and grandfather (a former collegiate baseball player) were his coaches, teaching him how to catch and throw, swim, dive, wrestle, shoot, and kick. Being an athlete helped him to build confidence at an extremely competitive high school, where discipline and perseverance practiced on the athletic field fueled his academic and future professional endeavors. As he got older, his experience playing sports helped him to break down barriers as a middle-class Jew in a predominantly Protestant upper-class school and community while embracing his own identity and heritage. As a collegiate soccer and lacrosse player, he became a keen student, facing the physical and psychological challenges of mastering those two sports. As a young teacher, his experience as a coach further crystallized his belief about how influential sports can be. He watched how high school boys and girls were transformed by sports experiences, gaining confidence, building relationships, and learning how to work through adversity. These benefits resonated with him as he chose to devote his career to clinical and sport psychology, helping many young athletes navigate the challenges of performing their best while deepening and enriching their personal and professional development.

For **Amy Baltzell**, sports were a crucial lifeline from the start. As a child orphaned at the age of 10, sports became her family, her passion, and a place where she belonged and mattered. She competed in tennis, field hockey, lacrosse, sailing, rowing, and basketball; in college, rowing became her sport, and she eventually became a member of the U.S. Rowing Team. Her fierce will, intense drive, dedication, equally driven coaches, and fear of failure produced remarkable results; though she lost a key race, she still won a place as an alternate on the U.S. Olympic Team.

Amy certainly should have been proud of her accomplishment, but she was emotionally drained, and her identity had become completely wrapped up in getting a place on the first team. Eventually, she grew in strength and wisdom from the painful lessons of her adversity and success. Amy Baltzell went on to become a member of the first all-woman yachting crew vying for the America's Cup. She is currently a professor in sport psychology at Boston University and a practicing sport psychologist who has helped hundreds of high school and college athletes. She is intensely committed to helping young athletes love what they do, win or lose, and learn to be proud of themselves.

Growing up in a city neighborhood, **Steve Durant** benefited from a rich mixture of organized and informal sports. Kids were always available for playing pickup games. He feels particularly blessed to have played varsity football at a Jesuit high school with caring coaches and loyal teammates who taught him the importance of dedication, sacrifice, and teamwork. In college and for the following thirty-plus years, rugby has given him immeasurable joy and taught him invaluable life lessons. On a crystal-clear day one October, he experienced one of those magic moments of sublime sports elation when he, his 70-year-old father, and his 15-year-old son played as teammates in a rugby match in Division 3 of the regional men's league. He had heard that the Native American Mohawks put a lacrosse stick in the cradle of the tribe's newborn boys as a way of passing on their passion for their traditional game, and on that day he profoundly understood the beauty of that tradition.

Sports form a bond within his nuclear and extended family and have given his wife and himself a great teaching tool for their kids. All four of his children have enjoyed robust, rewarding sports experiences. His work as a clinical and sport psychologist has been dedicated to helping parents and children seek answers about their experience in sports and ways to gain mastery in all aspects of their lives.

This book is a continuation of the collective internal and external dialogues of these three authors as psychologists, athletes, and parents. It reflects the worthy struggle to cultivate all that is good in competitive sports in order to build emotionally healthy people of character.

Index

Academics
    and ADHD, 45
    and college sports, 96, 101, 104, 105–6
    decline in students' grades in, 194,
        203
    developing confidence through, 52
    disciplining athletes who fail to meet
        standards of, 6
    parents who value, over sports,
        144–46
    undervaluing of, by organized
        sports, x
    See also Scholarships (athletic)
ACL injuries, 96, 97, 110
Acne, 250, 255
Activity. See Physical activity
ADHD (attention deficit disorder with
    hyperactivity), 45, 144, 179
Adolescence. See Teenagers
The Adonis Complex (Harrison), 250
Adversity. See Perseverance; Self-
    control
Alcohol abuse, xii, 280–81
    See also Drug abuse
Amenorrhea, 239, 240
American Obesity Association, 226
Anabolic steroids. See Steroids
Androstenedione (andro), 247–48
Anemia, 244
Anorexia nervosa, 85, 239–41, 250

    See also Eating disorders
Apathy, 192
Art, 52
    See also Music
Artest, Ron, 171
Ashe, Arthur, 130
Assault. See Violence
Athletes
    applying adult standards to child,
        17–29, 48–49, 55, 73, 194, 223
    bad behavior by professional, x, xi, 5,
        171–73, 175
    balanced life needed by, 98, 194,
        197–200, 203, 204–5, 280
    becoming professional, 12–13
    breaking rules for exceptional, 57
    college recruiting of, 279–80
    corruption of, 99–100
    pressure on young exceptional,
        190–94, 204–5
    reasons for being, 257
    self-absorption by, 99–100
    as worthy people regardless of per-
        formance, 96, 99, 101, 115, 154,
        182–83, 231, 244, 254, 255, 264, 266,
        267, 270, 280
    See also Children; Female athletes;
        Male athletes; Nonathletes; Orga-
        nized sports; Scholarships (ath-
        letic); Teams; Specific sports

Made in the USA
Lexington, KY
22 October 2011